EMERGENCY ANIMAL RESCUE STORIES

TRUE STORIES ABOUT

PEOPLE DEDICATED TO

SAVING ANIMALS FROM DISASTERS

TERRI CRISP

Prima Publishing
3000 Lava Ridge Court • Roseville, California 95661
(800) 632-8676 • www.primalifestyles.com

PRIMA PETS and colophon are trademarks of Prima Communications Inc. PRIMA PUBLISHING and colophon are trademarks of Prima Communications Inc., registered with the United States Patent and Trademark Office.

The stories in this book are all based on actual events. I have learned, though, that during disasters it is especially easy to lose track of time; events sometimes fall out of sequence, and a lot of the details become a blur. Whenever possible, I contacted the people we included in the stories, and between all of us, we remembered what happened as best we could. I apologize for forgetting the names of some of the people; so in those cases, we came up with new names. To disguise their identities, several other people mentioned in this book were given other names too.

Insert photos taken by United Animal Nations staff and volunteers.

Library of Congress Cataloging-in-Publication Data
Crisp, Terri.
     Emergency animal rescue stories : true stories about people
dedicated to saving animals from disasters / Terri Crisp.
         p.   cm.
     ISBN 0-7615-1706-5
         1. Emergency Animal Rescue Service. 2. Animal rescue—
United States. I. Title.
     HV4763.C75   2000
     636.08'32'06073—dc21   00-058888

00 01 02 03 HH 10 9 8 7 6 5 4 3 2 1
Printed in the United States of America

How to Order
Single copies may be ordered from Prima Publishing, 3000 Lava Ridge Court, Roseville, CA 95661; telephone (800) 632-8676 ext. 4444. Quantity discounts are also available. On your letterhead, include information concerning the intended use of the books and the number of books you wish to purchase.

Visit us online at www.primalifestyles.com

To those that I leave behind when I go to a disaster:
My husband, Ken, and daughters, Jennifer,
Amy, and Megan—plus the critters who make
our family complete. Without their unwavering
love and support, I could not do what I do.

CONTENTS

INTRODUCTION

IN MY first book, *Out of Harm's Way*, I explained how I got started helping animals during disasters. It's not what I had intended to do when I grew up, even though I've loved animals for as long as I can remember. I have come to realize that rescuing animals is what I was meant to do, and now, 17 years later, I look back on the remarkable experiences I've had and realize how glad I am I didn't become a high school art teacher.

I've been on an incredible journey that continues to amaze me. It began in 1983 with a flood in Alviso, California. An innocent desire to keep dogs and cats from drowning drew me to something that would change the course of my life, or at least the one I had planned for myself.

In 1987, an ad in the *San Jose Mercury News* provided a vehicle for my dream, one that had grown out of my awareness that people were failing animals during disasters. They died because individuals, shelters, and animal organizations were not adequately prepared to save them. That ad introduced me to United Animal Nations (UAN), a national nonprofit animal welfare organization headquartered in Sacramento, California. I owe a great deal of thanks to the founders for having the idea for the Emergency Animal Rescue Service (EARS), and allowing me to develop the program. We shared the common realization that animals were the forgotten victims of disasters for too long.

Nurtured with the right blend of the organization's vision, the staff's dedication, the volunteers' long hours, and my unwavering passion to ensure that animals get the help they deserve during disasters, EARS has grown into a model national disaster response and recovery program for animals.

I have been the director of EARS since September 1993, following five years of working as a part-time consultant. In January of the following year, I began training people to become volunteers with the program. Without volunteers, I realized EARS would never be able to grow into what it had to become if the job of helping animals during disasters was going to be done right. As of May 2000, there are just over 3,300 individuals comprising the dedicated and talented team of volunteers that has made EARS such a success.

My journey has taken me to 46 disasters of every type but a volcanic eruption. I have learned a lot from the people I met during each of these events. They have enriched my life beyond anything I could have ever imagined. I believe each one of them has come into my life for a reason and I thank them for what they have taught me. They provided stepping-stones to the next thing I had to learn or understand in order to keep EARS headed in the right direction.

What I do has resulted in awards, media recognition, and the title of hero. I never asked for or expected any of this. I thank the people who feel I deserve the recognition, but I would have been content with nothing more than the personal satisfaction of knowing my life has made a difference to animals. Each dog, mouse, cat, guinea pig, snake, bird, horse, fish, rabbit, pig, ferret, cow, turtle, goat, hamster, frog, and iguana I have saved brings me a more lasting satisfaction. It is my hope that I will be able to continue to do what I do for a very long time, as I cannot imagine ever doing anything else.

Out of Harm's Way focused on three disasters to which EARS responded: the Exxon *Valdez* oil spill in 1989, Hurricane Andrew in 1992, and the Midwest floods in 1993. All of these were major disasters, taking the lives of thousands and thousands of animals, both domesticated and wild. At the same time, with each disaster, EARS was able to save more animals. These were disasters that captured the attention of people around the world, in part because the news media kept the stories alive. There were many other less-publicized disasters, all of which had similarly devastating effects on animals.

When I started to think about writing a second book, I faced a dilemma. There had been too many disasters since my first book. Between November 1994 and September 1999, EARS participated in the rescue work of 29 disasters. I realized that I could write an entire book about almost every fire, flood, hurricane, tornado, and earthquake. How was I going to be able to pick and choose which ones to include, knowing that I would have to leave out some really important stories?

I finally decided I would begin by telling the stories from two of the lesser-known disasters—ones that didn't make the national news for more than a few nights before they were replaced with something more exciting or sensational. Just because the media stops covering a disaster doesn't mean it's over. People and animals suffer for weeks, months, and sometimes years, as they struggle to regain some semblance of the life they knew prior to the disaster. I wanted to give these people and animals the recognition they deserved for surviving and remember the ones who tried so hard and didn't make it.

The two disasters I've chosen may not even be ones most people will remember. They are Tropical Storm Alberto, which struck Georgia in July 1994, and the relentless rain that drenched the state of Texas in October of that same year, causing widespread flooding in the Houston area. The stories from these disasters are day-to-day accounts of the struggles, successes, miracles, mistakes, tragedies, lessons learned, and the people who cried and laughed with me as I held the position of director of EARS. And, of course, there are the animals. This book is a collection of their stories that will bring you tears and joy, and, in the end, make you more aware of what animals go through as they struggle to survive.

Following the stories from these two disasters, I share some of my recollections from several of the disasters that happened after the flood in Texas. These stories come from the 1994 earthquake in Kobe, Japan, the 1996 wild land fire near Wasilla, Alaska, plus the floods in Northern California and in Grand Forks, North Dakota, in 1997. I have carefully selected them to give you a blend of the realities that the EARS volunteers and I encounter during disasters.

I feel fortunate to have the opportunity to write this second book. Writing is something I love almost as much as I love animals, and it has happily provided me with another way to reach people who may never have given a thought to what happens to animals during disasters. I will consider this book a success if you the reader learn from it and take the necessary steps to protect your animals from disasters. You owe it to them, and I know this book will help you understand why.

Each disaster, each person, each animal, has taught me something, and I continue to learn. It is this knowledge that I want to share. I also made promises to the animals who didn't survive. I have no choice but to continue diligently trying to prevent the same kinds of tragedies that took their lives. I hope this book helps to fulfill those promises.

To those of you who have read my first book: *Thank you!* I received so many thoughtful notes, letters, postcards, and e-mails from people like me who are passionate about animals. I apologize for not being able to respond to all correspondence personally. I want you to know how much I appreciated all the kind words, and how pleased I was when you wrote of the inspiration you gained from reading my book and the steps you took afterward to do something to help the animals in your community. Every person's effort, no matter how big or small, *does* make a difference, whether it's for one animal or a whole shelter full.

Words, too, have an amazing power. The positive ripple effect of the first book proves this. That is why I've written a second one—so the ripples will reach even farther.

EMERGENCY ANIMAL
RESCUE STORIES

CHAPTER ONE

Changes

I NEED A one-way ticket from Denver to Atlanta," I explained, wedging the phone between my shoulder and ear so I could stretch across the unmade bed and grab my jeans. A quick inspection of the pants confirmed they needed to be washed, but there wasn't time.

"When do you want to leave?" the ticket agent asked as I stuffed the dirty jeans into my duffel bag. I had learned from a previous phone call that I should have been in Georgia the day before, but later that afternoon would have to do. "Some time after two o'clock today," I responded, realizing that I would have to live up to my reputation of having a lead foot on the gas pedal if I was going to get to the airport in Denver on time.

"There's a flight at 2:15 that'll get you into Atlanta at 9:25 P.M.," the agent informed me after a lengthy pause that gave me enough time to locate my work boots and drop them in my bag, on top of the dirty jeans. "I'm afraid it's a pretty full flight," she said. The sound of fingers tapping on computer keys let me know further information was coming. "But there are two seats available in the back."

"I'll take one of them," I blurted out, as if bidding for a prized treasure at an auction. Having secured seat 32B, I dumped the contents of my cluttered purse onto the floor, knowing I was about to be asked for my American Express number to pay for the ticket. I cringed when the woman on the other end of the phone told me, almost apologetically, what the fare would be. Once again, Mother Nature proved she has no clue as to what last-minute airline tickets cost. If she could only give me a heads-up 14 days in advance of doing a major demolition job on the landscape, it would save EARS a nice sum of money.

Mother Nature's latest handiwork was Tropical Storm Alberto. This Gulf-born storm had come ashore near Destin, Florida, on the afternoon of July 3, 1994, and was meandering through the western and central parts of Georgia, occasionally sidestepping into Alabama. Two days later, the storm decided to stall, and not a square mile of the Peach State escaped the drenching rain. One of the towns hardest hit was Americus, where 21 inches of rain fell in 24 hours. In other parts of the state, rain totals were between 8 and 15 inches. The Ocmulgee and Flint Rivers were rapidly rising as the rain continued to fall, with no reprieve on the horizon.

As Mother Nature was busy producing her first major storm of the hurricane season, I was secluded in Vail, Colorado, hoping for no disasters. I had set aside a much-needed week to complete more chapters of my first book, *Out of Harm's Way,* in a place where I thought there would be no interruptions, including the Weather Channel.

Hurricane season starts the first of June, but the category fours and fives that can be so destructive usually don't arrive until later in the six-month season. For my scheduling purposes, I hoped July would be uneventful, but it seemed Mother Nature had decided she'd get to work early.

After hanging up from my call to the airlines, relieved to have gotten on a flight during this busy travel time, I returned to my hasty packing job. Scanning the bedroom for what I still had to grab, I knew I was in trouble. I would be heading off to Georgia with clothes that were more suitable for a writer, not someone who was about to go boating in disgusting floodwater, searching for stranded animals. I was sure to be overdressed for the occasion, so at some point I would have to stop at K-Mart to buy some jeans and red T-shirts, the official EARS uniform.

The call that alerted me to the situation in Georgia came on July 6. My husband, Ken, and two younger daughters, Amy and Megan, had just left the morning before. They had driven me from our home in Santa Clara, California, to Vail, and had stayed for the town's spectacular Independence Day celebration. I spent the day of their departure switching gears, going from being a mom and wife to a writer, focused on nothing else but telling a story. The following morning, I rose early and biked into town, stopping at a health-food store for a tall glass of a fruit and vitamin concoction that was supposed to stimulate the brain. I was hoping it would take direct aim at my creative side, which had been a little sluggish the day before.

Feeling recharged and ready to get down to work, I settled in at my computer. But before my brain even produced one cleverly written page, I was interrupted by my beeping pager. Having told everyone that under no circumstances could I be disturbed, except a major disaster or a family emergency, I knew right away the pager was the bearer of bad news. Something horrible was happening outside my secluded world that I suspected would delay my writing, again.

I didn't recognize the phone number displayed on my pager. I dialed it and stood looking out the picture window at the aspen-covered landscape, wondering who would answer the phone on the other end. After three rings, I heard "Hello," and knew right away who it was.

I had met Shirley Minshew two years before when we were in Florida cleaning up after Hurricane Andrew, one of Mother Nature's most destructive performances. Our friendship began during the long hours we spent nightly, trying to rescue frightened cats struggling to survive in the ruins of

Homestead's mobile home parks. We stayed in touch after that. When I began to teach the EARS Disaster Preparedness workshops in January 1994, Shirley asked me to do a workshop that May in Macon, Georgia, where she lived and also worked as the director of the Animal Rescue Kennel in nearby Warner Robins.

"You better be calling about a disaster, or else you're in big trouble," I joked. The tone of our conversation changed as soon as Shirley responded, "I am. And his name is Alberto."

Staring now at my blank computer screen, I listened as Shirley summarized what she knew. "It's looking real bad for the animals," she explained. "I've done a few rescues so far with the help of one of Warner Robins' animal control officers, but there have to be a lot more animals that need help." Her sentence ended with a muffled yawn. "Sorry," she began when she could talk again. "It was a long night and I think there are going to be some more very long days ahead. I know you're supposed to be writing, but can you come down at least for a few days?"

As it began to sink in that I was probably not going to be spending the next week writing about past disasters, but rather participating in a new one, my January manuscript deadline suddenly seemed right around the corner. Disasters can happen at any time, but there's a much greater chance for activity during the summer months, whether it's an East-Coast hurricane or a wild land fire in the West. Considering it was still only early July, there was a good chance there'd be more disruptions before the summer was over, which wouldn't leave me much time to make up for the week I was going to lose.

After getting as much information as I could from Shirley, I hung up with the promise to call her back as soon as I talked to Deanna Soares, vice president and controller of United Animal Nations (UAN). The practice had been that Deanna and I decided jointly when to mobilize EARS.

"You know what it's going to cost to get me to Atlanta?" I injected, as Deanna and I began our discussion about Alberto and the effects he was already having on the animals in his path. EARS was still in its infancy at this time and every penny had to be spent wisely. A ticket to Atlanta would make a major dent in our meager budget.

"I know it's going to be expensive, but what choice do we have?" Deanna replied, with concern in her voice, not only for the animals, but also for what this disaster could end up costing. "We have trained volunteers in Georgia now who will be expecting us to respond. You've got to go."

So the decision was made.

WITH MY bags packed and a car rented for my race to Denver, I said good-bye to my writing partner, Samantha Glen, who had opened her home to me in anticipation of us spending a week hard at work on the book that she so deeply believed in, too. She would do what she could in my absence, but we both knew we were running out of time. Either Mother Nature would have to take an extended vacation, or I might have to sit out a disaster or two. My gut feeling told me that Alberto was one that I could not miss. After all, for the first time, the very first time, I actually had trained EARS volunteers awaiting my arrival. A very important part of the plan was finally falling into place.

I made the drive from Vail to Denver in record time. I figured I was able to escape a speeding ticket as I descended from my mountain hideaway for one of two reasons. Either a guardian angel who loved animals watched over me or all the state troopers along Interstate 70 were out to lunch.

Managing not to get lost, a mistake that would have cost me precious seconds, I whisked past the "Welcome to the Denver Airport" sign, with a whole 39 minutes to spare. I calculated this was all the time I needed to drop off my one-way rental car; sprint to the TWA counter (accounting for my overstuffed duffel bag, which would slow me down); take possession of my expensive ticket; clear security; call Ken and in two minutes break the news that I'd had a slight change in plans; and, if all went well, board the 2:15 flight. It was an optimistic calculation, but I was determined to make it to Georgia before day's end.

Hot, and breathing like I had just run a marathon, I had 11 minutes to spare when I finally landed in my middle seat, wedged between a woman who shopped at Pretty and Plump and a pimple-faced teenager who'd crammed his mouth full of watermelon-flavored bubble gum that he chewed with nervous enthusiasm all the way to Atlanta.

A sigh, mingled with relief and amazement, signaled I'd made it and could now relax. I leaned my head against the seat and closed my road-weary eyes in hopes that I'd quickly doze off. I knew there wouldn't be much time for sleep once I got to Georgia. There never is in disasters. In a short time, I would be exhausted, wishing I could figure out a way to stockpile sleep during the respites from a lifestyle that seemed to have less and less downtime, and then borrow from this reserve when I ran low. With no surplus of sleep to draw from, adrenaline becomes my ally. So often, it's what sustains me, and I can almost always count on it to kick in during the crucial times. But even adrenaline eventually runs out. So any sleep I could grab on the plane, before the demands on my mind and body began, would hopefully give me a few extra hours of energy.

No matter how hard I tried, however, my mind would not shut down. There were endless questions that crisscrossed through my head, but I was still an outsider to this disaster, so the answers would have to wait until I got to Georgia. By the next morning, I would most likely be inundated with information, from which I would have to find solutions for the animals' survival. Extracting what I needed to know to do my job, I would slowly begin to compile the pieces of those solutions, which would direct how EARS responded. Until that process began, I'd have to be patient, and that's not easy, knowing as I do that delays can cost more animals their lives.

"We'll be on the ground in 30 minutes, folks," the pilot announced as we started our descent into Atlanta. I looked at my watch. We were arriving right on time. I'd apparently fallen asleep, but the break had not been long enough. Looking past the pimple-faced kid, I could see only darkness punctuated by the blinking light at the end of the plane's wing. For one last moment, I leaned back and closed my eyes. "For the animals' sake, please don't let me make any mistakes," I pled to whoever might have some influence on the decisions that I would be faced with. Hopefully, that guardian angel, who I think had something to do with me not getting a speeding ticket in Colorado, had flown with me to Georgia.

WHEN I knew the trip was a go, I had phoned Shirley to give her my arrival time and some instructions to prepare for what I could only anticipate lay ahead. While I was en route, she was contacting the local volunteers and arranging for them to meet with us the following morning. There were not a lot of them, but it was more help than I'd ever had before, and I was thrilled.

I spotted Shirley right away as I exited the muggy jet way, where I could hear the rain pelting the metal roof. Her face confirmed that the disaster had already begun to take its toll on her. She greeted me with a hug and a recognized weariness in her voice. "It's good to see you. I'm only sorry it's for this reason and that it's taken you away from your writing."

"Same here," I whispered as we stepped apart and went to retrieve my bags, which actually contained a whole lot of stuff that I wasn't going to need.

For just a brief moment, I thought about all the chapters I still had to write. This book was so important. More than anything I wanted it to make a difference for animals in future disasters. It was the animals in the present that I needed to focus on now, though. I knew all too well there had to be hundreds of them struggling to stay alive above the rising waters as the rain continued to cause some of the worst flooding Georgia had ever seen.

A sense of urgency—a life-and-death mission—hurried us along as we wove our way through the terminal packed with summer travelers who had nothing but fun and relaxation on their minds. In Shirley's truck, we listened to the latest news on the radio as we headed south on Highway 75 toward Macon. What we heard was discouraging. One reporter told of livestock that had drowned because owners didn't have enough time to move them to safety. In the talk that followed about more evacuations, river levels, locations of human shelters, and weather predictions for the next few days, there was no mention of pets, which was not unusual. Once again, pets were not important enough.

It was half past midnight when we pulled into Shirley's driveway and unloaded my luggage. We were both wiped out and collapsed on the living-room couch. Shirley's husband, Mack, had the news on. The three of us watched without saying a word. The pictures were unbelievable. Alberto was a nasty storm, and what I saw confirmed we had our work cut out for us.

Shirley finally broke the welcome stupor that had given our overstimulated brains a brief reprieve. "Well, you think we should get some sleep? If we don't, I know we'll regret it in a few hours." I could only nod in response.

It was 1:15 when I turned off the bedroom light. My mind fought the need to sleep while my body welcomed the rest. Laying still in the darkness, I listened to the ceiling fan rotating overhead and the relentless rain outside the closed window. Normally, it was a duet that would lull me to sleep. Now the rain only scared me. There had been no break in the storm yet and the rivers were continuing to rise above their banks, covering everything within their expanding reach. Tears escaped from my closed eyes as I thought of those animals who were still alive, having to wait another night to be carried to safety. I hoped we'd find them before it was too late.

⁓

I WOKE in response to a soft knock on my door, and Shirley's announcement that it was 5 A.M. The wake-up call had come too quickly, but I was up and dressed, with bed made, within 10 minutes. Shuffling into the kitchen, my nose welcomed the aroma of brewed coffee. "Where are the cups?" I asked Shirley, anxious for the jump-start the caffeine would provide.

"Grab one of those travel mugs by the stove," Shirley replied, as she continued to fill water dishes for her birds. "I'm just about done here, and then we can go."

"Have you listened to the news yet this morning?" I asked, pouring coffee into the biggest mug I could find.

"No, I couldn't. I figure we'll see it for ourselves soon enough."

It took us little time to load our gear into Shirley's red Dakota pickup and tarp the bed to keep its contents from getting wet. The rain had stopped at some point during the night, but the gray clouds overhead confirmed we'd not seen the last of Alberto. Confident that we had everything we needed no matter where our adventure would take us, Shirley and I headed for downtown Macon, where we were to meet with the EARS volunteers.

"This is it," Shirley announced, as we pulled up in front of the single-story humane services building on Hardeman Avenue. Edwina Barnes, an EARS-trained volunteer and a devoted friend to the animals in Macon, had started this haven to help reduce animal suffering. Though she was out of town, she had insisted that we use the building, so we'd have a place to work until we figured out what we would be doing.

When we walked in, I took a quick inventory of what I saw. I immediately recognized three of the people gathered there; it was only 67 days before that they had been trained to do what they were doing right now. I saw new faces in the group, too. People who knew Edwina had shown up to help. The energy in the room was contagious, and the animals were going to be the ones to benefit from it.

Donna Mosely, one of the trained volunteers, sat at a cluttered desk with a black-and-white cat weighing down the mess. "Yes, we've gotten a lot of dog food donated," I heard her say into the phone. "But we could use some puppy food." I smiled immediately. She'd listened to my stories during the workshop, which described the overwhelming quantities of dog and cat food we receive during disasters, but how no one ever thinks to bring food for puppies and kittens, and all the other types of domesticated animals and birds. "And, if you want to bring formula for nursing puppies or kittens, that would be great." Donna looked up just then, saw me, and grinned. I responded with a thumbs-up and said, "Good job!"

"It's great of Edwina to let us use this place," I told Shirley as she came up beside me. "I hope she gets back into town before I leave so I can thank her."

Shirley agreed, and then proceeded to tell me that, thanks to her local media contacts, information had already gone out to the public announcing what we needed. The growing assortment of food, cages, and other supplies that I saw confirmed that people were once again responding—doing what they could for animals.

"Before I call everyone together, Shirley, can you contact the Emergency Operations Center and get an update?" I looked at my watch. It was 6:45. Considering that there was a disaster going on, everyone's day was sure to have started as early as ours. Shirley disappeared into a back room to use another phone while I proceeded to greet the volunteers, which included a hug for each of them. The bond was beginning to form and, before this disaster was over, all of us would have friends we'd never forget.

When Shirley returned, I asked everyone to gather near the entrance to the building, where there was an assortment of overused chairs. I watched like a proud mother as the volunteers stopped what they were doing and found a seat.

In front of me sat the beginnings of a team, three of them with special qualifications. Amy Chappel, Diane Tatum, and Donna were the first graduates of an EARS workshop to respond to a disaster. None of them had ever done this before, but I trusted that what they'd learned at the workshop and what they'd learn in the next few days would make them experts real fast. In addition to them, there was a handful of other people who couldn't just sit at home and do nothing when animals were in trouble. Considering the magnitude of this disaster, it was great to have the extra help.

While everyone took a turn introducing themselves, I remembered what it felt like to be in their place. When I responded to my first disaster, I was broadsided by a rush of emotions. I went from feeling mad to scared to nervous to impatient, back to being mad, and more than anything, I felt sad for the animals that couldn't be saved. A lot of those same emotions were stirring in me as I began to speak to the anxious faces before me. Only now I knew more of what to expect, and I had the experience of 11 disasters to fall back on.

"The animal control shelter in Macon was evacuated the day before yesterday," I began. "What I want to do first today is find out where those animals have been taken. It doesn't appear as though animal control has a disaster plan, so I suspect if that's the case, they really had to scramble to find a place to put the animals."

"Did they have to euthanize any of them?" Amy interrupted. I knew from the expression on her face that it was a question she needed to ask, but she was afraid of the answer I'd give her.

Shirley responded to the difficult question, and I was confident that she'd know what to say. "I've heard that some animals were put down." She paused as Amy, who'd been the one with the guts to ask the question that was on everyone else's mind, stared quietly at the tiled floor in front of her, tears welling up in her eyes. "But it could just be a rumor," Shirley added, in hopes of softening the blow. "I've learned from the two disasters that I've been to that information can get misconstrued very easily, so that's why Terri and I are going to find out for ourselves if this is true or not." Others around her just shook their heads, confirming the unfairness if animals had been destroyed because it was the easy thing to do.

As Shirley continued to answer questions that other volunteers had, I half listened. My attention had strayed to the scene outside the window. The rain had started again. It hammered the saturated ground, searching for somewhere to go, but the earth turned it away. Eventually, the water would find its way to the Ocmulgee River and only add to the misery that had disrupted the lives of all the victims in its path.

This disaster, like others before it, would cost animals their lives. Some of the deaths would be unavoidable, but I struggled with the possibility that animals had been euthanized at the shelter. Choosing at the last minute to kill animals instead of coming up with alternatives that would have saved their lives cannot be an option when disasters happen. Planning ahead can prevent the killing. The possibility of a repeat of what had happened too many times before made me sick.

I could not let this group of innocent volunteers see my frustration, though. I wanted them to hold on to their hope for as long as they could. We would all learn the truth soon enough, a truth I feared would break each of our hearts. The anticipation of yet another example of how people fail animals could have pushed me into thinking about quitting, but giving up was no longer an option.

The volunteers were counting on me for guidance, so I searched within myself for that anger-fueled determination that I have come to count on so often during disasters when I feel discouraged. That's what gets me through the tough times.

There would be new memories from this disaster, some of which would leave scars. They would be added to the others that I keep pinned to my mental bulletin board. I hang on to them, not to torment my emotions, but rather to remind me not to give up. The memories return often, sometimes just as vivid as when the event itself happened. When I revisit these memories, it's for the benefit of the animals who are still alive. If I were to forget, more animals would die. For this reason, I'm glad that I've learned to live with the memories and that they are never far from my thoughts.

"Terri, anything you want to add?" Shirley's question interrupted my thoughts, bringing me back to the present.

"There is only one thing," I said, as I searched for the right words. "In the workshop, I told you that helping animals during a disaster is unlike anything you have probably ever done. This is your chance to make a difference. The animals need each and every one of us now and I know *we* will not let them down."

CHAPTER TWO

Removing the Blinders

F RIENDSHIP ANIMAL Hospital," the woman on the other
end of the phone answered. She already sounded like she
had talked to one too many people that morning. I could
only imagine the number of desperate calls the hospital must
have received from pet owners who had been forced to evacuate and suddenly found themselves scrambling for a safe
place to put their animals.

"By any chance are the dogs and cats that were evacuated
from Macon animal control two days ago at your clinic?"
This being the eighth call I had made, I was more than ready
to be told I had finally tracked them down.

Shirley's earlier phone call to the Emergency Operations
Center in Macon had confirmed that an unknown number of
animals had been moved to a veterinary clinic, but the public
information officer didn't know which one, so my fingers
had been jogging through the Yellow Pages.

"Uh huh, they're here," she responded, with some reser-
vation in her voice. I took that to mean that I was not the first
person to have made this inquiry.

"That's great," I said with relief. "May I ask how many
animals there are?"

"Well," she paused. "I'm really not sure. I'd have to go in the back and count, and right now I'm the only one here. Excuse me a minute." The woman put me on hold to answer another call.

I placed my hand over the phone's mouthpiece and whispered to Shirley, who was sitting on a chair next to the desk, assembling an airline crate. "They're at Friendship Animal Hospital, but the lady doesn't know how many there are. She is the only . . ." My sentence was cut short when I heard the voice on the other end ask, "Are you still there?"

"Yes," I assured her, anxious to get more information before we were interrupted by another call.

"Sorry I had to put you on hold," the woman said, sounding slightly overwhelmed, "but like I said, I'm the only one here right now. Dr. Miller is with the National Guard, and when the flooding started, he got called to help with the evacuations."

"You must have your hands full taking care of the shelter animals, on top of everything else," I concluded.

"Things aren't all that bad. With it flooding and the doctor not being here, a lot of our appointments got canceled, but the phones have been pretty busy. By the way, are you one of our clients?" the woman asked.

"No. My name is Terri Crisp and I'm the director of the Emergency Animal Rescue Service, from Sacramento, California. A team of trained volunteers and I are here because of the flood. When we heard that the animals from the shelter were moved, we wanted to find them so we could offer our help if it was needed."

"You came all the way from California?" the woman exclaimed.

"Yes," I responded, anxious to get back to my reason for calling. "So can we help in any way? There must be animals who need walking, cages or runs that need cleaning, and I suspect it must be getting close to feeding time." I fully expected the woman to interrupt me and say, "Great. When can you be here?" But she didn't.

"Well, that's real nice of you, but you shouldn't have to do that. We can take care of the animals." Before I could respond, she was interrupted by another call, which gave me a chance to think up another persuasive tactic. It wasn't that I didn't trust the woman. In her mind, I'm sure she thought the situation was under control. My concern was the result of conversations I'd had with people during previous disasters who thought the same thing, and when I checked things out myself, the situation turned out to be anything but okay. Somehow I suspected this was the case again.

"I'm back," the woman announced, and before she could say anything else, I jumped right in.

"I was wondering, where'd you find room to put all of the animals anyway?"

"Oh, they're out back," she replied, sounding confident that the accommodations for the animals were suitable.

I wondered what "out back" meant. Were the dogs tied up? Did the cats get put into some type of makeshift cages, or were animals sharing common space—maybe even running loose in a fenced area? With it still raining off and on, and the temperature brutally hot and humid, I hoped some type of protection was available for the animals. These questions gave me more reason to push for answers.

"So how are you keeping them confined?" I asked the woman.

"They're in the old kennel," she said, further explaining that at one time there had been a boarding facility behind the hospital, but it had not been used for that purpose in years.

"When animal control called and asked if we had room, the doctor said they could use the kennel. It's not in the best shape, but when the officers dropped the animals off, they thought it would work just fine."

"They must have been desperate."

"I know they were," the woman responded.

"I bet they couldn't bring any food, litter, or other supplies with them. From what I understand, they barely had
enough time to grab the animals."

"Right," the woman answered. "We've been using our
stuff."

"Well, why don't I bring you some food and litter? We've
had a lot donated and there are some cleaning supplies that
I'm sure you can use." This had to be an offer she could not
refuse, and if she accepted, it would get us in the front door
of the hospital, and maybe farther.

"I suppose that would be okay," the woman said, hesitantly. "I'd ask Dr. Miller first, but I'm not sure when he'll be
checking in. And I guess those animals are going to need
some more attention before long, considering we haven't
seen anyone from animal control since Wednesday and here it
is Friday already."

Before she could change her mind, I told her we were on
our way. I wanted to make sure the doctor didn't incur any
expense as a result of the shelter evacuees staying in the vacant kennel. If the animals became a problem, I feared what
the solution would probably be.

An hour later, six of us walked into the lobby of the
Friendship Animal Hospital, loaded down with bags of dog
and cat food, plastic jugs of litter, feeding dishes, and cleaning
supplies. Joining our team were Bobbie Thompson and some
other volunteers from the Animal Rescue Foundation in
Milledgeville, Georgia. We'd left a skeleton crew of volunteers at Humane Services to answer the phone and collect
more donated supplies.

The woman behind the counter at the hospital, whose
face I immediately matched with the voice on the phone,
seemed amazed that we actually showed up. I wondered if
her disbelief came from other offers of help that hadn't mate-
rialized, or it could have been that she wasn't quite sure how
to deal with the big responsibility that was dropped in her lap
and the sudden disruption it brought her routine.

"Hi, I'm Terri," I said, extending my hand in response to her welcome. "I'm afraid I didn't get your name when we were on the phone."

"Barbara Howell. And this is my daughter, Kim, who came to help me." She put her arm around the teenager standing next to her.

"So where do you want us to put this stuff," Shirley asked, once everyone had finished introducing themselves. Kim led us to a storage room that was nearly empty. Unless there was more food kept somewhere else, our reinforcements had arrived just in time. Making repeated trips to our vehicles, we were able to stock the room with more than enough supplies to take care of a lot of animals for at least a week.

"This is unbelievable," Barbara said to me after I dropped off my last load of food in the storage room and returned to the lobby. "One of your volunteers told me a little bit about EARS. What you do is great. I don't think animal control knows about you guys, but they should. Maybe if they had, they wouldn't have had to euthanize any of the animals."

"So animal control didn't get all the animals out of the shelter." I watched Barbara's face. The momentary glance down the hall, followed by a deep breath and sigh, confirmed we were headed into a conversation that neither one of us wanted to have, but I needed to know what had happened, and so did the volunteers.

"I heard they had 140 animals on the property when they realized the water was getting too close. If they didn't act fast, there was a good chance the animals would have drowned in their cages. That's how serious the situation had become. They had less than half an hour to do something, so the decision was made to euthanize the older, sick, and aggressive animals. The rest were moved," Barbara explained, as she picked up a pen and began to tap it against the wooden counter. I knew that if I could have seen her eyes, I would have seen them filled with tears.

In my head, I understood the selection process. The three officers, whose job it was to move the animals, were working against the clock, so of course they would be limited in what they could do. In my heart, it was hard to justify the decision. I couldn't help but feel how unfair it was to the animals. Once again, they were paying the price for people being unprepared. My only solace was knowing that none of the animals had been left behind, still alive, to drown in their cages. That would have been unforgivable.

"How did they end up bringing the animals here?" I asked, trying to distract myself from thinking about the animals who were either too old, too sick, or too mean to be saved.

"They loaded the animals in their trucks, cramming them in anywhere they could find room. There were even some big dogs riding shotgun. I would have liked to have seen them when they drove off. They must have looked like the modern-day version of Noah's Ark." Barbara laughed. The image brought a much-needed smile to my face, too.

"They already knew there were a lot of people in the community scrambling to find safe places for their own pets, so it wasn't going to be easy to find a place to put this new group of displaced animals." She motioned with her hand to a door at the end of the hall, behind which I could hear a chorus of barking dogs. "Heck, we were full up two days ago with animals who belong to some of our regular clients."

"So what did they do?"

"They drove to the nearest phone booth and, with their engines running so the air-conditioning would keep the animals cool, they started down the list of kennels and vet clinics in the Yellow Pages, hoping to find some space."

"And they got lucky and found this place," I interjected.

"Yeah, I don't know what they would have done if we couldn't have taken them. Maybe they'd still be driving around town with their trucks packed full of barking dogs and meowing cats."

Without saying it, I think we both knew that wouldn't have happened. Those animals would have run out of time, too.

"Did they give you any idea how long the animals might be here?" I asked, certain that no one knew.

"No," Barbara said, putting down the pen that she'd been tapping against the counter, so that she could reach for a Kleenex. "When they left here, I heard they got assigned indefinitely to distribute drinking water, since animal control is part of the police department, and that's one police responsibility. That means the city of Macon is without the services of animal control. And considering the shelter flooded, they'll have a mess to clean up before the place can reopen. So I don't know what's going to become of these animals."

As I listened to Barbara describe the situation, I glanced out the front window where Shirley and the volunteers were now sitting under a shady tree, anxiously awaiting further instruction. Seeing them, I realized again why they were so valuable. At a time when the animals' needs were so great, the people whose responsibility it was to take care of them were unable to do their job. If the volunteers were not willing to give so generously of their time, more animals would undoubtedly not survive this disaster.

"Did you have a chance to find out how many animals there are?" I asked, reaching for a bottle of water that I had set down in a chair earlier.

"My guess would be something close to 75."

"Are they mostly dogs or cats?" I asked, already knowing the answer.

"Dogs, mainly," she said, confirming my suspicion. "There's a couple of puppies, too, which the other vet tech and I brought into the hospital so we could treat them for coccidia. They were in pretty bad shape when they arrived, but they're doing much better now."

"Can I see the lucky survivors?" I asked, as I massaged my lower back. I was beginning to feel the physical effects of hauling 50-pound bags of pet food, and my emotions had already had a workout, too. After some quick calculations in my head, I figured as many as 65 animals could have been euthanized at animal control. I tried not to think how they had done it. Given the time limitations, I guessed the most efficient way was to inject them in their cages and then leave them where they dropped.

"Sure, I'll take you back there," Barbara replied. "Do your volunteers want to come, too?"

I knew they were just as anxious as I was to see the animals that we'd been waiting all morning to help, so I tapped on the window and signaled for them to come inside. Following Barbara, we walked single file through the door that she had pointed out to me earlier. As we continued on toward the back door, we passed cages containing evacuated dogs and cats who were fortunate to have owners who cared about them. These were ones we didn't have to worry about.

Stepping out on a cement driveway, we could see straight ahead a neglected cinder-block building. The roof was sheets of badly rusted corrugated metal, which had to make the inside of the building feel like an oven in the summer and a refrigerator in the winter. Some of the windows were broken and the ones with glass still in them were closed, most likely sealed shut with layers of paint that coated the wooden frames. The entrance door, having suffered the effects of being exposed to too much rain and changing temperatures, was warped and required a few hard tugs before Barbara was able to get it open. When the door finally relented, the nine of us quickly covered our noses and mouths with our hands to block out the nauseating stench.

Cautiously, we entered the dark building that housed the cats. The only light came through the front windows and some smaller, dirty windows at each end of the narrow room. As we waited for our eyes to adjust, we listened to the pitiful cries of the cats housed in wall-mounted wooden cages and some smaller metal ones, stacked in the leftover space. Each cage, meant to hold just one adult cat, contained two or three.

Taking a quick look around the room, I noticed to the right of the front door an elevated bathtub, designed for bathing animals. The white porcelain was a blend of green- and rust-colored stains. Above the tub was a shelf with an assortment of partially filled plastic bottles, their labels worn off from repeated exposure to the water. I assumed they contained pet shampoo. On a counter lining one wall, a dozen or so cans of cat food were haphazardly arranged, and on the floor next to the counter were several stacks of yellowed newspaper. Nowhere did I see any litter or litter boxes.

The only sound in the room was that of meowing cats, as all of us moved from cage to cage, reaching through the bars to touch the felines, who needed our affection as much as we needed to give it. Some of the cats responded with contented purrs, while others continued to meow loudly, voicing their discontent. A few cats stayed against the back of the cages, their big eyes watching our every move. They had decided not to trust us yet.

⤙⤚

IT WAS probably more shock than anything that left us speechless for those first minutes. I hoped the volunteers were remembering what I had told them at the workshop: "During a disaster, our focus is the animals. Period. It is not our job to judge."

Once again, this was not the time to point fingers and complain. Getting these animals taken care of was how we needed to direct *all* of our energy, and without a doubt that was the best thing we could do for those cats at that moment.

The uneasy silence, mixed with meowing cats and the sound of nearby barking dogs, was interrupted when Barbara's daughter Kim opened the hospital door and yelled to her mom that she had a phone call. Barbara excused herself, and we were left alone. Knowing the volunteers were ready to explode, I knew I better do some defusing once Barbara left. She'd given us permission to clean and feed, which was good.

"It's bad, no doubt about it, but it could be worse," I emphasized, as the volunteers turned to look at me, each face revealing their torment. "These cats are the lucky ones. They survived the cut and we *have* to focus on that."

"But there are too many cats in each cage," blurted out one volunteer. "And there aren't any litter boxes or food dishes," added another one. "But heck, where would you put them? There's no room." Her voice revealed her disgust.

I listened patiently to the group, while each of them voiced their anger, concerns, and deep-felt sadness. This was not fair to the animals, and all of us were struggling with the harshness of what we'd just walked into. The shock was harder on the volunteers, though. In other disasters, I had seen animals living in such pitiful conditions. The volunteers hadn't. For this reason, it was important for them to share their feelings and to hear collectively what everyone else was feeling. The exchange could not be allowed to get out of control, however. We had a job to do and, if we were going to do it well and be allowed to continue to take care of these cats, we needed to put our personal feelings aside temporarily.

It took some persuading, but the volunteers finally put their feelings on hold, and as a group, we agreed to tackle the mess. When they made the decision to become volunteers 67 days earlier, I'd warned them it wasn't always going to be easy. They now believed me.

"Okay, the four of you work in here," I said, feeling like a coach trying to rally her team when morale was down. "Shirley and I will be back to help as soon as we check on the dogs." Seeing the dogs right then would have been too much for the volunteers. They needed a little time to recover from the shock of finding the cats in the conditions they were in, and they also needed to feel the incredible satisfaction that would come from making that situation right. Once they felt that, I was confident they'd be ready for the dogs.

I paused for a minute in the doorway, listening to the volunteers discuss where to start. As their plan slowly began to take shape, I knew it was all right to leave them alone.

Stepping outside, Shirley and I breathed in the fresh air as we made our way toward the sound of the barking dogs behind the cats' building. Before we even reached the back of the building, our noses gave us the first hint of what we'd find when we turned the corner. It no longer smelled good outside. We paused to remove our bandannas from around our necks and used them to cover our noses and mouths. The stench was worse than what we'd had to breathe in the cat room.

The kennel was about the size of a three-car garage, completely enclosed with a chain-link fence, partially woven with vines. On the side closest to us were four long, narrow dog runs intended to hold one or two dogs. A center walkway separated these runs from a larger exercise area. On top of the structure was more rusted corrugated metal. The concrete slab floor was now covered with feces and urine.

It was difficult to count the moving dogs, ranging in size from a Yorkie mix to a hefty-sized Rottweiler. We counted 32 dogs divided among the four dog runs, and 18 in the exercise area. It was too many animals in too little space, but I had to remind myself that at least they were alive. We'd counted 31 felines in the cat room, so there were a total of 81 animals who'd survived this disaster so far. Barbara's earlier guess was close.

The excitement of having visitors caused a tangle of movement as the big dogs and the little dogs vied for a spot where they would be noticed and, if lucky, chosen to get a much-needed pat on the head. An occasional growl could be heard in the uproar, as one dog challenged another for a prized spot.

We were stunned by the conditions. "Oh my God!" was all I could say, when I finally sat down on a nearby dirt-covered cinder block. I pressed my bandanna closer to my face and realized the effort to block out the stench was pointless.

"There's not a one of them that's not covered in crap," Shirley said, standing frozen in the same spot. "And tell me, how are we going to get them all cleaned when there's no running water in the city of Macon right now?"

"Next downpour, we'll take them out, one by one, and let Mother Nature clean them up," I said, managing to find the energy to laugh. "It's what we did during Hurricane Andrew and it worked."

"Yeah, but dirt is a whole lot easier to wash off than caked-on dog crap," Shirley responded. "Do you know what we're going to smell like when we get done?"

"Crap," I said, as I stood up to go look for Barbara.

You'd have to be blind and have no sense of smell to think that these animals were being properly taken care of. I didn't blame Barbara, though. She'd already proven to me that she cared about the animals. One person would have had a hard time keeping up with the care of so many animals. When a person feels overwhelmed, one way to survive is to ignore the problem. Barbara's eyes were no longer closed. We'd made it okay for her to open them, by promising her we'd take care of the animals.

WHILE I went to K-Mart for some serious cleaning supplies, Shirley returned to the cat room to help the volunteers clean. I was right. It would have been too much, too soon, for the volunteers to see the dogs. Besides, we didn't have enough help to adequately tackle both the dog and cat area at the same time, so we decided we'd get rid of one mess before we moved on to the next.

This was a job that required a tremendous love for animals, and a strong stomach. The cleaning process was slow, delayed by everyone's need to go outside from time to time for air when they'd feel the dry heaves coming on. At no time did anyone complain though, or talk about quitting.

I returned from my shopping spree with a truckload of stuff, including waterproof overalls, knee-high rubber boots, ventilator masks, and latex gloves. These items became our official cleaning uniform. On my way to K-Mart, I had passed a shopping-center parking lot, where the National Guard had set up a public water-distribution site. This would become our source for water, which was far more reliable than Mother Nature. I assigned one of the volunteers to water hauling, and she made continuous trips in Shirley's truck from the hospital to the shopping center to fill up the plastic garbage cans I had bought.

I was pleased when I returned to the cat room to see the volunteers hard at work. They weren't saying much as they went about scrubbing, filling litter boxes, washing cats, scooping food into dishes, and cuddling the grateful cats in their arms. I was certain each of the volunteers had their own conversation going on in their head. Repetitious tasks give you time to think whether you want to or not. I wished that I could have heard their thoughts, but I knew there would be time later for them to tell me.

The system the volunteers had set up was working great. In the short time I had been gone, they had made steady progress, as they tackled one cage at a time. They were using the airline crates that we'd brought with us as temporary holding cages, so the dirty cats could be removed while volunteers pulled out the disgusting, wet, shredded newspaper and scrubbed and disinfected the filthy cages from top to bottom, bars included. Without a litter box, the cats had no choice but to use the floor of the cage. In such close quarters, they couldn't avoid stepping in the waste, so naturally everything in the cage, including the cats, ended up getting coated.

While one person was cleaning, two people struggled to bathe the cats, a job that resulted in a few scratches but, amazingly, no bites. The cats would probably have been a whole lot less cooperative if it weren't for the fact that they undoubtedly knew how badly they needed baths. Without any running water, all the rinsing had to be done with a plastic water jug, the top of which we'd sliced off. It took 25 to 30 scoops of water from the garbage can to bathe and rinse each cat completely.

While we were cleaning, Cindy Foster, an EARS volunteer from Athens, Georgia, arrived with more cages from her local humane society, so that each cat would have its own permanent cage, complete with a litter box plus a food and water dish. We also provided each cage with a fleece square, so each cat could lay on a soft surface. I'm sure they all felt as if they'd moved into a four-star hotel.

When we placed the last cat in her cage, we stepped back and looked at what we'd accomplished. The cats were no longer meowing loudly, begging to be removed from a dirty, overcrowded cage. Instead, the 31 cats were busy eating, drinking fresh water, grooming their clean fur, or sleeping, stretched out to take full advantage of the two fans we had directed at them. We guessed it was probably the first sleep they'd had in two days.

Barbara had come out to check on us several times while we were working, each time thanking us repeatedly for our help. One of the times she came out, I looked at my watch. It was already four o'clock.

"So when do you go home?" I asked Barbara, while I held a very relaxed and wonderful-smelling cat in my arms. "We still have to clean the area where the dogs are and that's going to take awhile."

"I talked to Dr. Miller and, first of all, he wanted me to thank you for all your help, and he said to keep the hospital open for as long as you need," Barbara said, reaching over and scratching the head of the cat in my arms. "As soon as I'm finished with the animals up front, I'll come back and help you guys."

"Great," I replied.

So our team grew by one. The extra person definitely came in handy once we started cleaning the dog area, which was an even bigger challenge than the cat room had been. We cleaned the dogs and the runs in much the same way as we had the cats. We emptied one of the runs by doubling up in another. We then cleaned the empty run, step one being to shovel out the piles of feces. Since the animals were stressed, many of them had the squirts, so step two was to pour buckets of water mixed with bleach on the concrete, followed by buckets of rinse water. We used push brooms to move the standing water and waste into the drains. It was a time-consuming, smelly, backbreaking process, but we did it, figuring if we didn't, who would? The look of relief on the dogs' faces kept us going.

While the cleaning was underway, we put a leash on the dogs, one by one, and led them to the cemented driveway where two volunteers washed the dogs, using the best-smelling, heaviest duty pet shampoo I could find at K-Mart. The dogs were a lot more cooperative than the cats had been.

"I want to know who's going to give *us* a bath when we're all through?" I overheard a volunteer ask, after an unwelcome shower of water from a shaking dog who was not even close to being clean yet.

"I've got a swimming pool," another volunteer offered. "When we leave here, we can go for a dip, clothes and all."

"Sounds good to me," I interjected. "I'd hate to be your pool man, though."

It was just after nine o'clock when we put the last clean dog back into a spotless run. We'd been at the hospital for 10 hours. We were a very smelly, soggy, bone-tired group, Barbara included, but we were still able to find enough energy to say good-night to the animals, one at a time. They thanked us with wonderful, juicy kisses. We were really dragging as we walked to the parking lot, some of us realizing for the first time that we hadn't eaten all day. The last of our energy had been spent on the dogs though, so food would have to wait until tomorrow.

"Thank you," I said to the volunteers, after they'd pulled off their overalls and boots, thrown them in the back of Shirley's truck, and found a spot to sit on the parking-lot curb. As I stood in front of them, a mixture of fatigue and emotions made it hard to get more words out. "This is the way it should be," I managed to say. "Good people doing good things for animals. You saved these animals' lives."

"We couldn't have done it without you," Amy said. "You brought us together, which has allowed all of us to make a difference, so we should be thanking you."

I was touched by Amy's kind words, and all I could say in response was, "There are 81 animals that are really glad that *all* of us were here today."

———

AS WE said our good-byes before heading home for some well-deserved sleep, there were hugs, tears, and more thank-yous. We would all be back in this same parking lot in less than eight hours for a repeat of what we'd done that day. Only this time, the job would be easier.

When I crawled into bed that night, I felt good in spite of how difficult the day had been physically. What we had accomplished brought comfort that compensated for the soreness, but I knew the relief was only temporary. We'd made a difference for the shelter animals. For a few minutes, I allowed myself to think only about them, but I could not ignore for long the fact that they were not the only animals that would need our help.

On our way back to Shirley's house, we had listened with interest to the news updates on the radio. Alberto had been tough on Macon, but it sounded as though there were areas that were in for a lot worse, especially a town called Bainbridge, located in the southwestern part of the state. Water from up north was headed toward this community of 27,000 people, unfortunate enough to be located right on the Flint River.

"Evacuations have been ordered and officials predict that the river will be at least 20 feet above flood stage," the reporter warned. "It's going to be bad."

If it was going to be as bad as they thought, we'd be there—for the animals.

CHAPTER THREE

Moving Ahead

SATURDAY MORNING, we had the luxury of sleeping until six o'clock, but it still took three cups of strong coffee to get me moving. While I laced up my work boots, I watched the morning news. The predictions we'd listened to the night before on the truck's radio had been accurate, but now the anticipated crest of the Flint River was 48 feet above flood stage rather than 20. That was a whole heck of a lot of water.

As Shirley and I drove to the Friendship Animal Hospital, we debated whether to stay in Macon or take the volunteers and head to Bainbridge. Since the water was already starting to recede along the Ocmulgee River, we decided to relocate to Bainbridge. The volunteers from Milledgeville had offered the night before to continue caring for the animals at the hospital for as long as we needed them to. We decided to take them up on their offer, which would free us up to leave.

Our plan was to spend the morning taking care of the animals at the hospital, then return to Humane Services to pack up the supplies we'd need and leave for Bainbridge first thing in the morning.

When we walked into the hospital lobby, Barbara greeted us with some good news. Dr. Miller had arranged with the local fire department to have one of their trucks come by the hospital, starting the next day, to provide on-site water until the city water was turned on again. Eliminating the repeated trips to get water from the National Guard would save time and reduce the number of volunteers needed to keep up with the cleaning.

The dogs and cats were really excited to see us as we stood outside their cages getting dressed in our cleaning outfits. We were pleased to see that the desperate, worn-out expressions we'd seen on their faces less than 24 hours earlier were gone. On our way to the hospital, Shirley and I had stopped to pick up some more donations that had been dropped off at Humane Services. We arrived this time with treats and toys, which we divided among the eager animals. It was great to watch them playing and behaving as though they no longer had a care in the world.

It took a mere three hours to clean both the dog and cat areas and give everyone their breakfast. This was a big improvement over the 10 hours it had taken the day before. Barbara helped us when she could, but she and the other veterinary technician were busy up front as people began to come back to retrieve their pets. These were the lucky folks, whose homes the Ocmulgee River had not touched. With fewer animals in the hospital and the other technician back at work, Barbara said she'd have more time to help the volunteers with the daily cleaning and care. Knowing this made it easier for us to move on.

After we'd been hard at work for an hour, Barbara found me in the kennel where I was playing tug-of-war with a toy I'd given to a Shepherd mix. "Guess who just called?" she asked.

"I don't know," I responded, as I ended the game with the dog so he could return to his run for a big drink of water, something I realized I needed, too.

"One of the animal control officers."

"Really," I said, wiping the sweat from my forehead. It was not quite 10 o'clock and already it had to be 95 degrees.

"He wanted to know how the animals were, and he also apologized for not being able to come back to help take care of them. He said it would probably be a couple more days before he and the other two officers were released from their water duties."

"Did he say whether they'd been by the shelter to see what kind of damage was done?"

"He said they hadn't, but he didn't expect it to be too bad. He guessed it would only take a day or two to clean it up. And just before he hung up," Barbara said with a grin, "he offered to try and make it by to help with the cleaning. I was happy to be able to say that wouldn't be necessary. When I told him you were here and we had all these volunteers helping, he was pleased."

"Good," I said, glad that our help was taking some of the pressure off the animal control officers.

When we had finished the cleaning, we said our good-byes to the animals to whom we'd become very attached. We knew that until animal control was ready to return them to the shelter, they would be well cared for and spoiled. What would happen to them after that depended a lot on luck, something these animals seemed to have. There were some great dogs and cats in the group, so we had to hope that people looking to adopt a pet would see this too and give them a new, permanent place to live.

"Well, it's been a pleasure," I said to Barbara, as we stood alone in the lobby of the hospital. "Thank you for letting us help."

"I don't know what I would have done if all of you hadn't shown up." She paused, and took a deep breath. "I'm afraid I would have ended up letting the animals down, and that would have killed me."

"You did good," I said, as I gave Barbara a hug. "And I can't imagine you ever letting an animal down."

"Thanks," she said, as her eyes filled with tears.

We estimated that it would take us four to five hours to reach Bainbridge, still getting us there before the water that was headed their way. Accompanying Shirley and me on the journey would be Diane, Amy, Cindy, Donna, Terry (Donna's boyfriend), and Warner Robins' animal control officer Greg Langston. The city had agreed to loan Greg to us for a week. In addition, Wendy Borowsky, an EARS coordinator and a veteran of the floods in the Midwest the previous summer, had flown in from St. Louis, Missouri, after Deanna said I could ask her to join us. She'd more than compensate for not having as many trained volunteers as I'd liked to have had.

We gathered at Shirley's shelter in Warner Robins just after 5 A.M., did some last-minute loading of supplies that she had collected, and then decided on the caravan order for our five trucks. Shirley and I would take the lead and Greg would bring up the rear. In between would be Diane's truck with a camper on the back, Terry's truck pulling a flat-bottom boat, Amy's truck with a load of dog and cat food, and a third truck, which had been loaned to Cindy by Hugh's Acura dealership in Athens, filled with cages. We lined up and pulled out of the shelter driveway at exactly 6 A.M., our first stop: Thomasville, Georgia.

⌒

THE PREVIOUS afternoon we'd received a phone call at Humane Services from Laura Bevans, southeast regional director for the Humane Society of the United States (HSUS). Shirley and I had worked with Laura during Hurricane Andrew and had been in touch on and off since then. Laura was calling from Albany; she was with Nick Gilman from the American Humane Association (AHA), another veteran of Andrew. We could hear the desperation in her voice as she described the worsening situation. Before the conversation ended, she asked for our help. We agreed to meet with her and Nick on our way to Bainbridge.

It wasn't quite yet 11 o'clock when we pulled into the parking lot of the Shoney's restaurant on Highway 19 in Thomasville, our rendezvous spot. This was going to be the first time that the three groups, HSUS, AHA, and EARS, would meet during a disaster to determine how to distribute our resources better. During the previous year, I had met with representatives from the two organizations several times to work on a plan that would facilitate us working together during a disaster. I was hopeful that our first attempt to do this would be the start of a tradition.

Over lunch, we decided that Nick would return up river to Albany to work with the local humane society, and EARS, along with HSUS, would position ourselves in Bainbridge, which had not yet flooded, but was still expecting a 48-foot crest within the next few days.

"Is there any kind of animal shelter in Bainbridge?" I asked Laura, as we began to figure out what we were going to do once we got there.

"Yes, there's a small animal control shelter. Actually, it's referred to as the pound. In fact, a sign near the front door says, "This pound is for city animals only.""

"Meaning it may not be an adequate facility?" I questioned.

"Right," Laura responded. "Plus, it's sitting dangerously close to the river, which is the reason the animals have already been removed."

"Where did they take them?" Shirley asked.

"The one animal control officer, whose nametag reads 'Dogcatcher,' opened the cages and shooed the animals out the front door. It was all she could do before she got assigned to other duties with public safety."

"Is there a county shelter?" I asked, trying not to think about the freed animals. I tried to convince myself that letting them go was definitely better than leaving them to drown in their cages, but trying to survive on their own during a flood would be hard.

"No, the city shelter is all there is," Laura said.

"Well, then it looks like we are definitely going to be busy." I pushed back my chair. "I suggest we get over there and see what's going on."

Our first stop in Bainbridge was the emergency operations center, located at a fire station just off Shotwell Street. Before Laura and I went in to talk with the director of public safety, I divided the EARS volunteers into two groups and instructed them to scout the neighborhoods that were expected to flood. On two maps that I had obtained at the command center, I highlighted the areas I wanted each team to cover. For future rescues in these areas, it would make it easier for the volunteers to find their way around if they'd seen the neighborhoods before they disappeared under water.

As they drove around, I wanted them to talk to the people, find out who had animals, and what their plans were for them if they had to evacuate. If a person didn't know what they were going to do with their pets, the volunteers were to hand them my business card, which had the 800 number for United Animal Nations (UAN) in Sacramento on it, so the people would have a way to reach us later and find out where we'd set up the temporary shelter.

After the two teams departed with Shirley in charge, Laura and I went to find Larry Funderburke, the public safety director, who we hoped would welcome our assistance. We didn't have to wait long to see him, and were immediately pleased by his enthusiastic response to our offer of help.

"The experts are predicting the floodwaters will encircle the city, cutting it off from the county, and once that happens, people and supplies will not be easily moved back and forth," Larry explained, pointing to the areas involved on a large map tacked to the wall. "Here in the city, there will be plenty of resources, but the county will not be so lucky. Out there, people are going to have to be self-sufficient."

A man from the Red Cross momentarily interrupted Larry to let him know they'd just had to open a second evacuation shelter.

"Now where was I?" Larry asked, as he refocused his attention on the map. "Oh yeah, so what makes sense to me is to have two shelters set up for the animals, one in the city and one in the county."

"Any idea where we might be able to set up these shelters?" I asked.

"Here in the city, the old K-Mart building can be used. It's been vacant for some time, but the outside garden area would work quite well for housing animals, I imagine." He looked at Laura and me for acknowledgment.

We agreed it sounded perfect.

"The area is enclosed with a sturdy chain-link fence, and I can easily get the water and electricity turned on. Whoever sets up there can stay at the YMCA. It's not the Hilton, but they do have a swimming pool and a spa, which would feel real good at the end of a long, hot day."

"We'll take the city," Laura volunteered immediately.

Knowing EARS was prepared to face the challenges of opening a shelter in the county, I eagerly accepted the other choice. Larry referred me to Kenny King, his counterpart at the other emergency operations center, which was set up at the Decatur County Fire and Rescue off Highway 84 on a street called Fourth Ramp. "Follow the signs to the airport, and you'll know you've made it when you see the water tower, which is in a field across from the airport," Larry instructed. "The fire station is at the airport."

"Do you have any idea where we might set up a shelter in the county?" I asked, while Laura went to find the bathroom.

"That fenced-in field across from the fire station might be suitable for a temporary shelter," he said, "but Kenny will have to let you know if it's available."

Before we left, Larry promised he'd let everyone at the afternoon command briefing know about both organizations, and he'd do everything he could to get the same information to the people in the community who might need our help.

Laura and I parted company in the parking lot of the emergency operations center, agreeing to stay in touch and offer whatever assistance we could to the other. With over an hour to wait until the volunteers returned from their scouting mission, I decided to use the phone booth I had spotted across the street and get caught up with my calls. The first one was to Deanna at home.

"So we have the county," I told Deanna, concluding my full update on the activities of the last two days. "It was obvious Laura wanted the city, which is okay because I would have asked for the county anyway, since EARS has a whole lot more experience at setting up and running temporary shelters." I used my shirtsleeve to wipe the sweat from my forehead. "I suspect we're going to be working in some pretty primitive conditions."

"Do you think you'll have running water or electricity?" Deanna asked.

"I doubt it, but we've worked around these obstacles before, so we can do it again." Of course, no electricity meant no air-conditioning, which would have felt real good when it got to be 98 degrees in the middle of the afternoon.

"How are you doing on money?" Deanna asked.

I quickly summarized what I had spent so far, the biggest expense after my airline ticket being my shopping trip to K-Mart. What it was going to cost to set up and run a temporary shelter was guesswork at that point, but I did have a pretty good idea of what we would need, and I was certain that a lot of it we could get from donations. What I was more concerned about was getting some additional help. That I couldn't buy at K-Mart.

"Can I bring Dara Hoffman down from St. Louis?" I asked Deanna, as we began to discuss my need for more people. Dara had proved her value when we worked together the previous summer during the Midwest floods, after which I had asked her to become an EARS coordinator.

"Yes, she can come," Deanna agreed. "And there's someone else who wants to come and help, too."

"Who?" I asked, trying to guess.

"Pam De La Bar from the Cat Fanciers' Association," Deanna explained. "CFA will buy her ticket from San Antonio and rent her a car, plus they're sending a check to help cover some more of the expenses we'll have."

"Great! Tell her to get here ASAP," I responded. "And tell her to bring as many wire collapsible cages as she can."

Following my conversation with Deanna, I got hold of Dara.

"Are you ready to rescue some more animals?" I asked, when I heard her voice on the line.

"Sure!" was her immediate response.

I instructed her to book a flight to Tallahassee, which was a lot closer to Bainbridge than Atlanta, and once she got there to rent some kind of four-wheel-drive vehicle.

"How will I find you?" she asked.

"Get a map and head north. Once you get to Bainbridge, follow the signs to the airport and you'll see, and probably hear us, right across the road."

My next call was to Ken, who I hadn't talked to since I had left Denver.

"Hi," I said, when I heard his voice, competing with the sound of cartoons in the background. "How are you?"

"Fine," he responded. "How are you doing?"

"Okay. I have some terrific volunteers and that *really* helps. It sure beats doing this by myself."

"Where are you?"

"I'm sure you've never heard of it, but I'm in Bainbridge, Georgia."

"Doesn't sound like a vacation destination to me," Ken said with a laugh.

"You're right. It's not Vail," I said, remembering the wonderful place where I'd been just three days before.

"When are you coming home?" Ken asked, no longer needing to compete with the TV that he'd turned off, much to Amy and Megan's annoyance.

"I'm not sure," I answered, which Ken was used to hearing.

We spent the next 20 minutes on the phone, updating each other on what our last few days had been like. Mine had definitely been hard, but Ken didn't have it easy either. Taking care of three girls while trying to work full time was no easy job, but he never complained, which was one of the reasons I loved him so much. I got to talk with the girls, too, and all they wanted to know was how many animals I was bringing home.

"None!" was Ken's immediate response in the background.

With no one else to call, I walked back to the emergency operations center, thinking how nice it would be to find a quiet spot and take a nap. I had noticed a pot of coffee in the fire station kitchen earlier, so I helped myself. It was just the boost I needed. While I sipped the strong coffee and waited for Shirley and the volunteers to return, I sat in a folding chair I found in a corner and watched the commotion around me. There were a lot of important people, busy doing all kinds of important things. To the casual observer, however, it might have looked as though no one knew what they were doing, but I knew better. It was organized chaos, something I would be experiencing soon.

We ended up assembling our shelter in a treeless, fenced-in lot about the size of two football fields lined up side by side. The area was a patchwork of grass parched by the summer sun, and asphalt scarred by cracks with weeds growing out of them. To the right of the property was a municipal golf course, and to the left, a cluster of single-story wooden buildings surrounded by a tall barbwire-topped chain-link fence. Behind us was a dense line of trees. According to Kenny King, the Decatur County Fire and Rescue department had at one time used this property for training exercises.

As I stood at the gated opening surveying the piece of land for the first time, it reminded me of the horse pasture where we had set up the "MASH" unit during Hurricane Andrew to care for the animals from that disaster, only this was much larger. Remembering how a whole group of dedicated people had transformed that empty horse pasture into a shelter for animals, I knew it could be done again. Even in its primitive state, this field had endless possibilities. There was room for hundreds of animals, including livestock, if they needed a place to stay.

"Will it work?" Kenny King asked, when I found him back at the county fire station, sipping a tall glass of iced tea.

"We'll take it," I said, as I shook his hand. "It's perfect!"

Our team of nine spent the rest of the afternoon building our shelter from the ground up. With the approval of the emergency operations center, the National Guard loaned to us a 30-foot-by-30-foot tent. Much to our relief, the tent came with five guys to put it up. We decided to use it to house the cats and the supplies it would take to care for them.

At K-Mart I had purchased a 20-foot-by-20-foot tent, which became our command center. Within a couple of hours after our arrival, a man named Doug Brandt had arrived to set us up with a phone, a convenience we had not expected. It was Kenny King who saw to it that we would have a reliable way to communicate, and it wasn't long before people knew to call 246-9887 if they had an animal problem. We would coordinate animal intake from this tent as well, because we were limited in space that was protected from the wind and rain, two things that can quickly ruin paperwork!

Donna and Terry had brought their bright yellow and green, two-room camping tent that became home to them and three other volunteers. In the front room, we stashed most of our equipment that needed protection from the rain. In the back room, we lined up the cots that the Red Cross had loaned to us. Diane had brought her camper, which was where she and Wendy would sleep, along with hundreds of small black ants who decided that it was their home, too. Shirley and I shared a smaller dome tent that we set up next to the command center so we could be close to the phone if it rang after everyone went to bed—which it did.

"Where are we going to put the dogs?" Amy asked. Four of us were struggling to figure out how to put up the two-room tent; the instructions had been lost two camping trips before, according to Donna.

"We'll do what we did during Hurricane Andrew," I replied, just as I found two support poles that actually fit together. "The chain-link perimeter fence is in good shape, so we'll tether the dogs to it, and then fasten a tarp to the fence with metal shower-curtain rings and stake the other side to the ground. Each dog will have his own lean-to, which will protect him from the sun and the rain. After we get this tent put together, if we ever do, we'll start on the dog area."

It was after dark when we realized we had done as much as we could for one day. We had accomplished a great deal in just six hours, including getting the two-room tent put together, thanks to the National Guard guys who gave us a crash course in tent construction. I knew everyone was hungry, so I sent Shirley and Wendy into town to see what they could scrounge up from the Red Cross. They returned with a stack of Styrofoam containers, each containing a scoop of cold green beans and a mound of macaroni and cheese, plus warm fruit cocktail, all staples of a disaster diet. To drink, there was good ol' Southern iced tea, with enough sugar in it to make it taste like syrup. I opted for a can of warm Coke.

Following our flashlight-illuminated dinner, Shirley and I made one last trip across the road to use the men's bathroom at the fire station. As we waited for a guy to finish up in the bathroom, we watched the news on TV, which we hadn't seen since the previous morning at Shirley's house. All the rain that had fallen up north was still flowing straight toward Bainbridge, and was expected to arrive by this time the next day. We'd have to hustle our butts off the next day to be ready for the animals that were about to be moved from their homes. I wondered how many of them we'd have to take care of.

Shirley and I said good-night to the volunteers when we got back from the fire station. With everything secured for the night, we disappeared into our tent. Still in our shorts, sweat-soaked T-shirts, and muddy boots, we collapsed on our narrow, squeaky cots. It felt so good to lie down.

"Do you feel like we're back in Hurricane Andrew?" I asked Shirley.

"In a way, but in that disaster we were never in bed before midnight," she said, laughing.

"Yeah, but somehow I think bedtime will come a lot later tomorrow night once we have animals to take care of."

Neither one of us spoke after that. I think it was the anticipation of how much work we had ahead of us that made the thought of sleep that much more inviting. With my eyes closed, I listened to the chatter in the tent next door. Our neighbors had no idea what they were in for over the course of the next few days. If they did, they would have been just as silent as Shirley and me. The last thing I remember hearing before I dozed off was the sound of a mosquito buzzing around my ear.

CHAPTER FOUR

Coming Together

YOGI WAS the first animal to come through our front gate. She belonged to a family to whom the volunteers had talked the day before when they had been driving through the neighborhoods closest to the Flint River.

"I called your 800 number in California and they said to bring my dog here," the woman said, as she handed the leash with the brown-and-white Springer Spaniel on the other end to Wendy. "You promise me you'll take good care of her."

"She'll be in good hands, I promise," Wendy replied, as the woman and her five children bent down and each gave Yogi a kiss on her nose.

When Yogi arrived, we were as ready as we were ever going to be, so it was time to hang up the "United Animal Nations Disaster Relief Services" vinyl banner, along with the set of 12 informational signs that instructed the public in big bold red letters: Incoming Animals, Animal Food/Supply Distribution, Foster Information, Volunteer Sign In, and so on. I'd had these signs made up following the floods in the Midwest when I realized how important it was to provide disaster victims with easy-to-read and understandable signs that would point them in the right direction when they walked into our temporary shelter. When the signs went up, the community knew we were "open for business."

Our next arrivals that Monday morning were four boisterous Coonhounds who belonged to Tommy, an 80-year-old Georgia native. He had told the volunteers the day before, "If I has to, I'll put my rocker on the roof, along with my dogs, and let God decide what happens. I ain't going to leave them alone. They's all the kin I've got left."

The volunteers gave Tommy my business card, too, and told him that he and his dogs would be a lot better off not sitting on his roof, watching the flood rise around him. If he brought us his dogs for safekeeping, he could then go stay at the Red Cross shelter. This gentle man, who so loved his dogs, had obviously decided this was the smart thing to do.

By 8 A.M., our population included nine mosquito-bitten, sunburned volunteers and the five animals who had been entrusted to our care. For three hours prior to their arrival we had worked our tails off getting the shelter ready. One of my jobs was to call Larry Funderburke in town to give him the exact location of our shelter so that he could pass the information along at the morning command briefing. I followed that call with one to the local radio station, so they could put on the air information pet owners needed to know. The most important message: *Animals left behind in a disaster may not still be alive when you return, so don't leave home without them.*

For the rest of the morning, there was a steady procession of people pulling up to our front gate in cars and trucks packed full with precious belongings they had chosen to remove from homes that were already filling up with water. Often seated on the laps of their owners were the dogs and cats who mattered enough to be evacuated, too. Volunteers were at the gate to welcome all our guests who needed as much TLC as their animals. The look of disbelief on their faces was the first reaction to the effect this disaster was having on their lives.

Wendy and Diane worked in Animal Intake, which was where each arriving animal was taken. Before the owner left, they completed paperwork on each pet, so we would have all the details we needed to ensure that when it came time for the animals to go back home, they'd leave with the right person. They also took a Polaroid picture of the animal with the owner for the same reason. To complete the intake process, Wendy or Diane put a temporary collar and ID tag with the pet's intake number written on it on each pet.

Intake then handed the excited dogs over to Amy or Donna, and they would find a completed lean-to along the fence and tether them. Cindy took the cats and got them settled in cages inside the tent on loan from the National Guard. Meanwhile, Greg, Terry, and Shirley were trying to stay one step ahead of the housing needs, assembling cages for the cats and securing tarps to the perimeter fence to create more lean-tos for the dogs. The latest report we'd heard was that the water was still rising, so we were expecting a lot more animals to arrive; therefore, my job was to get on the phone and get more help. Dara was the first of the reinforcements to arrive.

"You found us," I said, throwing my arms around Dara's neck as she stepped out of her rental car. "Boy, is it good to see you."

"I can't believe I made it," Dara said, brushing her wind-blown hair out of her eyes. "It poured almost the entire way. I kept thinking to myself, *The road's going to flood and I'm going to get swept away.* I kept saying out loud, over and over, 'Okay, God, keep me safe for the animals.'"

We were lucky to have stayed dry so far, but the sky to the southwest was beginning to indicate that was about to change. Quickly, I showed Dara around, introducing her to everyone, animals included. I told each of the volunteers as I made the introductions to get everything that shouldn't get wet covered up. It was time to batten down the hatches. This would become our routine every afternoon between three and four o'clock as that day's thunderstorm passed overhead, bringing with it buckets of water, something this community did not need any more of.

We survived our first thunderstorm, which stayed for an hour and then left as quickly as it had arrived. It actually felt good to get drenched. The moisture cooled us off, and the dogs seemed to enjoy the break from the heat, too, getting soaked as they stood next to their lean-tos instead of seeking cover under the tarps.

As I waited out the storm inside the command tent, hoping we had hammered the stakes far enough into the ground for the tent to stand up to the wind, I watched an expanding puddle form around my boots from the water dripping off my sopping wet clothes. The dirty jeans I had tossed into my duffel bag in Vail were finally getting washed, thanks to Mother Nature. This was not the first time I had appreciated her help with my laundry. Using my wet T-shirt sleeve, I removed the drops of water cascading off my nose, but my drenched hair continued to supply more annoying droplets, so I just gave up.

"This is not going to be a good hair day," Dara announced, as she pulled back the tent flap, joining me inside.

"Yep," I replied. "Ain't none of us going to want to look in a mirror for a while."

The phone rang. I reached across the two aluminum folding tables, which were the centerpiece of the tent, careful not to let any drops of water fall on the pile of animal intake forms that Wendy had brought inside and dumped on the desk for safekeeping. I'd be in big trouble if I ruined her paperwork.

"Emergency Animal Rescue Service. Can I help you?" I said, working my way around the table to an ice chest, which was our only chair in the tent.

It was Kenny King calling. "Just wanted to make sure you guys were okay over there," he said.

"We're fine. Now that we've had a shower, we're real happy campers."

"If y'all want a hot shower instead, you're more than welcome to use the one here at the fire station," Kenny offered.

"That would be real nice," I said, looking at Dara. "I think all of us will be ready for a real shower in a day or two."

The smile on Dara's face confirmed the truth of this.

"The other reason I called was that the Red Cross came by earlier to let us know they're going to be coming by the command center, starting tomorrow, to drop off meals for us. I asked if they could also swing by and feed all of you, too."

"That would be great." The mention of food made me realize that I hadn't had anything to eat since the night before, aside from a bag of sunflower seeds.

"If there's anything else you need, let me know," Kenny offered.

"There is one thing," I said, wasting no time. "Any chance we could get a port-a-john so we don't have to keep running to the fire station?"

"I'll see what I can do."

Peak's Septic Tank Service from Climax, Georgia, delivered our port-a-john the next morning and showed up every day after that to service it, much to everyone's delight.

The relief the rain had brought from the heat was short-lived. Once the sun came out again, we were back to working in a sweatbox that seemed hotter and muggier than before. We needed more shade in the field, but the National Guard could not spare any more tents. This essential commodity got moved to the top of our growing wish list. First thing the next morning, we'd have to go do some more shopping.

⌒

LEAVING WENDY in charge, Dara, Shirley, and I drove into town to be at the stores when they opened. Shirley had some ideas as to where she might be able to get a tent or two, so she went off in her truck. Dara and I, in her rented four-wheel drive, went to the new K-Mart store. We bought lanterns, propane canisters, citronella candles, toilet paper, sunscreen, dog chains, metal shower-curtain rings, rope, buckets, two more ice chests, individual bottles of drinking water, and a battery-operated weather radio so we could get updates on the flood and warnings of any storms headed our way. The store manager noticed our EARS vests and, after asking us what we did, gave us a 25 percent discount on everything we bought.

"K-Mart is helping out the people," he said. "I think we should help the animals, too."

With Dara's car packed full, we made one last stop before we left town. We found the old K-Mart store, so we could check to see how Laura and her team were doing setting up the city shelter. She told us they had not received any animals yet, primarily because they were still trying to round up more cages and volunteers. Several humane societies were going to send some of their staff, but they hadn't arrived yet. We couldn't stay long because we had enough to do ourselves but, before we left, I told Laura, "Holler if you need any help."

When we got back to the field, we saw that more animals had arrived in our absence. Our population as of Tuesday morning had grown to 29 dogs and 9 cats, all of whom had been brought to us by owners fleeing the tide of floodwater. The time the volunteers spent on Sunday talking to people as they were preparing to evacuate had paid off. It made me wonder how many of these animals might have been left behind if we had not been there to give their owners an alternative.

"Guess what I found?" Shirley announced as I walked into the command tent, with stuffed K-Mart bags hanging off each of my sunburned arms.

"I hope you're going to tell me a tent," I said, handing to Wendy three of the bags that contained the office supplies she had requested.

"You guessed it, but they aren't enclosed tents. They're the awning type, but I thought they'd work just fine."

"How many did you get?" I asked with growing excitement.

"Six!" Shirley beamed.

"Where did you find six tents?"

"You'd never guess where they're coming from," Shirley said, her laughter confirming she was just as amazed as I was probably going to be. "Would you believe two of the funeral homes in town?"

"You're kidding!"

"Nope. The ones from the Cooper Funeral Home will be delivered at two o'clock and the people from Ivey will be here to set up theirs before four o'clock. And each of the six tents are 20 feet by 20 feet, so we have ourselves a whole bunch of shade now."

"How'd you get them?"

"I was on my way to a rental company to see if maybe they'd loan us one of those big white party tents, but when I passed the cemetery, I had a change in plans."

"Great job," I said, giving Shirley a hug. I knew where she had learned to be so resourceful. It was an essential skill that both of us had depended on during Hurricane Andrew.

Our next newcomer was Pam De La Bar. She arrived with the collapsible cat cages I had requested, and the names and phone numbers of several cat fancier clubs in Georgia who she thought for certain would loan us some of the cages that they used to house felines during cat shows. Her rental car was a mini cattery, stuffed full of other items we needed, such as disposable litter boxes (compliments of Johnny Cat), something we were really needing.

"Good to see ya," I said, giving Pam a hug. The last time I had seen her was 25 days earlier at the Cat Fanciers' annual meeting in Traverse City, Michigan. Pam had invited me to give a talk to the general assembly on disaster preparedness, followed by a condensed version of the EARS workshop for a smaller group of participants. When we parted company in Michigan, little did we know that our paths would be crossing again so soon, and that the reunion would take place in a town of which neither one of us had ever heard.

"This place is amazing," Pam said, as she surveyed the property. "Do you have any cats yet?"

"I think there are nine," I informed her. "But let's go see. I'm sure you're anxious to get busy taking care of them and I know that Cindy, one of the trained EARS volunteers, will be pleased to see you. She's been staying real busy trying to keep the cats cooled down."

I left Pam in the cat tent, confident that the kitties were in the hands of an expert who would do a super job of taking care of them. As I walked back to the command tent, I thought to myself, *This is really working.*

When I came through the tent opening, Dara was seated on the ice chest at the aluminum table, talking on the phone. I could see that she was filling out a "Request for Rescue" form, the person on the other end of the phone providing the information.

"Can you give me some kind of landmark that you think might still be visible above the water? Like a billboard, the color of a two-story house, a distinct-looking tree tall enough to still be seen," Dara asked. Having been responsible for rescuing many animals during the floods in the Midwest, Dara knew the right questions to ask. She had learned during that disaster that street signs and house numbers are not always going to be visible, so landmarks become your backup when trying to find the property where stranded animals are located.

"Okay, that's great," she said. "We'll send someone out this afternoon to get your cat."

And so the rescues began.

Most of the 129 animals that we ended up taking care of arrived during the first four days our shelter was set up. Owners brought the majority of them to us; the rest we rescued. Many of the rescued animals were not ones that someone had called and asked us to go get. We found them by accident.

Shirley, Terry, Dara, and Greg made up our first rescue team. They took the "Request for Rescue" form that Dara filled out, and with Terry's boat in tow, pulled out of the gate early Tuesday afternoon in hopes of finding a black and white kitten named Sylvester.

While they were gone, I had two very important jobs to do. First I had to find a veterinarian for us. Already the volunteers were reporting that some of the animals had diarrhea and there was a mixed Collie that I noticed had not eaten since she was brought in. Using the Yellow Pages the phone man had given us, I started calling the local veterinarians. It was Dr. Ed Height who ended up treating most of our animals at his clinic. The doctors and staff were great, often seeing injured and sick animals on very short notice.

In addition to him, Drs. Larry Helm and Kitty Remington came to the shelter and donated their time, giving vaccinations, doing routine exams on each animal, and treating minor medical problems, such as ear mites and skin irritations. It was Dr. Helm who figured out why the Collie mix was not eating. When he examined her, he discovered a twig in the roof of her mouth, wedged between her teeth. Once the twig was removed, she made a real pig of herself.

To help pay for some of the more serious medical problems and injuries that the animals sustained as a result of the flood, EARS volunteer Lisa Yackel, who worked as the office manager for Dr. Case in Savannah, facilitated a donation from the Georgia Veterinary Medical Association. Since the EARS disaster fund was quickly dwindling, we greatly appreciated the donation.

With the animals' medical needs taken care of, I still had one more very important job to do before I got back to the other tasks that were on my very long "to do" list. I had to find us another source of water. There were no spigots in our field, so the National Guard was supplying us with gallon jugs of water that we stored under one of the tents. The dog tied nearby liked this setup, since he chose to lay on top of the water bottles to stay cool. We had to have a better solution for our water needs, though. We emptied the jugs too fast when the water was being used for both drinking and cleaning. In addition, it was becoming a waste management nightmare dealing with the growing pile of empty jugs. I had asked the man who brought us the water if the Guard had a water buffalo, which is what they call a water truck, that they could park at the shelter. Unfortunately, the few they had were already being used.

While I was on the phone with Dr. Height, Wendy placed a scrap of paper in front of me that read, "Someone named Ollie Brown is waiting outside to talk with you when you get off the phone. He says it's important." Five minutes later, I walked out of the command tent to find out what Ollie Brown needed.

"Hi, I'm Terri. Can I help you?"

"Hi," he responded. "Actually, I'm here to see if I can help you. I'm the facilities manager for Industrial Park."

On either side of Fourth Ramp, the road leading to our shelter, were warehouse-type buildings that housed a variety of businesses. Ollie explained that it was his job to maintain the exteriors of these buildings and the surrounding landscape, all of which belonged to Industrial Park.

"I have a lot of resources at my disposal and I thought you might be able to use some of them. I love animals and I'd like to help you out," Ollie offered.

"Do you know where I can get a continuous supply of water, instead of what we're getting delivered in gallon jugs?" I asked, fully expecting him to say, "You don't want much, do you?"

To my surprise, he immediately turned and pointed to the golf course, "Right over there. I can connect some hoses together and hook them up to the closest spigots. With a nozzle on your end of the hose, we can leave the water on, and when you need some water, you can control the flow. No big deal."

"They won't mind?" I asked.

"Heck no. The guy in charge over there has dogs. He'll be happy to help. And besides, he owes me a favor," Ollie said with a wink.

When Ollie went over to talk to the guy at the golf course, he not only got us our water, he also got us a golf cart.

"This is a pretty big piece of property and with all the walking around you end up doing in a day, the guy thought you might like a golf cart to use. It'll save everyone a few steps," Ollie said, handing me the keys.

The following day, Ollie got electricity hooked up in the field, which took the place of the noisy generator on loan from the Red Cross. Each day, conditions improved a little more, thanks to our facilities manager.

With my two major jobs for the afternoon accomplished, I decided to check to see how Pam was doing in the cat tent. When I walked inside, I was knocked back by how hot it was inside, in spite of the side, front, and back flaps being rolled up.

"This is horrible," I said to Pam, who had sweat just pouring down her forehead. "We've got to find a way to cool this place down or the cats are going to get cooked, not to mention you and Cindy."

"Is there any place to get some ice?" she asked, as she was using a dampened paper towel to wipe the face of an orange-and-white Tabby cat who was panting. Cindy was doing the same to the cat two cages over. "And we'll need some small sealable sandwich bags."

"I can run to the store and get both," Cindy said.

"I'm afraid all the ice may be gone already. Why don't you go to the store and get the bags, and I'll make a call about the ice."

As Cindy got in her truck and drove out the front gate, I got on the phone in our command tent and called Kenny King.

"I need to talk to Kenny King," I said to the man who answered the phone.

"He's in a meeting right now. Is there something I can do to help you?" he asked.

"Maybe so. This is Terri Crisp and I'm the director of the program that is taking care of the animals across the road from the fire station."

"I kinda gathered that," he said. "I can hear the dogs barking in the background."

I laughed, and then got back to the reason for my call. "We have some very hot cats and we need a way to cool them off. Any chance you've got some ice over there that we could have?"

"There's a whole semitrailer full. How much do you need?"

This was too easy.

Within 15 minutes, two uniformed men in a Humvee delivered 20 bags of ice to our front gate, along with half a dozen Styrofoam ice chests. Shortly after that, Cindy returned with the sandwich bags, which she and Pam filled with ice and laid flat on the floor of each of the cat's cages. It wasn't long before the weary cats slowly stood up, sniffed this new thing that had been placed in their cage, and then decided it was okay to lie down on top of the bag. The ice bags did the trick. Whenever we needed more ice, all we had to do was call the command center. We kept trying to find a sealable bag the size of a mattress for all us hot humans to lie down on, too. That's about the only thing we wished for that we never found.

BEFORE OUR afternoon thunderstorm hit, the rescue team returned with Sylvester and seven very noisy geese. The kitten had been inside the unlocked house where his owners had left him, still high and dry. He was sitting on top of the refrigerator, meowing loudly when the team located him. This was the only remaining high spot in the entire house. When

Sylvester's family came to reclaim him, they told us that the water in their house had risen to eight feet. There's no way Sylvester would have survived.

Dara handed the cage, with Sylvester in it, to Wendy who took over from there. The first thing Wendy did was call the owners to let them know their cat was safe. Delivering that kind of news made the volunteers feel great, and all of us needed the joy it brought. The good calls helped compensate for the bad ones.

One of the team of volunteers had spotted our first feathered guests on Sunday when they were scouting the neighborhoods. The geese were in a slapped-together pen that was visible from the street. The volunteers stopped to see if the owners were home. Their knocking brought no response, but an elderly woman who lived next door poked her head out her screen door and asked in a southern twang, "Can I hep you?"

The four volunteers stepped off the wooden porch of the small bungalow and explained to the neighbor who they were and what they were doing.

"They's already left," the woman said, referring to the owners of the geese. "They's got family up near Moultrie they's staying with till this all passes."

The volunteers looked at one another, knowing what the others were thinking. The pen was no more than waist high and there were wooden planks covering the entire top. Certainly, once the flooding reached this street, which was only a few blocks from the Flint River, the water would be deeper than the top of the pen. With no way to get out, the geese would be trapped inside.

"Do you think your neighbors would mind us letting their geese out?" Amy asked. "We're afraid if we don't, they'll drown."

"I reckon it'd be okay," the woman said. "I's surprised they didn't do it the'selves."

So the volunteers freed the seven geese. As they walked back to their vehicles, Cindy said, "Now that they're free, those geese are going to have themselves a grand time swimming around in all this floodwater."

Waterfowl are about the only living creatures that actually welcome a flood.

While Shirley and Terry were unloading the crated geese from the back of Terry's truck, they told me that they'd gone back to check on the geese after they'd gotten Sylvester. When they pulled up in the driveway, they encountered quite a commotion. The geese were being chased in all directions through a foot of water by two brown Chows.

"That was when we decided we'd better bring them back here before they became those dogs' dinner," Terry explained.

"What happened to the Chows?" I asked.

"They took off as soon as they saw us," Shirley said. "There was no way we could catch them without a trap."

"How did you catch the geese? That couldn't have been any easy task either."

"We got our gloves on, herded them into a corner of the yard, started grabbing, and, amazingly enough, we caught them all. It helped that the dogs had already worn them out."

As Greg and Shirley put together a makeshift pen for the geese, I sent Terry to K-Mart to get them a wading pool.

I waited out Tuesday afternoon's storm inside the cat tent with Pam and 10 felines, asleep on their ice beds, not the least bit startled by the resonating claps of thunder that made Pam and I jump a few times.

"They sure seem happy now," I said to Pam, looking at the peaceful felines. I was a bit envious of their ice-filled plastic bags and the sleep they were getting. As predicted, we hadn't gotten to bed before midnight the night before. It was 1:45 when Shirley and I practically crawled into our tent, and we woke at 5:30 when the dogs sounded the alarm that it was time to get up.

"Any word on more cages?" I asked, sitting down on a stack of cat-food bags placed on a wooden pallet to keep the one on the bottom off the ground. We had discovered during the storm the day before that the tent was not completely leak-proof.

"Yeah, the southern region cat clubs are going to loan us a total of 50 cages," Pam informed me. "They should be here sometime tomorrow."

"Perfect. With that number of cages, we can take care of a whole slew of cats."

It wasn't long after the rain stopped that one of the mobile feeding trucks from the Red Cross pulled up to the gate. The meals that Kenny King had told me were coming had finally arrived. A waterlogged, hungry team of volunteers slowly gathered at the window on the side of the truck to wait their turn to be handed a Styrofoam container with today's dinner inside. When we pulled back the lids, we discovered more cold green beans and another pile of warm fruit cocktail, but instead of macaroni and cheese there was some kind of meat goulash.

Being a vegetarian, I asked the woman inside the window if by chance there was any macaroni and cheese left.

"No, I'm sorry," she replied. "We passed the last of that out at lunch today."

"Well, in that case, could I possibly have some more green beans and fruit cocktail, because I don't eat meat." I couldn't believe I was asking for more helpings of my two least favorite canned foods, but I was hungry. I had reached the point that I'd eat most anything, meat still being the standing exception.

"Certainly," she said, handing me another Styrofoam container, which I stacked on top of my other one.

"Thanks," I said. "We really do appreciate you bringing us food."

"That's what we're here for, and we'll be back in the morning with breakfast."

I could hardly wait.

I didn't wake up to the sound of barking dogs on Wednesday morning. Instead, it was a muffled voice from outside my tent. I couldn't imagine who had enough energy to be getting up with the sun. At first I tried to ignore it, but whoever it was sounded like they needed help.

Poking my head out the tent flap, with only one eye barely open, I thought I saw Wendy standing near the camper with her back to me, but it couldn't have been. I tried to focus on my watch and finally determined that it was only 6:30. Again, there was no way it was Wendy outside. I had learned during the floods the previous summer that Wendy *does not* do mornings. There was no way that she could be up before everyone else, including the dogs.

"Someone help me," the woman pleaded in a weary voice.

Struggling to get my boots on, minus socks, I stumbled out of the tent. *God, it's already hot out here,* I thought to myself as I walked toward the woman. When I got closer I stopped dead in my tracks. It was Wendy.

I will forever have embossed in my memory the picture of her that morning. The woman who I had *always* known to be impeccably dressed and coifed, had done a kind of Clark Kent-in-the-phone-booth wardrobe switch during the night. No wonder I hadn't recognized her right away.

Standing smack-dab in the middle of the property, Wendy had on a pair of loose-fitting turquoise shorts, something she *never* wears, and a white T-shirt that had printed on it, "St. Charles Humane Society." Both sleeves were rolled up, in the manner truckers use when they need a place to stash their smokes. The top of her head was covered with a brand-new, lopsided, tan fisherman's hat with the price tag still dangling on one side—true Minnie Pearl style. On her feet were someone else's too-big, knee-high rubber boots folded down to her ankles. When she heard me stomping toward her, she turned slowly. That was when I noticed she didn't have on her glasses, which she wears instead of her contacts during disasters. Finally, I spotted, clutched in her hands, a single blue dog leash. Certainly Wendy had not gotten up this early to walk the dogs, who were being kind enough to let us sleep in past 5:30.

My attention was diverted at that moment when I caught sight of three loose dogs in the field, having a good ol' time romping with one another in the wet grass. That, I realized, was what Wendy needed help with. She was trying to catch the dogs while she was still half-asleep, unsuitably dressed, and unable to see clearly.

Wendy proved to me that morning, and I think to herself, too, what she's willing to put up with to help animals.

～～～

AS PROMISED, the Red Cross feeding truck returned just as we finished walking the last few dogs and giving them their breakfast.

I was still laughing to myself about the earlier episode with Wendy when I walked up to the red and white truck and said good morning to the woman I recognized from the night before.

"Please tell me you've got some coffee," I said, as I leaned my elbows on the ledge outside the truck's serving window.

"Sure do," the woman said, handing me a cup of what turned out to be lukewarm coffee. In spite of it not being hot, there not being any half-and-half, and the only sugar available was the diet stuff in the pink package, it tasted great.

"Do you want some breakfast to go with that?"

"Sure," I replied, reaching out to take another Styrofoam container. A peek inside revealed watery scrambled eggs, two biscuits with a mound of rounded sausage in between, and a spoonful of white stuff that I guessed was grits.

I looked up at the woman and tried to say with true appreciation, "Thanks."

Before I walked away she hollered out to me, "We'll be back at lunch with a surprise for you."

I could only imagine.

～～～

I SPENT most of the morning on the phone inside the sweltering command tent, making calls and answering the multitude of questions from people who had called in either looking for help or wanting to do something for the animals. The local newspaper and radio station, plus the media from Atlanta, were starting to call for interviews, which I knew would generate even more phone calls.

One of the calls that I had to make was to locate some dog runs to keep our escape artists from getting loose again. We discovered how that morning's escapees had gotten free. They somehow had managed to slip out of their collars. Maybe they, too, were losing weight.

Fortunately, we had closed the front gate before we went to bed the night before, so they couldn't escape beyond the fence, but during the day it would be hard to keep the gate closed with all the people coming and going. It didn't take but two phone calls before I reached ABC Fence Company who agreed to let us use enough chain-link panels to assemble 20 dog runs. The panels arrived at 11 o'clock on the back of a flatbed truck. Volunteers spent the rest of the daylight hours assembling dog runs and moving the dogs who thought they could outsmart us.

I was once again stuck in the command tent, answering phones, because Dara had to go help Shirley with another rescue. While I was talking to a woman who wanted to know if we had rescued any black Chows, of which there seemed to be an abundance in this town, I noticed near the front gate a very nicely dressed man and woman.

Instead of an animal in tow, the man had three brand-new garden hoses encircling his forearm. The couple didn't look like they were prepared to volunteer, so when I hung up the phone I went outside to see if I could help them. Our guests turned out to be Mr. and Mrs. George Daniel. Mr. Daniel was the mayor pro tem of Bainbridge.

"I heard about the great stuff you were doing out here, so we had to come see, and I assumed you might need some hoses," the mayor said, handing them over.

"Your timing couldn't have been any better," I replied, remembering that a volunteer had asked me no more than 15 minutes earlier if we had any more hoses. It seems one of ours had sprung a leak. With three new hoses to replace that one, I could check one thing off my latest K-Mart shopping list.

I spent the next few minutes being a tour guide, showing the Daniels our shelter and introducing them to the volunteers, who were hard at work, and the animals, who kept all of us busy. Before they left, Mr. Daniels gave me his number at city hall and said to call if there was anything else he could do.

It was nearly one o'clock when the Red Cross feeding truck returned. Lunch had arrived.

"You guys hungry?" the woman who'd promised a surprise asked me and a couple of other hungry volunteers.

I really was, considering I'd had only enough time to drink the lukewarm coffee for breakfast, but somehow I didn't think lunch was going to be a smorgasbord of edible delights that would silence my growling stomach.

Instead of handing me another Styrofoam container, this time I was given a disposable coffee cup with steam coming out the top. *Another liquid meal,* I thought, as my stomach growled in protest. Inside was something that looked like watered-down vegetable soup.

"I felt bad that you vegetarians weren't getting enough to eat," she explained, "so I had the kitchen make you up a pot of vegetable soup."

I was dumbfounded. It was such a thoughtful thing for her to do for me and the other two vegetarians, considering the cooks at the Red Cross had the enormous task of feeding thousands of people who were counting on them for their next meal.

"Now, if I were making it at home, it'd taste a whole lot better. But all they could find to make the soup were cans of Veg·all, to which they added water and some seasoning," the woman said, handing me a package of saltine crackers to go along with the soup.

"That was so nice of you," I said, just as I was about to take my first sip.

Considering it was 98 degrees outside, soup would have been one of the very last things I would have ordered for lunch if I'd had a choice, but I drank the entire cup and asked for a second serving.

My new friend's name was Billie, and she and her husband, Bill, spent as much time with us as they could before they moved on to their next stop. They were both from Texas and had become full-time Red Cross volunteers after they retired.

"You know, this helping animals during disasters is a pretty neat thing," Billie said, as we took a few minutes to visit with some of the dogs. "Maybe next disaster we'll come and help you."

"That would be great. Just be sure to remember the soup," I laughed.

Everyday after that, we had Veg·all soup for lunch, and sometimes for breakfast and dinner.

BY WEDNESDAY night, we had 110 animals on the property. There were almost an equal number of dogs and cats, and our seven geese had been joined by 14 chickens brought to us by their owner.

"I didn't want to leave them at my place, even though they probably would have been okay on their own," he said, pausing for a moment to reposition the chew in his mouth. "But there's too many hungry people looking for something to eat now, and I'm afraid my chickens might end up on someone else's plate. I'm going to need them to feed my family when this is all over."

So we took care of the 14 chickens that would feed the Murphy family after they got back home.

It had been four days since most of us had enjoyed a hot shower, so I decided it was time to take Kenny King up on his offer. On the agenda for Wednesday evening were showers at the fire station. Two of us went at a time, thinking it was probably smart if one person took a shower while the other person stood guard at the door. This was a bathroom where the men weren't used to knocking before they barged in.

"They only give you five minutes in the shower," Wendy said, when she and Dara returned from the fire station smelling really good. "It normally takes me that long just to rinse the shampoo out of my hair."

"And don't even think about shaving your legs," Dara added. "I think the hair on my legs is almost long enough to braid."

Even two minutes in the shower would be enough, I thought, as I gathered what I needed to take with me.

By the time Shirley and I got to the fire station, the late news was on. I sat in an overstuffed recliner in the station's air-conditioned TV room, where I could see the door Shirley had disappeared through and still watch the TV. The threat of the city getting cut off from the county had passed, but it had come darn close to happening. This didn't mean Bainbridge was out of the woods yet. The last thing I remember the newscaster saying was that the Flint River had not risen any more that day, but it had not started to recede either, and with more rain on the way, who knew for sure what would happen next. Mother Nature probably had a clue, but she wasn't volunteering any information.

A gentle tap on my shoulder startled me awake. It was Shirley, with a towel wrapped around her head.

"You're a great guard," she said, laughing. "Falling asleep on the job."

"Sorry," I said. I slowly raised myself out of the chair, feeling as though I had been drugged. I was actually tempted to fall back into the chair and skip the shower, but I elected to smell better.

As I turned the shower faucet, I considered hopping in the shower with all my clothes on, which were as dirty as I was, but I decided the clothes could wait to get cleaned during tomorrow's storm. Much to my surprise, there was still some hot water left, and it felt fantastic. To finally remove the accumulation of sunscreen, bug repellant, and grime felt as though I had shed a whole layer of skin. The presence of shampoo in my hair made me feel human again. I walked out of that bathroom, seven and a half minutes later, feeling like half a million dollars. What would have made me feel like a million bucks was some clean clothes.

Having had our showers on Wednesday night, we decided to bathe the dogs on Thursday morning. With an endless supply of water now, we thought the dogs would appreciate getting cleaned up, too. Some of them had been swimming in the floodwaters when we found them. Raw sewage, petroleum products, and pesticides are just some of the substances mixed in with the water. The animals really didn't need that nasty stuff on their fur. This time I went to K-Mart to get three more wading pools for us to use as big round canine bathtubs.

We took turns cleaning the dogs, enjoying the spray of cool water as much as they seemed to. Following their baths, we combed and brushed each dog under the shade of the funeral home tent, where we ate our meals and had our daily briefings. As a finishing touch, we trimmed all the dogs' nails and gave them each a new, permanent collar from our growing supply of donations.

When we were down to the last few dogs, we were starting to get tired. Bathing and sprucing up 52 filthy canines turned out to be a major job. I was sitting under the funeral tent combing a longhaired black Labrador mix when Diane walked up. "There's some military guy over near the command tent who needs to talk to you," she said.

"Do you know what he wants?"

"Nope. He just asked to speak to the person in charge."

"Well, I guess that'll be me," I said, standing up. "Diane, do you mind putting our friend here away. He came from the run next to the pen with the three puppies."

"Sure," she replied, taking the leash from me.

Rubbing my hands against my jeans to remove the black fur stuck to my damp skin, I headed for the command tent.

"Hi, I'm Terri. Can I help you?" I asked, assuming I was speaking to the right party, given that he was the only uniformed person in sight.

He extended his tanned arm, saying softly, "I sure hope so." After shaking my hand, he asked, "Do you need any help walking dogs?"

This was not the question I was expecting, so I hesitated for a moment before I responded, "Well, yes."

"Good," he said with relief. "Would it be okay if I spent a little time walking a few of them? I guarantee you I have experience."

I wouldn't have been a bit surprised if he'd whipped a resume out of his back pocket to prove his credentials.

"You'd be doing me a big favor," he added, with a slight look of desperation on his face.

"No problem. Let me show you which dogs need walking."

"Thank you," he said with a big smile. This was definitely not the same look he had had on his face when I first started talking to him.

After some brief instructions on where to walk the dogs and how to dispose of their waste, our uniformed dog walker got down to business, while I returned to the shade of the funeral tent to brush another clean dog. As I watched him lead one dog after another around the dog-walk area, I remembered that I had seen this man several times at the emergency operations center. He was always surrounded by people asking him one question after another. I assumed he had to be someone important.

It wasn't until almost an hour later that I saw the man again. He wasn't walking dogs anymore, but helping another volunteer bathe the last dog, a Setter mix who Wendy had named Howard. While the volunteer rinsed the dog, the man held the dog's leash. I could hear him laugh when the dog decided enough was enough and shook, water and fur flying every which way, a good part of it landing on the uniformed handler. But it was clear that he couldn't have cared less.

"So you've graduated from dog walker to groomer," I said to the man when he brought Howard to me for brushing.

"Hope you don't mind," he said, sitting down on a folding chair next to me. "The volunteer was looking for another pair of hands and mine were available."

"That's fine," I assured him. "We appreciate the help."

He said nothing, just stroked Howard's fur.

"Well, I better get back," he said with a sigh, handing Wendy the leash with Howard on the other end. "Or else they'll have the troops out looking for me."

"Does this mean you're AWOL?" I asked with a grin.

"Something like that."

"Come back any time," I said, offering him my hand. "You're always welcome."

"I'll keep that in mind the next time it gets totally crazy across the road." He glanced toward the fire station that was a constant hub of activity.

Then the uniformed man looked me directly in the eyes, and said, "You don't know what a lifesaver this has been for me."

And I replied, "Oh, I think I do."

CHAPTER FIVE

New Ways

FRIDAY BEGAN with a frantic phone call. We'd just started our morning briefing, accompanied by another breakfast of cold biscuits and black speckled grits when I heard the phone ringing.

"And so our day begins!" I jumped up and ran to the command tent, reaching the phone on the fifth ring. "Emergency Animal Rescue Service. Can I help you?" I said, as I successfully swatted a mosquito that had landed on my arm, deciding I'd be his breakfast.

"Oh, I hope so." That's all the woman could say before her voice trailed off and she started to cry.

"Ma'am," I said, after giving her some time to cry before I tried to get her to talk again. "I can't help you if you don't stop crying."

Still, all I heard on the other end of the line were the sobs of a disaster victim who was losing control of her emotions. My heart went out to her, as I tried to help her tell me what she needed to say.

"Do you need help with an animal?" I asked. I barely heard her response of yes. "Okay. Don't worry, we'll do what we can," I said softly, hoping to reassure her.

When she finally calmed down enough, she explained why she was calling. "We have three dogs. When our neighborhood started to flood, we gave them to a man in Newton who my husband works with. He agreed to take care of them, never thinking his house would end up being threatened by the flood, too."

When I had been at the fire station the afternoon before picking up more ice for the cats, I'd overheard a conversation about this town 50 miles northeast of Bainbridge. The townspeople were losing their battle with the Flint River, their human-built wall of sandbags no longer able to stand up to the strength of the river. Mother Nature was winning again.

"Now he has to evacuate, he has nowhere to take our dogs, and all the roads into Newton are flooded, so we can't go get them." The woman started crying again. Between sobs, she managed to tell me, "And . . . if we . . . don't get them . . . I'm afraid they are going to . . . die."

"When did you last talk to the man?" I asked.

"Just before I called you," she told me, stopping to blow her nose.

I proceeded to ask the woman for the information I needed to complete the "Request for Rescue" form. It took a while, but when I was finished, I told her I'd do everything I could to find her dogs and bring them back.

"Thank you," she said softly. "They're my whole life. I'd be devastated if I lost them."

The woman and her family had moved into the Red Cross shelter at the Jones Wheat Elementary School. Before we hung up, I promised her that as soon as I had any news, I would call her there. More than anything, I hoped when I made that call that I would be able to say, "I have them!"

After I hung up the phone, I remained seated on the ice chest in the command tent, staring out the front door, as my mind worked to come up with a way to get a rescue team to Newton. More than likely a boat wouldn't do the trick, which was too bad because we had several of those parked right outside. If we waited until the roads opened, that would probably be too late. There seemed to be only one solution. We'd have to fly to Newton. But considering that we didn't have a helicopter parked alongside our small fleet of boats, this plan needed more work.

Suddenly, it dawned on me. It might be a totally crazy idea, but heck, it was worth a try. At the airport across the road from us were three Air National Guard helicopters, just sitting there, going nowhere. Maybe, just maybe, I could convince someone to fly us to Newton. And I knew just who to ask.

Going to my tent, I put on my EARS vest. I thought the gold-star badge, which always gets the right people's attention, might come in handy. Looking as professional as was possible, I returned briefly to the funeral tent where the volunteers were finishing up breakfast, and announced I had an errand to run and would be right back.

Taking the golf cart, I crossed the field to the fire station, my mind rehearsing what I would say when I found who I was looking for. Hopefully, he'd still be around. I'd heard the National Guard was scaling back now that the local evacuations were completed.

Once again, it was a circus when I stepped into the large room that served as coordinating headquarters for the county portion of the disaster. I ducked inside the door and stood against the wall, out of the way, looking for that familiar face. It took a while, but I finally located him at the far side of the crowded room, surrounded by three men. Their conversation did not appear to be casual chitchat. I decided this was not the time to interrupt.

Watching their exchange with interest, I wondered if the man at the center of it would look away momentarily and notice me. But he didn't. He was oblivious to everyone in the room but the three men. Deep creases in his forehead indicated the seriousness of whatever they were discussing.

Just then the door I had come through a minute or two earlier opened and another very important looking man entered the room, followed by an entourage of military personnel. The three men across the room looked up from their conversation and excused themselves a few moments later. I figured this was my chance. Before the opportunity slipped past, I made my way through the crowd.

"Excuse me," I said, standing in front of the man I had come to see. He was reading what looked like some kind of report but, when he heard my voice, he looked up, a smile replacing the frown lines.

"Did you come to walk some of my people? I hope so, because some of them need to go for a *very* long walk," he said.

We both laughed. "Actually, I came to ask you a favor." I told him about the dogs and their desperate owner, talking quickly since I didn't know how long I would have him to myself. When I finally had to stop and take a breath, he spoke up.

"Let me understand this. You need to be flown to Newton in one of our helicopters so you can locate and bring three dogs back to Bainbridge." He'd heard me correctly. "When do you want to go?"

"For this woman's peace of mind, the sooner the better," I said, crossing my fingers behind my back.

"Can you be ready to leave in an hour?" he said with a smile.

"We can be ready in half an hour."

My high-ranking military friend, who knew the comfort of surrounding himself with dogs, had come through. I thought about giving him a hug to show my appreciation, but that probably would not have been appropriate, present company considered, so I shook his hand. The look on his face told me that he knew how much his help meant to me.

I controlled my excitement until I was in my golf cart, and on my way back to the shelter. Then I mumbled to myself, "I did it. I really did it."

I CHOSE Dara and Diane to go with me to Newton. Neither one of them had ever been in a helicopter, so they were thrilled, but at the same time not quite sure they were ready for this new experience several thousand feet above the flooded landscape.

"I don't even do roller coasters!" Dara told me as we gathered what we needed to take with us.

I reassured both of them that they were in for an experience of a lifetime. The first time I had flown in a helicopter was when United Animal Nations sent me to Barrow, Alaska, in 1988 to participate in the international effort to save the three gray whales who were trapped among the ice floes. In order to get to where the whales were we had to fly in by helicopter. Remembering that time, I was really looking forward to flying again.

With the help of several of the volunteers, we located three medium unassembled airline crates for the smaller mixed-breed dogs we were going after. In addition, we grabbed a catch pole, a pair of animal handling gloves, a 20-pound bag of dog food, and three collars and leashes. We stacked the crates inside one another and then packed everything else in the top one. My friend had told me to travel as light as possible, and we'd done just that. It was 38 minutes later that Dara, Diane, and I returned to the airfield, ready to go.

The weather was perfect for flying. There was not a cloud in the mid-morning sky as we took off, circling over our shelter twice before we headed north. The crewman who sat in the back with us asked if we wanted to keep the side door open so we could take pictures. Dara and Diane weren't quite sure they liked the idea. On being reassured that their seat harnesses would keep them from getting sucked out, they agreed to the unobstructed view, and were glad they did. We got some incredible pictures of the flood, amazed at how large an area it actually covered. It was a sobering look at what Mother Nature was capable of doing. I couldn't help but wonder how many of the homes below might still have animals trapped inside.

We landed in Newton 20 minutes later and, as I predicted, Dara and Diane were glad they'd come along.

Before I left the shelter, I tried repeatedly to call the man in Newton who had the three dogs, but no one answered his phone. I could only hope that we could locate him once we reached our destination. Considering that there were no roads open into Newton, there weren't any coming out either, so the man would most likely still be somewhere in town. Shirley had informed me that Newton was not very big. I decided the best place to start looking for him would be the Red Cross evacuation shelter, which is where our helicopter landed.

As we were unloading what little we'd brought with us, the helicopter pilot informed us that he had just received word that they were to return to Bainbridge. Something unexpected had come up and the helicopter was needed back ASAP. He explained that we could return with them, or stay and take our chances that they would be able to return for us sometime later that afternoon or evening. We decided to stay.

It didn't take us but half an hour to locate the man we were looking for at the Red Cross shelter. When we asked him about the dogs, he told us he had let them go. *Great,* I thought, *now they're running loose in a flooded neighborhood they're not familiar with.*

When we pressed for more information, we learned that his house was a little over two miles away from where we were. We headed in that direction on foot, hoping we would get lucky and find the dogs running beyond the reach of the floodwater.

We hadn't walked much more than a mile when I spotted a dog coming toward us down the middle of the street. "That looks like one of them," I said. The dog matched one of the descriptions on the rescue form. When he got closer, we could see the Frisbee-sized black spot in the middle of his white back. We knew for sure then that we had found one of the woman's dogs. I don't know who was more excited, him or us. He came trotting up, his tail just a-wagging.

After a round of juicy kisses, we fed the hungry dog. When he had finished inhaling the food, we put a collar and leash on the wet pooch and went in search of his friends. After more than an hour of walking the perimeter of the flooded neighborhood where the dogs had been turned loose the night before, we came up with nothing.

The absence of animals puzzled us. Either people had evacuated them before the situation got out of hand or all around us in the flooded homes and yards were animals that had not survived.

Unsuccessful in our search, we decided it was time to return to the Red Cross shelter. The brutal midday sun was taking its toll on all of us, the dog included. Before we headed back, we dumped the rest of the dog food we had with us in a spot close to where we'd found the dog and where it would be protected from the rain. If the other two dogs were hiding somewhere nearby, maybe they would find it after we left.

We also had to start thinking about hitching a ride back to Bainbridge. The idea of spending the night in Newton didn't appeal to any of us. We'd seen a helicopter pass overhead about 45 minutes earlier, so we were hoping that maybe our copter had returned and it would be parked and waiting for us—but no such luck. When we reached the blistering-hot asphalt parking lot, which had served as a temporary heliport, there was not a copter in site, just row after row of cars packed full of people's belongings.

Before I called Shirley to see if she could run over to the command center and hopefully make arrangements to have us picked up, Diane and Dara went inside the shelter to get us something to drink. Since animals were not allowed inside, I stayed outside with the dog, who was as anxious for a drink of water as I was.

I found a spot for us under a nearby tree, out of the scorching sun and off the asphalt, which I knew had to be hot on the dog's pads. Sharing the shade with us was a Georgia State Patrol car, with an officer leaning against the passenger door, drinking a Diet Coke.

"Howdy," he said, as I walked up.

"Hi," I replied, as I plopped down on the ground, thinking how good it felt to sit down.

"Who's your friend?" he asked, directing his attention to the dog beside me, who was now sprawled out in the much cooler grass, his eyes closed.

I told the trooper the dog's story and how disappointed we were that we couldn't find the other two. I explained that we'd had to give up our search because of the heat and the need to figure out a way to get back to Bainbridge before it got too much later.

"I can give you a ride to Bainbridge."

"I thought all the roads in and out of here were flooded."

"Nope. You can still drive to Bainbridge. It's not a real direct route, but it's still possible to get there by car."

So we returned to the shelter in the caged-in backseat of a state patrol cruiser, stopping along the way to pick up a tortoise just starting across the busy highway, slowly fleeing his flooded habitat.

After thanking our chauffeur for the ride, I led the sleepy dog to the command tent. While I waited for Pam to get off the phone, I briefly filled Wendy in on our trip to Newton.

"The dog's owner must have called here 10 times wondering if you'd gotten back yet," Wendy told me. "She'll be so excited when you tell her you found one of the dogs."

"I know. But, boy, is it going to be hard to tell her we couldn't find the other two," I said, moving toward the phone that Pam had just hung up.

"Any luck?" Pam asked.

"We got one." I pointed to the dog who now lay at my feet, too exhausted to move even a whisker.

I dialed the number the woman had given me that morning. After getting a busy signal six times, I finally got through. While I waited for someone to answer the phone, I reached down and patted the dog's head, wondering where his buddies were. I refused to believe they were dead.

The owner was seated within earshot of the pay phone. When she said hello and then heard me ask for her, she blurted out, "Well?"

"We got the black-and-white dog," I told her, hesitating long enough for her to enjoy the news before I told her the rest. "I'm afraid we never saw the other two, though, but we'll go back tomorrow."

After a silence, the woman asked in a faint voice, "Do you think the other two drowned?"

All I could say was, "I sure hope not."

The woman and her family were at the shelter in less than 30 minutes. Watching that reunion gave me one of my best memories from this disaster. Luck had definitely been on our side with this one, or maybe it was that guardian angel from Colorado again.

A team returned to Newton by truck three times over the next two days to search for the dogs. Upon their return on the first day, they excitedly reported that they had spotted the dogs not far from where we had found the first dog. In spite of patient attempts to gain their trust, the dogs were too frightened to be caught. It was Shirley, Amy, and two new volunteers, Lyn and Alan Rees, who finally succeeded in capturing the two holdouts. When I made the call to tell their family the good news, it was my turn to shed tears.

Lyn and Alan were great additions to our team. Lyn, a veterinary technician, had seen me interviewed on their local news, and at that moment decided she was going to come and help us, no matter what. She announced to her husband, who thought she'd lost her mind, that they needed to go to the sporting-goods store to buy a pair of waders and a sleeping bag.

"But you're not a roughing-it kind of person," Alan said, trying to persuade his wife to stay home and just send a donation to help the animals instead. "You know there's probably going to be snakes crawling all over the place down there."

Even that didn't dissuade her. Lyn had made up her mind.

It took little time to shop and pack her Trooper. Just before Lyn was ready to walk out the door, Alan stopped her, and said, "Hold on. Let me make a call."

Taking time off from work, Alan reluctantly joined his wife and they left Lawrenceville on Thursday evening, headed for Bainbridge to save animals. When it came time for them to return home three days later, Alan admitted it had been an incredible experience, one on which he came very close to missing out. As Lyn put it when we were saying good-bye, "What happened here has sunk deep into our hearts and we will never forget this time."

Just before they pulled out the gate, Alan rolled down his window and yelled to me, "Be sure you call us next time."

"Believe me, I will."

Dara had to leave us, too, and returned to St. Louis on Saturday. We'd had her with us for six days. She'd made a huge difference for the animals and she'd been a tremendous help to me, which is part of the reason why I had picked her to fill one of the EARS coordinator slots. She became part of a carefully selected group of individuals who would continue to go with me to disasters, gaining more and more valuable experience. The coordinators would become a team of experts, and their expertise would ensure that EARS got better and better at helping animals during disasters.

As I walked Dara to her rental car, she confessed that she had been really scared coming down to Georgia for the first time, alone, but had made herself do it because of the animals. "When Deanna told me to bring a pillowcase that zipped so a snake couldn't crawl inside and hide, I almost unpacked my suitcase," she said, laughing. "But I'm glad I didn't."

"Me too," I said, giving her one last hug.

As I waved good-bye to Dara, I felt an incredible sense of accomplishment. EARS was becoming what I had always wanted it to be, an ever-growing network of talented individuals who genuinely loved animals. I was no longer a team of one, and I was thrilled to be in such great company.

CHAPTER SIX

Going Home

I HAD SOME catching up to do when I returned from Newton. I left Shirley and Wendy in charge, and they did a
great job of filling in. After dinner Friday night, they updated
me on all the day's activities.

"It's a whole lot more fun being an Indian than being the
chief," Wendy commented.

"No kidding!" I said, enjoying Wendy's revelation.

During my absence, there were no major crises, but
rather the normal ups and downs that make disasters anything but boring. Every day is a constantly changing combination of animals and people who test your patience, teach
you new things, challenge you to try harder, and give you
plenty of reasons to laugh and cry. From what Wendy and
Shirley told me, Friday was no different.

Some of the dogs had gone back home in the afternoon,
Tommy's four Coonhounds among them. I was disappointed
I didn't get to say good-bye to our noisy tenants. We kept
them tethered under one of the funeral tents at the back of
the property, but that was still not far enough away from our
sleeping quarters. It was their deep-throated barks that I
heard first thing each morning as my mind tried to convince
my still-tired body to get moving. At night, their barks

would be the last sound I heard before I finally conked out. Even though they were rarely quiet, I would miss them.

"The water got within an inch of going inside Tommy's house," Shirley told me later that night as we were getting ready for bed in our tent, which should have had a sign over the door reading, "Condemned—Unsafe for Human Occupancy."

"He was mighty lucky," I said, peeling off my soaking-wet socks, which had gotten drenched during that afternoon's downpour. I tossed them in the pile of other equally disgusting mildewed socks under my cot.

"You should have seen how excited Tommy was when he saw his dogs. And the four of them! Oh, my God . . . they just about pulled down the tent trying to get to him."

It was a reunion I was sorry I missed.

In my absence, more volunteers had arrived, and I was really glad to see them. Pam and Cindy had left during the week. The new recruits, who had an abundance of energy, would get us through to the end. Tim Gainous, Sara Corville, and Maggie Mercer, all untrained volunteers, had decided, just like Lyn and Alan Rees, that they wanted to help. They made a big difference, as did a handful of Bainbridge residents who were fortunate to escape the reach of the Flint River. They felt that they needed to do something to help those who had lost everything. Besides helping us with the animals, they mowed the grass in our field, brought us pizza when we couldn't handle another bowl of Veg•all soup, and helped us find our way around Bainbridge when we rescued animals. They initially provided foster homes and, eventually, permanent homes for some of the unclaimed animals.

The combination of trained and untrained volunteers worked well. A total of 50 people spent some very long days and nights taking care of the animals' needs. It was their willingness to do whatever had to be done that made the EARS response to this disaster such a success, and I couldn't have been happier.

More supplies had arrived on Friday from the Midwest, filling up the area under one of the tents. The networking that was going on outside the state was incredible. Stacy Elders and Nadine Carter, two EARS volunteers from Friends of Companion Animals near Kansas City, plus Sherrie Harper, one of our volunteers from the Madison County Humane Society in Illinois, had called us earlier in the week to see what we needed, and they'd come through big time.

Humane cat traps, which the St. Charles Humane Society let us borrow, also arrived on Friday. They were the same traps we had used the summer before to catch cats during the flood that had struck their community. EARS volunteer Connie King, who worked for Burlington Air Freight, arranged through her employer for the free shipping of the traps and some of the other supplies, which helped to make up for what my airfare to Georgia had cost.

As I helped Wendy open boxes and distribute the supplies on Saturday morning, I asked her, "You haven't by any chance seen a box big enough to hold a washing machine, have you?"

"I'm afraid not," she laughed. "Believe me, if I had, it would have been the first box I opened."

"Oh, well," I said, handing a stack of clean towels to a volunteer who needed them to dry off some cats who had arrived the evening before desperately in need of a bath. The whiff of laundry soap from the stack of remaining towels teased my nose and made living in dirty clothes seem suddenly that much more unbearable.

We had been set up in the field for one day short of a week, and during that time we'd been wearing the same few clothes, which by now were all totally disgusting. I joked the night before that I thought all of my jeans could stand up by themselves. The rest of the group admitted that jeans were not their only garments that looked as though they'd been overstarched. All I could say was, "I guess it's a good thing we're living outdoors."

More than once we gave some thought to finding a Laundromat, but there was never time to follow through with the idea. The days passed, and we all came to the conclusion that we would have to wait until we got home to have the pleasure of wearing clean clothes again.

Sunday mornings are always the quietest time of the week for us. People don't fill out any rescue requests, they don't show up to reclaim pets, local volunteers are scarce, and picking up and dropping off food and supplies for animals gets forgotten until later. Instead, people are sitting in church, thanking God they survived Mother Nature's wrath, while we use the time to catch our breath.

When everyone started to wander out of their tents at seven o'clock, still half-asleep, I announced that breakfast was on me. Instead of letting them start another day with a bellyful of biscuits and grits, I would send them into town for a real breakfast.

"Now, you have to promise you'll bring me back a stack of pancakes, smothered in butter and maple syrup," I said.

The group scattered to get ready to go. I hadn't seen them move that fast in days. As the last of the three trucks pulled out of the gate, Amy rolled down her window and asked, "You want *hot* coffee with those pancakes?"

"Yes, ma'am," I said, giving her a thumbs-up. "And don't forget the half-and-half."

I had somewhat selfish motives for sending everyone away. It was going to be wonderful to have at least an hour to myself, with no questions to answer, complaints to listen to, or problems to solve. Plus, I hadn't called home in five days, so I thought this would be a good time to find out, without any interruptions, what my family had been up to.

"Hi," I said when I heard Ken's sleepy voice. I had forgotten about the time difference. Looking at my watch, I subtracted three hours and realized it was still only 5:25 in California. "I'm sorry I woke you."

"Don't worry about it," Ken said after yawning. "How are you?"

"Doing okay, especially now that I've got the place to myself."

"Where is everyone?"

"I sent them out for breakfast."

"And you didn't go!" I could hear the disbelief in Ken's voice. The last time I had talked with him I mentioned what I'd been surviving on, so it was hard for him to believe I passed up a meal that wasn't being prepared in massive quantities by the Red Cross.

"They're bringing me back something," I assured him. "Instead of eating I wanted to call you and the girls, who, I take it, are all still asleep."

"Right. If I'm lucky, they'll be asleep for another hour or so." He sounded tired, and it wasn't just because I'd woken him up. He definitely had his hands full keeping up with Jennifer, Amy, and Megan, not to mention our menagerie of animals. I would owe him big-time when I got home.

Ken and I only talked for a couple more minutes. Before I hung up, I told him to be sure to kiss the girls for me and tell them how much I loved them. He didn't ask, but I did tell him just before I said good-bye, "I think I'll be home by the end of the week, but I'll call as soon as I know for sure."

"That would be good because we all miss you, animals included."

After I hung up the phone, I sat in the chair that had replaced the ice chest, which was the only thing to sit on in the command tent until a local volunteer showed up with three white plastic chairs. Keeping me company in the tent was a two-month-old Chihuahua mix named Chico, who was being very quiet. Part of the reason for his impeccable behavior was that he had discovered on his own how to stay cool. The cap covering the drain on the ice chest was cracked, therefore it leaked—cold water. Chico would lie right under the drip, allowing the water to soak his fur. He was the only one—among both the people and the animals—who never complained about the heat.

I thought about taking some of the dogs for a walk, but they were quiet right now. Besides, it was starting to get too hot to exert that much energy. I looked over toward my tent and considered doing some housecleaning. Some of the volunteers joked that if a prize were awarded for the messiest tent, Shirley and I would get first place. Well, they could continue to think we were slobs because I didn't feel like spending what was left of my hour of solitude doing housework.

I finally decided that what I really wanted to do was visit with the cats. There was an absolutely adorable marmalade kitten who had been brought to us by a man with the Department of Natural Resources. He had found the kitten in a tree when he was helping some friends move back into their partially flooded home. I left Chico to his drips and headed for the cat tent, which was a lot cooler since we had hooked up three fans.

As I was passing the front gate, a car came toward me across the field that separated us from the fire station. *There's actually someone besides us who's not in church*, I thought, as I waited to see who would get out of the car.

It was an older woman, maybe in her late seventies, who walked with the help of a cane. *Certainly, she's not coming to volunteer*, I concluded. *She must be missing an animal or maybe she wants to make a donation*—those were the logical choices.

"Hi," I said, walking to greet her. "Can I help you?"

"Oh dear, I don't need any help," she said in a gentle voice. "I just love animals so much, and I just had to come and see all your kitties and doggies."

She reminded me of my grandmother, and I decided that spending some time with someone like her would do me as much good as playing with the marmalade kitten.

"Well," I said, "let me show you who we've got staying with us."

Slowly we made our way around the perimeter of the field, stopping so she could say a few words to each of the dogs, who greeted us with wagging tails. I'd grabbed a box of treats as we passed the supply tent. The woman and I took turns giving each dog a handful, their first of the day, but most definitely not their last. If the dogs in our care were going to die of anything, it would be from overdosing on treats.

Once we visited with all the dogs, we moved to the cat tent and made the rounds in there. When we put the adorable marmalade kitten back into her cage, the woman said to me, "You have been so kind to take the time to show me around."

"My pleasure," I responded, tickling the head of another kitten, who was working so hard to get my attention with her persistent meows.

"I wish there were something I could do to help," she said. She paused on her way toward the door. "If I were just 20 years younger, I wouldn't hesitate getting on a boat and going and saving some of the animals. It makes me so gosh darn mad to hear there were people who left their animals behind when they evacuated."

I found myself, too, wishing the woman were younger. She would have been a great addition to our team.

"How about I drive into town and buy some kitty or doggy food and bring it back?"

I wanted to say, "Oh, please don't," because we already had enough donated food to feed half the dogs and cats in Decatur county for the next six months. As I thought about it, though, there really didn't seem to be a lot of ways the woman could help and she would be extremely disappointed not to have done something. I was just about to say, "Okay. That would be very nice of you to bring us some pet food," when I had a much better idea.

"You may think this is a strange request," I began. "But you see, people have already been extremely generous, so we have more than enough food for the animals. What would help, though, and this is not something that's actually for the animals, but I think they'd agree that the volunteers need to be taken care of, too." I paused for a moment, aware of the puzzled look on the woman's face. I wondered what she would think when I told her what we really needed. "Would it be too much to ask for you maybe to do some laundry for some of the volunteers who have been here the longest, myself included?"

"You need your laundry done?" the woman asked.

"Well, yes. Most of us have been wearing the same clothes for a week and having clean clothes to wear would be absolutely wonderful," I explained.

"My dear," she said with a smile on her face, "You gather up those dirty clothes and I'd be real happy to take them home and wash them."

"Really?" I exclaimed, and gave her a hug.

"Yes, really," she said, patting me on the back.

I ran to the supply tent, thinking I better move fast before she changed her mind. Grabbing two extra-large black garbage bags, I disappeared into the three sleeping tents and proceeded to fill the plastic bags with dirty clothes, most of which were heaped in piles on the floor and under the cots. It reminded me of cleaning my kids' bedrooms. I grabbed socks, jeans, and red T-shirts, stuffing them all into the two bags. *It's a good thing I told the volunteers to put their names on their clothes,* I thought, as I continued to stuff, working up quite a sweat. When the bags could hold no more, I rejoined the woman by her car.

"You want me to put these in the trunk?" I asked, putting both bulging bags down on the ground momentarily. I decided while I was walking toward the car, holding the bags at arm's length, that putting them inside the car could be hazardous to the woman's health.

"That would be fine," she said, handing me the key to the trunk.

With the clothes packed away in the airtight trunk, I returned the key and thanked the woman again for being willing to do this for us. "You just don't know what a boost this will be for everyone," I said. "When you bring the clothes back, I know they'll all thank you."

"I'll get these done up this afternoon. There's a good breeze blowing, so they should dry in no time flat," she said, looking toward the west. "I'll just have to be sure I get them off the line before this afternoon's storm rolls in."

"I really hope this is not too much trouble," I said, feeling slightly guilty.

"Oh, it's no bother. I'm happy to do it," she said, getting into her car. "I had three sons, so I'm used to doing lots of grungy laundry."

Knowing that made me feel better.

"I'll have the clothes back to you by tomorrow morning, line-dried fresh."

I could hardly wait.

I stood at our gate, watching her back up and drive toward the road. Just before she disappeared out of sight, she put her hand out her window and waved good-bye.

When the volunteers returned with my breakfast, I felt like falling to my knees and thanking that guardian angel who kept making good things happen. She had outdone herself this time, seeing to it that I had a real breakfast and bringing me a laundry woman.

"Guess what?" I announced enthusiastically, when all the volunteers had gathered under the tent for the morning briefing that I had postponed until after breakfast. "As I speak, our clothes are getting washed."

"You're kidding!" Amy said in disbelief.

"Did someone bring us a washing machine?" Wendy asked, looking toward the garden hoses snaking through the grass from the golf course, thinking there might be a washer hooked to our end.

"No, I am not kidding, and no, there is no washing machine on this property," I said as I proceeded to explain what had happened while they were in town eating. We were all so excited that we considered having our own mini church service that morning, to thank God we had survived the week and to thank him for kind little old ladies.

As we went about our jobs the next morning, I saw everyone glancing periodically toward the front gate, anticipating the return of our clean clothes. I realized, as I caught myself doing the same a few times, that this was almost as exciting as when I was a child waiting for Santa to arrive on Christmas Eve.

When it got to be 10 o'clock, a few of the volunteers started to ask me, "What time did she say she'd be here?"

I responded in an optimistic voice, "She said sometime this morning."

There were still two more hours left in the morning, so she really wasn't late yet. Maybe she hadn't been able to get everything off the line before the storm the afternoon before, so she had to wait for everything to dry this morning. Or maybe doing our laundry turned out to be a bigger job than she thought it would be. After all, it had probably been a long time since she had done the laundry for her three sons. For the rest of the morning, I kept reassuring people, "She'll be here any minute now."

~~~

AT 2:30, our laundry had still not returned. When the Red Cross brought us dinner, we were still wearing the same dirty clothes, the only ones most of us had left to wear. When it was time for our showers, we went to a new place that Ollie had told us about—Mr. Pips Auto and Truck Plaza on Route 27. The drain in the shower at the fire station had backed up and the plumber couldn't be out until the next morning, so we had no choice. It turned out to be a good thing that we got away because it gave us something to do besides sitting around wondering what had happened to our clothes and the woman who vanished with them.

Showering at a truck stop was a new experience for the six of us who had not gotten clean enough during that afternoon's downpour. Mother Nature tried really hard to accommodate us, but her showers were never quite hot enough. We were ready for the real thing. Hanging out and eating junk food with a bunch of truckers, who were spotlessly clean compared to us, generated some lively conversations. We got to laughing so hard as we sat in the Formica booths in one corner of the mini-mart, that we thought for sure we were going to pee our pants, something we didn't want to do considering we didn't have anything clean to change into.

The tall, lean man behind the counter had us laughing the loudest all the way back to the shelter. He had only one front tooth left in his mouth, hence his nametag—Fang. When each of us headed for the shower in turn, he would look at that person, one eye going one way and the other in the opposite direction, and in his Southern drawl, say, "If ya needs your back soaped up, just holler." Then he would hand over the key to the shower room, a bar of rose-scented soap not much bigger than a postage stamp, one scratchy white towel the size of a doormat, and a light-blue Rubbermaid bucket (none of us could figure out what to do with it). As we got out of Shirley's truck, we all agreed that showers at home would definitely be boring after our adventure at Mr. Pips.

Greg, who had stayed behind, informed us that there was still no word on our laundry. I looked at the volunteers, all standing in their dirty clothes, and I didn't know what to say. I was even more shocked than they were.

As we sat under the Ivey funeral tent, our wet hair wrapped in towels and the darkness illuminated by a row of citronella candles, I said to the group, "You should have seen her. She looked like Aunt Bea from the *Andy Griffith Show.* No one could have looked more honest, and she was so genuine in wanting to help."

"What's her name?" Amy asked. "Maybe she's listed in the phone book?"

"I hate to say it, guys, but I didn't even get her name, or any other information, as a matter of fact," I said, rubbing my clean forehead that now smelled like roses. "It didn't seem necessary."

"Do you think she decided to keep the stuff for herself?" Diane asked.

"No way. There wasn't a thing she could have worn. She must have weighed 200 pounds," I said, shaking my head, still in total shock that this had happened.

"Maybe it was too much work, and she died of a heart attack," interjected Greg, who rarely said anything.

"If that happened, can you imagine what her family will think when they find her surrounded by mounds of jeans that are too small for her and a bunch of red T-shirts in all sizes?" Amy asked.

"And all those socks," Wendy said, adding to Amy's comment.

On Tuesday morning, having given up all hope of ever seeing the woman, I made a trip to K-Mart to replace some of our lost items. Thank goodness the manager was still giving us a 25 percent discount, or else that would have been a very expensive shopping trip.

Before I made my trip into town Tuesday morning, we had our briefing. I told the remaining six volunteers that it was time to start getting ready to go home. This would be our day to tie up loose ends. First thing in the morning, we would start taking down what it took us 10 days to put up. It was a job none of us were looking forward to.

We had provided the animals who lived in the county a safe and comfortable refuge; our guests had included 70 stray and 59 owned animals. All the animals with owners would be gone by noon the next day, something Wendy had been coordinating since Monday. She offered foster homes to owners who might not be set up to care for their animals yet, but all of them said they were ready to pick them up. One by one, we said our good-byes on Wednesday morning.

Of the animals no one claimed, we placed 36 of them in foster homes. (Most of these ended up being adopted by their foster family.) The remaining 34 animals that we couldn't find local foster homes for would return to Macon with us.

I talked to Laura from HSUS before they had pulled out three days earlier. They had stayed busy taking care of animals from the city, all of whom had owners and were reclaimed. Since we had rescued and picked up strays from the flooded areas, we knew our work would continue beyond the time we left Bainbridge. It's EARS policy to follow up with the animals until the very last one is placed in a good, permanent home.

Having shopped at the Bainbridge K-Mart for the last time, I decided as I was pulling out of the parking lot that I wouldn't return to the shelter right away. During our meeting in Thomasville 10 days earlier, Laura told us about the pound in Bainbridge. Before I left town, I wanted to see it—something I couldn't do until now because it had been underwater.

As I drove down Shotwell, I thought about the city dog-catcher freeing the animals. If she hadn't, there was no way they would have survived, trapped in their cages and runs. I'd heard from Nick Gilman that in Americus, which is where AHA ended up doing some rescues, at least 80 animals drowned in their cages at that animal shelter. The news stunned me and the rest of the volunteers.

When I spotted the sign I'd passed daily—City Pound, with an arrow below the words directing people where to go—I turned. I had gone about a mile when the black road disappeared under a thin covering of silt, left behind when the floodwaters receded. On either side of the road were tell-tale signs that water, rushing with tremendous force, had passed through there, bringing with it debris that had gotten tangled up in the shrubs and trees. Each refrigerator, bicycle, lounge chair, mailbox, and barbeque was a piece of someone's life that was swept away by the water and had come to rest in a strange new place. The people of Bainbridge had a real mess on their hands and it would take months for them to get their town back to looking like it did before.

As I got closer to the river, my nose recognized the nauseating smell that I had breathed during my first flood in 1983 and again the past July in the Midwest—that blend of sewage, mold, gas, decaying food, stagnant water, mildew, dead animals, and rotting vegetation, each odor intensified now by the summer heat. It would be a long time before this smell vanished.

When I saw the sign for the water treatment plant, I knew the shelter had to be nearby. In my travels around the country, I've been amazed at how many city and county animal control shelters are located next to the communities' water treatment plant. I guess the city planners figure they make good neighbors. After all, who at the water treatment plant will be bothered by barking dogs or possible smells coming from the shelter; certainly, the animals won't complain, even on those hot summer days when the wind is blowing in their direction.

Just after I passed the entrance to the water treatment plant, I spotted the shelter sitting in the middle of a grassy area that was lower than anything around it. *No wonder the place disappeared underwater,* I thought to myself. I parked in the middle of the dead-end road and got out of the car, my camera in hand.

There were still a few large swimming-hole-sized puddles around the shelter. In the areas where the water could drain, the ground was covered in clay-colored silt that was too deep to walk through. If I tried, I was sure to get stuck in the kind of muck that grabbed onto your legs and wouldn't let go. With so many obstacles in my way, I couldn't get any closer than 50 feet from the waterlogged building.

From where I stood, I could tell the shelter was an old, not very well-built wooden structure, which had not held up well to the flood. The place was not much bigger than a modest house. Its roof, which extended to the end of the dog runs lined up on either side, was covered in sheets of thin buckled metal.

Attached by hinges along the top of the outside dog runs were sheets of weathered plywood that had been raised, each section propped up with a two-by-four. I figured the wooden shutters were kept open to allow for more ventilation in the summer and, in the colder months, lowered to retain as much heat as possible. I saw no signs of heating or air-conditioning equipment. It was likely the animals were always too hot or too cold. It had been a makeshift shelter to begin with. Now that it had felt the full impact of the flood, it was an even sorrier sight.

On the other side of the shelter was a windowless aluminum prefab building that I guessed covered close to 3,000 square feet. It was still under construction. I wondered whether this might be a new shelter, to take the place of the dilapidated one that should have been torn down. It gave me hope that things were going to get better for the animals.

I took a few pictures of the old shelter to show at future EARS workshops. They would illustrate why it's sometimes necessary for us to set up temporary shelters. Even if the pound had not flooded, it would still have been necessary for us to create a temporary shelter. The 129 animals we took care of, plus the ones HSUS had, would never have fit in the existing building.

Returning to the car, I took one last look at the shelter, realizing I hadn't seen the remains of any animals or smelled any that had died when I was walking around outside. Maybe the dogs and cats that had been turned loose got far enough away before the swiftly moving water poured over the banks of the river with a force that would have easily swept them away.

I was careful when I backed up the car, not wanting to get stuck in the mud, out where no one would be passing by to help me get unstuck. Just as I straightened the car out and was about to drive past the entrance to the water treatment plant again, I noticed two men waving from the roof of the building closest to the road.

I stopped the car and the men crawled down a metal ladder attached to the side of the concrete building and headed toward me. Deciding I'd wait inside the car with the air-conditioning cranked up full force, I held off rolling down my window until the two stocky men were a half dozen steps away. When the hot, muggy air from outside clashed with the cool air inside the car, I thought, *It'll be nice to get back to California where it's a comfortable 80 degrees.*

"Hey, are we glad to see you," one of the men said when they were close enough for me to hear them.

I remained silent, anxious to find out why they seemed so glad to see me. It didn't appear they had been stranded out here.

"I don't know if you heard or not, but we had to evacuate the treatment plant three days ago, and we were just able to get back in today to check on things."

"It's a pretty big mess," the other man added.

"It looks like everything out this way got hit hard," I said, shooing away an annoying fly buzzing around my face.

"When we were going around checking to see what kind of damage was done to our buildings, we come across two kittens," the first man said. "They were real scared and hungry, so we gave them some pepperoni pizza we'd gotten from the Red Cross earlier and then we just left them alone."

Now the men had my full attention.

"And when we saw the sign on your car door that says 'Animal Rescue,' we thought you might want to come up and look at them. They're mighty scrawny. I suspect they's even too young to be away from their mama," the man said, with a concern that surprised me. Since we had been in Bainbridge, we hadn't found many people, men in particular, who cared a whole lot about what happened to cats.

"Where are they?" I asked.

"If you follow us, we'll show you," they said.

So off I went with the two men I didn't know, into the water treatment plant. The concern in their voices and looks on their faces, mixed with my gut instincts, told me I had nothing to be worried about. We climbed the same ladder that they'd come down minutes before, and walked single file along a railed metal plank with huge, open vats of some *really* disgusting water on either side. It was even worse than the floodwater and the smell was enough to make me feel like I was about to lose my breakfast.

"They're right over here behind this air-conditioning unit," the man in front said, pointing to a metallic box the size of a washing machine. "I doubt they've moved. Don't got the energy to, I reckon."

Sure enough, they were right where the men had left them, lying side by side on the cement, surrounded by scraps of pizza crust, minus all the slices of pepperoni. *Oh, boy, are they going to have a mean case of diarrhea,* I thought to myself, as I bent down to pick up the kitten closest to me.

The little boy was mostly white with blotches of orange on his head and down the middle of his back. His sister had less white, and some orange and black blended areas on her head and back. What was really unique about both of them was that their right eyes were an almost turquoise blue and their left eyes were light brown. I guessed they were about seven or eight weeks old.

"I heard the lady that works over at the pound turned all the animals loose before the place flooded, and we think these guys came from there, cause we'd never seen them before today," one of the men explained.

His theory made sense.

"So can you take them with you?" the man who seemed most concerned asked. "If they stay here, they probably won't survive, especially if we end up having to take them back to the pound when they open up that new building of theirs."

"Sure, I'll take them," I said, now cuddling both kittens in my arms, neither one of them purring.

The men helped me carry them down the ladder and to the car, at which time I realized I had nothing to put them in. The Chevy Blazer I'd borrowed from one of the volunteers was filled to the roof with junk that included the bags of new clothes and 25 blue Rubbermaid totes in which we would pack our supplies and equipment the next day. Shirley had agreed to store the totes in Macon, so we would have them for the next disaster down this way.

Surveying the inside of the car, I knew I'd have to do some major rearranging to find space for these two guys, in spite of how small they were. While I moved things around, trying to figure out a good spot to put my passengers, each of the men held a kitten.

When I was ready, the men gave me the kittens, one at a time. I was surprised when the little boy got a quick kiss on the top of his head before the man handed him to me. I thanked the water treatment plant employees, and drove off with both kittens curled up in one of the totes I'd secured in the front seat, with my yellow rain slicker providing some cushioning. As soon as I looked away, though, they jumped out, and scooted between the seats, disappearing into the mess spread out in the back. We were going to play a game of hide-and-seek when we got to Dr. Height's clinic.

I knew the kittens needed medical care. At the clinic, I left the engine running so the air-conditioner would keep the kittens cool, and crawled over the front seat. I started moving things around, careful not to place anything down on top of one of the kittens. I located the little boy first, grabbing him just as he was ducking inside one of my knee-high rubber boots. With him securely in my hands, I opened the rear door a crack and backed out.

"I've got two more patients for you," I said to the receptionist. "There's this little guy, and his sister is still hiding in the car. They came from the water treatment plant and they had pepperoni pizza for breakfast. Need I say more?"

"Oh, let me see him," the receptionist said, taking the frightened kitten from my hands. "Aren't you a cutie."

I left the kitten in the care of the receptionist while I went to search for his sister. She was a lot better at hiding, and it wasn't until I'd rearranged everything in the car that I finally found her inside one of the K-Mart bags, along with a bag of smashed Fritos that I had intended to have for lunch. She didn't hiss or try and swat at me, but she was not real pleased to be picked up and carried into the clinic.

"Can I leave them here and check back with you later?" I asked. "We're heading out tomorrow, so I've got to get back to the shelter."

"You're leaving already?" the receptionist and the technician standing next to her asked in unison. "We were hoping you'd stay forever. You've done so much for the animals in this community. That shelter you all built should become a permanent facility. Heaven knows it's needed."

"I'd love to stay, but I think my husband and children might have a few objections," I said, smiling.

I agreed to call back later that afternoon. By then I hoped I would figure out what to do with the kittens. It was not likely that someone would be looking for them, since I suspected they might even be borderline feral. With a little TLC though, I knew they could be easily placed. Their eyes alone would steal someone's heart.

Well, it was Deanna and Deb (two of my coworkers at United Animal Nations who share a house) and I who had our hearts stolen. I named the boy Flint, and he came to live with the Crisp family, bringing our cat total to eight. Georgia moved in with Deb and Deanna and their two dogs, Kallee and Lacey. The two little pepperoni-loving kittens were our final rescue during the Bainbridge flood.

Our last night was spent relaxing for a change. I figured we needed a night off before we tackled the enormous project that awaited us the next day. We would have help though. The two funeral homes were sending three men to take down their tents and the National Guard would be by sometime to dismantle and haul away their tent. In the morning, we would take down the sleeping tents, leaving just the command tent, which would be one of the last things we packed away for the next disaster.

On my way to K-Mart, I had stopped at the U-Haul dealer and arranged to rent a 20-foot truck and two U-Haul trailers. Even though we still had four pickups, we needed more room to haul everything back to Macon. Our gear now included the 20 chain-link panels that ABC Fencing decided to donate to EARS.

As we sat around under the funeral tent for the last time, trying to figure out how many drivers we would need to get all the trucks, trailers, cars, and our one boat back to Macon, we heard a soft humming sound coming from the direction of the fire station. If we weren't mistaken, the noise was getting louder and was headed our way.

Staring into the darkness, we suddenly could make out the outline of two golf carts speeding across the grass, with three of the National Guardsmen in each of them. It was the guys who'd done so much to help us over the past week.

"Can ya'll come out and play?" the guy driving the cart closest to the fence asked. "We want to see whose golf carts are the fastest, yours or ours."

You could tell the disaster was almost over. People who had been so busy days before, were starting to get bored, as some simulation of normalcy began to return to Bainbridge. In a day or two, the last of the National Guard troops would be going home, these guys included.

"Of course ours are faster," I responded. "We'll leave you guys in the dust."

"I don't think so," several of the guys said in unison.

"Come on, Shirley," I said, standing up. "We'll make these slowpokes regret they came and asked us to play."

We'd been given a second golf cart a day after we got our first one, so Shirley and Amy jumped in one and Diane and I got in the other one.

"I'll be the one to say 'go,'" Tim, a volunteer, offered.

Greg unlocked the gate and Shirley and I sped past him toward our challengers, who were way too confident they were going to win. Obviously, they had no idea of my reputation of having a lead foot when it came to a gas pedal. Of course, a lot depended on how much charge was left in both golf-cart batteries. We'd not used ours much that day, so I was hopeful that it still had lots of energy or at least enough to win one race.

We lined up side by side on the deserted road that separated us from the psychiatric care facility, which is what Ollie had told us all those buildings were behind the high chainlink fence with the barbwire on top. We waited for Tim's signal to go. The suspense was elevated by each side's cheering section, ours outnumbering theirs when we counted the barking dogs, whom we knew were rooting us on.

"On your mark. Get set," Tim paused for dramatics, then yelled out, "Go!"

And we were off, one of the guardsmen and I taking the lead. The finish line was the stop sign, where we would turn left to head into town. With my foot to the floorboard, and Diane and I leaning forward, we stayed in the lead. We were halfway to the stop sign when the cart alongside of us with the two guardsmen in it started to lose power. We left them in our dust, the driver yelling to his passenger, "I thought you said this thing was fully charged."

Shirley came in second.

We switched drivers, and this time only two carts raced, one from each side. The other guardsmen's cart had completely conked out. For half an hour, we raced up and down the deserted road, our laughter drowning out all other sounds. Our cart crossed the finish line first every time.

When the remaining three carts started to lose their steam, too, we quit. We had acted like a bunch of schoolkids, and it had been just what we needed. The experiences of the past 11 days would all be behind us by the next night, and this was a really good way let go of some of the stress we'd endured.

Packing took an entire day. Greg, Tim, Amy, Maggie, Wendy, Diane, and Shirley hung in until the very end. At 9 P.M., I drove the stuffed U-Haul through the gate and crossed the field for the last time, on our way to the fire station to return the key to the gate. The firemen who we had gotten to know over the past 11 days were out front, waiting to see us off. Kenny King was among them.

"I am amazed at what you did," he said, addressing all of us as we stood outside, the temperature still a warm 90 degrees. "When you all showed up here, I had my doubts that you could do what you said you could, but obviously you made a believer out of me."

"Our job was easier because of you," I said, extending my hand. "Thank you."

There were handshakes and hugs before we got into our vehicles to begin the long journey to Macon. Wendy and I got back in the U-Haul, both of us deep in thought. It was good to be going home, but at the same time it was difficult to leave.

Wendy broke the silence. "I can now tell people I've slept in a camper with ants, used a port-a-john, eaten grits speckled with gnats, showered with truckers, spent a night in a leaky tent, and won a golf-cart race."

"What more could you want out of life?" I joked.

"I think I need a plaque that says, 'I've been brain-fried in Bainbridge.'" Being from a cool climate, Wendy also found the heat of Georgia to be unbearable.

A plaque was my holiday gift to her that year. She had certainly earned recognition.

We took the 34 remaining animals to Shirley's shelter in Warner Robins to be spayed or neutered, and then made available for adoption. North Shore Animal League gave Shirley a grant to help cover the cost of caring for the additional animals. Diane took three young feral cats that we had trapped, to see if she could tame them and then find them homes, which she eventually did.

⌒〜⌒

WENDY AND I stayed at Shirley's house after we finished settling the animals into her shelter. Friday morning, we would head back to Atlanta with Georgia and Flint to catch our flights home. There would be no time to unwind, as I was running an EARS workshop for 46 people the next day in Placerville, California, and I had lots more writing to do if I was going to make my January deadline.

It was 3:30 when I crawled into the bed at Shirley's house where I had slept 12 nights before. That night, I had lain in the dark listening to the ceiling fan overhead and the rain outside the closed window. This time there was no rain. Alberto was long gone.

As I listened to the now-soothing sound of the circulating fan, my thoughts were much different than they had been nearly two weeks earlier. I wondered then what the days ahead would hold. Tears accompanied my fear that we wouldn't be able to do enough. Now I was back in the same bed and there were no more questions or doubt. They had been replaced with memories that were rich with friendship, teamwork, and the satisfaction of knowing that we had made a hell of a difference to some terrific animals. Yes, there were animals we could not save, but there were 129 in Bainbridge and 81 in Macon who survived because of what we were able to do.

A group of dedicated, hardworking, and compassionate people created a safe place for animals during this horrible disaster, with a little help, I think, from that guardian angel. I hoped she had plans to stick around for the next disaster, and the one after that, and the one after that. Without a doubt, we had a lot of good people on our side, and they weren't all just in Georgia.

If anyone doubts the effectiveness of volunteers, they have only to look at what the 50 volunteers who came together in Bainbridge were able to accomplish, and what they had to put up with to do it, and the doubts will disappear. These people went beyond doing what was easy, confirming over and over again their amazing commitment to animals.

With a smile on my face and an incredible joy in my heart, I fell asleep for the last time in Georgia.

CHAPTER SEVEN

Piece by Piece

I N THE three months following the flood in Georgia, I divided my time between writing my book, enjoying my
family, and nurturing EARS along, with the majority going
to the latter. My writing partner, Samantha, and I managed to
make up for the week we lost together in Vail, spending five
days writing at my home in Santa Clara and another week secluded in her permanent residence outside Washington, D.C.
I did nine workshops between July 23 and October 15, training 169 new volunteers. Somehow, I still found time to stay
acquainted with my husband and three daughters.

Fall is my favorite time of year, especially the month of
October when the leaves turn eye-catching shades of crimson,
gold, and harvest-moon orange. It's also the point in the six-
month hurricane season when I begin to watch the Weather
Channel less, as the most memorable hurricanes usually show
up and do their damage by the end of September.

THE 1994 hurricane season had been tame in comparison to
those of recent years. We had a couple of close calls, but the
only time EARS mobilized was in Georgia for Tropical

Storm Alberto. Appreciating the break Mother Nature had given me, I was able to get a lot of writing done on my own. By the middle of October, I was beginning to think it would be clear sailing through to January, when I could finally hand the manuscript over to my editor and say, "I'm finished!"

Then I got a call from Pam De La Bar.

One powerful storm after another had been hitting the gulf coast of Texas hard for days. Houston and its surrounding suburbs seemed to be getting the brunt of the severe weather, resulting in unusually high rainfall. I had been paying some attention to the weather, but the reports on my local news were not as disconcerting as those Pam was hearing in her home in San Antonio.

"It's not unusual for Houston to flood to some degree every year," Pam explained. "But this has far exceeded the norm."

"Are you aware of any local animal organizations that are prepared to respond?" I asked, hoping she would say yes.

"The only group large enough to deal with something on this scale is the Houston SPCA, but I suspect this is even beginning to extend beyond their capabilities," she said. "It's reaching clear up north into Montgomery County and east into Liberty County already and it sounds like things are going to get a whole lot worse before they start to get better."

Looking at a map I pulled off my bookshelf, I located Conroe, the city Pam said was in the most danger.

"According to the last news report I heard, they've already evacuated some of the neighborhoods closest to the San Jacinto River southwest of town and along the creeks that feed into it," Pam explained. Her detailed information proved she was really staying on top of the worsening situation.

"Do you know how many homes have been evacuated so far?"

"More homes than in Bainbridge," she told me.

If that many people were being affected, I decided I'd better call Deanna as soon as I hung up. It sounded like EARS would once again be needed, this time in the Lone Star State.

It didn't take long for Deanna and I to make the decision to mobilize EARS. This would be our third disaster of the year. Once again, Deanna said to me before we hung up, "Spend every penny wisely."

On the afternoon of Tuesday, October 18, I began making the phone calls that would put everything in motion. Joining me in Houston the next day would be Shirley Minshew and Diane Tatum, veterans of the flood in Bainbridge, in addition to recently trained volunteers—Warren Jones, a veterinarian from Kansas City, Missouri, and Abigail Lambert from Arlington, Virginia. Recognizing the fact that Texas has lots of cows, I decided to ask Mike Conant to join us as well.

Mike had helped develop a group called Emergency Animal Rescue, which was made up of a group of trained volunteers who were prepared to respond to disasters in Southern California. He and his wife, Patty, had invited me to a disaster-response planning meeting they held on January 16 in Ramona, located in the mountains northeast of San Diego. The following morning, 22 of us who had participated in the meeting found ourselves caravanning to the San Fernando Valley, 200 miles north of San Diego. Our destination was the city of Northridge, the epicenter of the devastating 6.6 earthquake that had fiercely shaken the ground under the Los Angeles basin at 4:31 that morning.

Forty-five trained EARS volunteers and I had spent 10 days working with Mike's group of talented and dedicated individuals who specialized in rescuing horses and cattle. During that disaster, I learned that Mike was a true cowboy. He shared a number of rescue stories from previous fires and floods he had responded to, where his group had saved hundreds of cows and horses. I expected to need his kind of expertise in Texas.

Samantha decided to go to Texas, too. What she knew about helping animals during disasters had only come from listening to my stories and working on my book with me. It was time, she said in her English accent, "to experience one for myself." I thought it would be great to have her along to give her the firsthand experience and to have her keep a journal of stories from this disaster for the book that I assumed would follow *Out of Harm's Way.*

I arrived in waterlogged Houston at 1:46 P.M. on Wednesday. A group of eager volunteers, all dressed alike in jeans and red T-shirts, met me at the gate. Diane, Shirley, Mike, and Warren had all arrived on earlier flights and, while they waited for my plane to land, they gathered their luggage, bought some maps of Texas, and scoured the *Houston Chronicle* for news of the flood. They learned that disaster declarations had been issued in 27 counties.

"We have to stop meeting like this," I said, giving Shirley and Diane a hug. "There must be another excuse besides a disaster for us to see each other."

"Yeah, it seems the only reason I go to airports anymore is to meet you as you're arriving for the latest disaster," Shirley laughed.

"Hi, Warren," I said, moving toward the first EARS-trained veterinarian, who was standing next to two overloaded luggage carts parked behind Shirley and Diane. Warren was a graduate of the Kansas City workshop I had just done in August.

"Good to see you again, Terri," he stepped forward and offered his hand.

"Nope. Nope. Nope," I said, shaking my head. "Once you're a volunteer, we do hugs." When I stepped back from giving Warren a quick embrace, I noticed he was blushing. As I turned to greet Mike, I thought to myself, *Our vet will get used to hugging.* It's such a comforting thing to do, and we do an awful lot of it during disasters. Hugs help us survive the tough times, and in moments of pure joy, giving those around you a hug is the first thing you think to do.

"I'll be happy to give you a hug," Mike said, wrapping his arms around me. "And thanks for asking me down here, director lady."

"No problem, my friend. You just better be as good a cowboy as you say you are," I said, patting him on the back.

Samantha was the next person arriving. Her flight was not due in for another hour, so the five of us went to get something to eat. The memory of surviving on Veg·all for more than a week in Bainbridge was still fresh in the minds of those of us who had done it. We had learned an important rule to survive disaster relief: Indulge your taste buds while you still can.

It was nearly four o'clock by the time we found Samantha and picked up two minivans from Thrifty. As we drove out of the rental car lot, I said to Diane, who was riding with me, "I can't believe six people from five different parts of the country showed up at the same airport on the same day, and not one of us was late."

"It's that guardian angel of yours again," Diane said with a grin. "Certainly no human could pull off such a miracle."

"Well, there were six humans who did something that was almost as amazing just a few minutes ago," I said, recalling how we had found room for 13 pieces of luggage and two bathtub-sized totes in two vans designed to hold half the stuff we had managed to cram in. And, on top of that, we still had enough room left over for us.

"Yeah," Diane said, realizing immediately what I was referring to. "After two disasters, I feel fully qualified to get a job working for a moving company."

It was indeed amazing what you learned during a disaster.

Pam had arranged for us to stay in Conroe that night at the home of Mike and Pat Lidell, members of the local cat fancier club. "They're far enough away from the river and creeks that you don't have to worry about it flooding," Pam assured me when I talked to her late the night before. "Pat apologized that they don't have enough beds for everyone, but there's plenty of carpeted floor space."

"Sounds great," I said, before hanging up to enjoy my last good night's sleep in my own bed for a while. I knew that for at least one night I would have a roof over my head in Texas, but after that it was anyone's guess what our sleeping accommodations would be. To be safe, I had packed one of the EARS tents.

Leaving Houston's Hobby Airport, we drove north on Highway 45 and, less than an hour later, got our first glimpse through the raindrop-speckled van windows of Mother Nature's handiwork. She had done a heck of a job of messing things up again. The vast expanses of muddy water, with partially immersed homes dotting the flooded landscape, brought back memories of the three previous floods I had witnessed.

"Here we go again," Diane said with a sigh, as we crossed into Montgomery County. "It's back to living in wet clothes and surviving on tasteless food dumped out of a can."

The Lidells greeted us like we were old friends. After a round of introductions, we rummaged through our luggage in the back of both vans and found what we would need just for the night. Then we hauled the basics indoors, sleeping bag included, and staked out our spots on the living- and dining-room floors.

"I haven't been to a slumber party since I was a school-girl," Samantha said with a giggle, as she was laying out her sleeping bag. "This will be fun."

"Nobody snores, do they?" I asked, eyeing the rest of my floor mates.

Everyone but Mike said no.

Dinner that night was at a place called Joe's Crab House. We ate as though we were condemned criminals partaking of our last meal, enjoying every morsel, especially the sinfully delicious mud pie each of us ordered for dessert.

At 6:30, I left everyone in the parking lot of the restaurant, each of them moaning and mumbling under their breath, "I can't believe I ate the whole thing," as they crowded into the other van. They returned to the Lidell house to consume large quantities of Alka-Seltzer and I headed back to the airport in Houston to pick up Abigail Lambert, who was coming in on the 7:16 flight from Virginia.

I had met Abigail in July in Harrisburg, Pennsylvania, at the EARS workshop that I did there. A group of us went out to dinner afterwards. Listening to Abigail tell of her animal experiences, I was particularly impressed by her knowledge of wildlife. Though EARS focuses mainly on domesticated animals, I knew Abigail's skills would come in handy at some point. In past disasters, there were a few occasions when we had to assist a wild animal or bird. I was pleased when Abigail called UAN's office in Sacramento to say that she was available to go to Texas. If we crossed paths with an armadillo that needed help, it was reassuring to know that we would have someone with us who would know what to do.

"Welcome to Texas!" I said, as I walked up to Abigail in the baggage claim area of the airport. "You bring your cowboy boots?"

"Nope, can't say that I did," Abigail replied, as she gave me a hug. "So have you guys roped yourselves any cows yet?"

"Haven't had time. Today was spent just getting all the people rounded up. Tomorrow is when we go after the animals." I grabbed one of Abigail's duffel bags and we headed for the exit.

"I am thrilled to be here," Abigail said, as we walked across the airport parking lot toward the van. "When I saw you interviewed last year during the Midwest floods, for the *ABC News* 'Person of the Week' segment, I'm ashamed to say you made me realize for the first time that people were not the only victims of disasters. I can't believe I'd never thought before about what happened to the animals."

"There are many of *us* who took way too long to realize what little chance animals have of surviving a disaster if there are not experienced people available to help them every time a natural disaster occurs," I explained. "Without that guaranteed help, no wonder so many of them died."

"*You* made me realize that," Abigail said softly, after we had settled into the van. "And you also made me realize that one person *can* make a difference. You're living proof."

"Well, thank you," I said, glancing at my passenger as I started the car. "But, Abigail, my dream would never have become a reality without people like you."

When we arrived at the Lidells' house, everyone was still up and complaining that they had been way too indulgent at dinner. "So how many boxes of Alka-Seltzer did you all go through while I was gone?" I joked, after I had introduced Abigail to the group of *pigs*.

"Well, we went through my stash," Mike admitted. "And if we're going to continue to eat like we did tonight, we'll have to make a stop somewhere and get more."

Diane and Shirley blurted out at the same time, "From here on out, it's disaster rations."

"If anything, you'll need some Tums," I added, laughing.

The last person to arrive on Wednesday night was Pam. She had driven over from San Antonio with some supplies. She had to be at work in the morning, so she could only stay the night. It was just about 9:30 when I saw her car pull up in front of the house.

"I see you brought everything but the kitchen sink," I observed, as I peeked through the open passenger window of Pam's overloaded vehicle.

"After Bainbridge, I've started living by the Boy Scout motto—be prepared."

"Howdy!" Shirley said, joining us. "Isn't that how you Texans greet one another?"

"Something like that," Pam replied. She came around the front of the car and gave both of us a hug.

"Do you need help carrying anything?" I asked.

"Yeah," Pam replied, handing me her sleeping bag.

As we walked toward the house, Pam asked how our accommodations were.

"This is the Ritz Carlton compared to our sleeping quarters in Bainbridge," I said, stepping over a tree limb that had fallen across the walkway during a storm earlier in the day.

"Oh, I almost forgot," Pam said excitedly. "Two friends of mine, Ana Sadler and Jody Garrison, who are with a cat club near Dallas, will be arriving on Saturday with 25 cages that we can use. And I talked to another friend of mine who works at the Dallas SPCA and he agreed to loan us two of their field staff. He said it would be great experience for them."

"When will they be here?" I asked, pleased by the news.

"They can be here anytime this weekend with a truckload of supplies. They're just waiting to hear from you. And I'll be joining you guys again for the weekend, too."

"That's terrific," I said, just as we were greeted at the front door by a pajama-clad Diane.

"Hey, stranger," Pam said. "Long time no see."

"Nice of you to have a disaster so we could come see you on your own turf," Diane said, giving Pam a hug and then stepping aside for us to come in.

Our team had grown to eight. Not bad for the first day, especially with the added bonus that four of us had previous experience. Joining us the following evening would be Sharon Maag and Marty Ferguson, two experienced and trained EARS volunteers who did a terrific job the previous summer taking care of cats displaced by the Midwest flood.

When I had called Wendy Borowsky in St. Louis to see if she was available to come down to help, she explained that she had previous commitments for the next few days, but could join us the following week if we still needed her. "Why don't you call Sharon Maag?" Wendy suggested, after we agreed that I would call her the first of the week to let her know what I needed her to do. "I'm sure she'd love to come down to help and you know she'll do a great job."

I'm glad I acted on Wendy's suggestion because Sharon and Marty were great additions to the team.

After Pam dropped her stuff in the dining room, we joined the noisy group in the living room for more introductions. There was one brief period of silence in the conversation that followed, which I knew meant everyone was thinking it was time to begin winding down. Before everyone got too comfortable, though, I decided to briefly explain the plans for the next day.

"Where we're going first is Montgomery County Animal Control. They are located in an area that has been hit hard by the flooding. We have a contact name already. Pat's going to have to help me out and remind me what the animal control officer's name is."

"Leann Plyes," Pat replied.

We all wrote down her name in our pocket-sized notepads.

I thanked Pat as I finished writing. "So, we'll be heading there to talk with her and see what help we might be able to give them. Plus, there's a humane society I want to check on and our contact there is . . ." I paused, again looking to Pat for help.

"Leon Neilson," she said, right on cue. "He's the executive director."

"You're good," I said. "And, by the way, we want to thank you and Mike for opening your home to us vagabonds and for all the phone calling you did before we got here. That was really helpful."

"No problem," Pat said. "We'd do anything for animals."

"So that's as much as I know now. By this time tomorrow, we'll undoubtedly know a lot more."

"How are we doing on supplies?" Pam asked.

"In addition to what you brought, I have two totes full of what we'll need right away. Shirley, tell Pam what's arriving on Friday," I said, with a smile for Pam to see.

"My husband, Mack, and Greg Langston, the animal control officer from Warner Robins who helped us during the floods in Bainbridge, are driving a 20-foot U-Haul truck here from Macon with all the supplies and equipment we had left over from July's flood."

"That's great," Pam said. "Sounds like we'll be in good shape."

"Yeah, it's the most stuff we've ever had starting out," I said. This was just one more indication that EARS was really making progress.

With the business out of the way, we spent the next hour or so reminiscing about our days spent in Bainbridge. It had been 13 weeks since that disaster ended for Shirley, Diane, Pam, and me. The memories of getting eaten alive by mosquitoes, being deprived of sleep, getting soaked to the bone every afternoon, and trying to function in that sweatbox had faded. What was now most vivid in our memories were all the successes, each a reason by itself to be grateful that we had been there for the animals in that disaster.

It was past midnight when we decided we had better call it a day. The group consensus was that we would be up, dressed, repacked, and on the road by seven o'clock, which meant reveille would be at 5:30. *Yep, I'm back in a disaster,* I thought, as I set the alarm on my watch.

There was the round of good-nights, Abigail not forgetting to include, "Good-night, John Boy," which was followed by a chorus of giggles, and then a few last thoughts shared in the dark. As people began to fade, the room got quieter and finally there was silence—except for Mike's snoring.

As I snuggled down in my sleeping bag, I regretted not having packed my earplugs. At first, I tried burying my head under my pillow in hopes it would quiet the snoring from the next room, but it didn't work. I uncovered my head so I could breathe easier, and then I rolled onto my back. Listening to the racket that vibrated the floor under me, I began to realize sleep was not going to come easy, in spite of how tired I was.

Since I couldn't sleep, I decided to revisit the events of that day. I felt good about what had happened so far. Even though we hadn't actually done anything substantial yet, mo-

EARS command center in Bainbridge, Georgia.

Me taking a call in my "office" in Bainbridge, Georgia.

Tommy and his
four boisterous
coonhounds, going
home from the
shelter in Bain-
bridge, Georgia.

Chico, the two-month-old Chihuahua mix who developed his own
method to stay cool by laying under the ice chest drain.

Bainbridge City Pound, after the floodwaters receded.

National Guard members, or should I say instigators, of the golf-cart race in Bainbridge, Georgia.

A magical reunion—
Dr. Davidson and his cat, Boy,
in Liberty, Texas.

Maggie, the blind Poodle
mix and first animal to
arrive to the shelter in
Liberty, Texas.

The Pug in Liberty, Texas,
who stayed on top of the
airline crate intended
to be her house.

The three-week-old Chihuahua brought to the shelter in Liberty, Texas, in a man's sock.

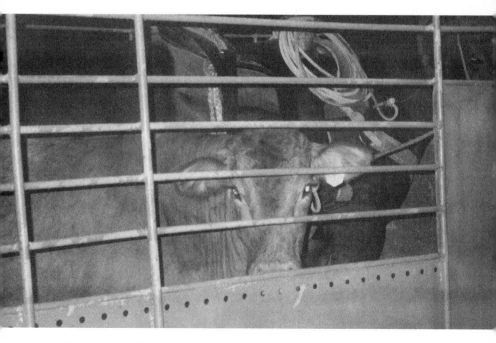

"The Obstacle" in Liberty, Texas, who was hoisted to safety.

Shirley Bollinger with her rescued dog, Libby, in Liberty, Texas.

Bobby French's surprise birthday party (left to right: Wendy Borowsky, Bobby French, Lawrence Hopkins, and me)

The impassable street caused by the earthquakes in Kobe, Japan.

A cat who sits atop an airline crate—just one of the many animals affected in this disaster in Japan.

A cat coming out of a dog house—an ironic sight in the midst of Japanese earthquake rubble.

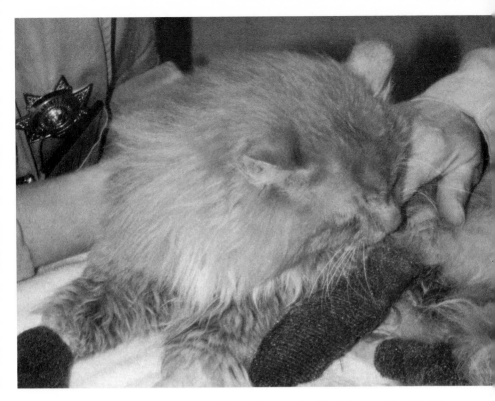

Bumpus, the "Fantastic, Fearless, Fireproof Feline" burned in Wasilla, Alaska, two days after Dr. Leach performed miracle surgery.

Bumpus
after his bandages
were removed.

bilizing seven people was no easy task. This first phase had passed, free of glitches, and the end result was that we had an excellent group of people ready to go to work.

As my mind gradually wandered to the uncertainty of the days ahead, I realized something was missing. The anxiety that I had always felt for the first day or two after arriving at a disaster site, while I obtained the information needed to clarify the role EARS would finally play, was absent. What I felt instead was an all-encompassing sense of peace. I asked myself, *What's different this time? Why am I not trying to figure out what's going to happen tomorrow and the next day, and worrying about whether I'll make the right decisions? And where is the fear that I won't be able to do enough?*

It would have been great to have had someone to talk with right then, to help sort out my thoughts, but it appeared I was the only person still awake, so I was on my own. As I thought more about it, the pieces began to fall into place, giving me the answers I was looking for.

One of the reasons I felt so much more at peace this time was that I felt confident with my continuously developing abilities to be a leader, to position EARS in the right place at the right time. After all, this was my twelfth disaster. In the 11 years I had been doing this, I had seen a lot, done a lot, and learned from all of it. I was determined not to make the same mistakes twice because, if I did, it would most likely be the animals who would pay for my errors.

It was also the people surrounding me at that very moment who enhanced the peace I felt. I was confident they would all do a top-notch job. I trusted the motives of each one of them, and their commitment to animals paralleled my own. There was no doubt that they would save lives, and I was already proud of these anticipated accomplishments. Certainly, I could never do alone what we could do as a group. *Teamwork is what has made the difference,* I said to myself.

It was the last thing I remember thinking before I fell into a peaceful sleep.

CHAPTER EIGHT

Hiding

I WOKE TO sunlight peeking through the living-room window above my head. It appeared the rain had moved on for now, and the news I could hear from a radio in another part of the quiet house said, "Expect clear skies through the weekend." This did not mean the threat of flooding had passed, though. There was still a lot of water on the ground in southern Texas, and it was going to go wherever it darn well pleased. More than likely, it would end up in places people didn't want it.

"Morning," I said, as I walked into the kitchen, wearing an oversize T-shirt and a pair of baggy sweats, my hair pulled up in a lopsided ponytail on top of my head. Mike and Pam were both up, seated at the table drinking coffee, which I desperately needed.

"Any more of that stuff left?" I asked, after I finished yawning.

"Just made another pot," answered Pat, who had walked into the kitchen behind me. She was already dressed and looking way too chipper for 5:45 in the morning. She handed me a mug with Siamese cats painted on it and proceeded to fill it with steaming coffee, which I diluted with half-and-half and sweetened with a scoop of sugar.

114

"Anyone else up?" I asked, after two sips of caffeine.

"The rest of them are stirring," Mike said. "May have to go in there and douse them with ice water to get them up, though."

"Hey, I'm up." Warren came through the kitchen door. "And I believe Abigail is in the bathroom getting dressed, so that's two less people you're going to have to douse."

Shirley and Diane appeared in the doorway not a minute later, and Samantha yelled from the living-room floor, "Does this hotel have room service?"

"Do you think you all will need a place to stay tonight?" Pat asked, pulling a pan of hot muffins from the oven. "If so, the floors are yours again."

"Thanks," I said, the kink in my back reminding me why I prefer to sleep on a bed. "Right now, I'm really not sure. Can I let you know later?"

"That's fine. You've got my number, so call when you know." Pat got plates out of the cupboard. "You're welcome to stay as long as you need to."

After a quick breakfast, everyone kicked into high gear, doing what they needed to in the bathroom and gathering up their few belongings in case we ended up staying somewhere else that night. We were all outside, packed up, seated in the two vans, and ready to pull away at 7:10, which was pretty darn good. We had missed our departure time by only 10 minutes.

"I'll page you tomorrow night and see where you are," Pam yelled, getting into her car for the drive back to San Antonio.

"Talk to you then," I yelled back.

Mike and Pat wished us good luck. "Call if we can do anything," Mike said.

"Thanks," I said, with a last wave good-bye.

Montgomery County Animal Control was less than 15 minutes away on South First Street, and we didn't encounter one roadblock or detour getting there, which was a good sign. The parking lot in front of the building had plenty of empty spaces, so we had no trouble finding two places side by side.

Gathering the group outside the vans, I shared with them what I had just determined from a first glance around. "My guess is that animal control is part of the police department." The sign in front of the building provided me with that clue. "And I suspect because we don't see or hear any animals, they don't have a shelter of their own. If that's the case, they probably have a contract with the humane society to house the animals they pick up."

"Should we go there instead?" Abigail asked.

"No. Shirley and I will still go in and see what we can find out, but I doubt if we'll stay long. As soon as we know anything, one of us will come back out and update you."

"Sounds good," Mike said, leaning against the van, smoking a cigarette.

When we walked through the front entrance of the building, we were in a small office area with a counter right inside the door. We could only see one person, and he was seated behind the counter, his attention focused on a pile of paperwork.

"What can I do for you?" the middle-aged man asked, looking up only briefly as we approached the counter.

"Is this animal control?" I asked.

"You're in the right place," he said, continuing to shuffle papers.

"We'd like to see Leann Plyes," I said, standing at the counter with Shirley beside me.

"She's out on a call," the man said.

"Do you know when she'll be back?"

"Don't reckon anytime soon."

"Is there any way to reach her or will she be calling in?"

"She has a radio," the man said, wadding up a piece of paper and tossing it in a waste can against the wall.

"Is it possible to call her and find out when she'll be back?" I asked, realizing we weren't going to get anywhere fast with this guy.

"I suppose so," he replied. "What's your name?"

I reached into my vest pocket and handed him one of my business cards, saying, "My name is on the card. If you wouldn't mind, could you tell Leann I'm here to see if she needs any help with the flood?"

"I can tell you right now we don't need no help," the man said, handing my card back to me. "We've got things under control."

"That's good to hear," I said, even though I didn't fully believe what the man was telling me.

"You might want to go over to the humane society though and see if they need help." The phone rang, but before he picked it up, the man added, "They're the ones that house our animal pickups."

I listened to his end of the conversation for a brief moment to determine if it might possibly be Leann on the other end, but it sounded more like a personal call, so I turned away from the counter. Shirley followed me to the door. When we were sure the man could not hear us, I whispered to Shirley, "I don't think this guy has any clue what's going on outside this office."

"I agree," Shirley said, looking over my shoulder at the man who was a whole lot more interested in talking on the phone than he was in us. "I think if we were able to talk with Leann, though, we might get a different story."

"Most likely," I said, looking out the window to where the volunteers patiently waited.

"So what do you think we should do?" Shirley asked.

"I'll get directions from him to the humane society and we'll go by there and see what's going on." I pulled my notepad out of my pocket. "Depending on what we find out, we may or may not come back here to see if Leann has returned."

"Sounds good to me," Shirley said. "You want me to go outside and tell everyone what we're doing while you get the directions?"

"That would be great." I went back to the counter to wait for the man to hang up.

"Can I get directions to the humane society?" I asked, as soon as he put the phone down. "We decided we'll run by there and see how they're doing."

The directions he gave me seemed simple enough. I slid my business card back across the counter in his direction and said, "When Leann returns, could you please give her my card and let her know that if she does need any help she can page me and the number is on the card."

All he said was, "Uh huh."

The humane society was just a few miles from animal control. When we pulled up in front, there was not much activity there either. While Shirley and I talked with Leon Neilson, who was extremely hospitable, the rest of the team walked through the shelter to pet dogs and play with cats.

"There's no threat of flooding where we are here, and there's plenty of room in the shelter for any animals that need a place to stay until all this passes. So we should be fine," Leon explained. "So far we've gotten just a few calls, which makes me think we're not going to get any busier."

"That's good to hear." I handed him my business card. "Just in case things change, my pager number is on the card. Don't hesitate to get hold of me."

"How long do you expect to be in town?" he asked, as we reached the front door, where the rest of the group was waiting.

"Don't know for sure, but I suspect at least another day or two."

"Well, I'll sure call if I need anything," Leon said, offering his hand in a farewell gesture. "Sure appreciate you stopping by."

Regrouping outside in the parking lot, I told the volunteers what Shirley and I learned from Leon.

"So does this mean we're done?" Warren asked.

"No," I replied. "We haven't gotten the whole picture yet."

"Do you think we'll really be leaving in a day or two?" Abigail asked, sounding disappointed.

"It's still too early to say for sure."

"You'll learn this is the way it is at the beginning," Shirley explained. "It's a lot of hurry up and wait, and then all of a sudden things start happening or else things turn out to be okay and we go back home."

"Mike, you got those maps you picked up at the airport yesterday?" I asked, after acknowledging what Shirley had just said.

"Yes, ma'am."

"Can you get them?"

While Mike retrieved the maps, I explained what I had in mind. "We're going to divide up into two teams and do some scouting on our own."

"Just like we did in Bainbridge, huh?" Diane asked.

"Exactly. Before we make any decisions about pulling out of here, I want to be sure we've seen for ourselves what's going on."

Using evacuation information from the morning paper and the maps we spread out on the hood of the van, we determined where the areas were that had already flooded. We used a highlighter to circle on two identical maps those areas that appeared to have the highest concentration of homes. If there were animals that needed help, that was where most of them would be.

"Shirley, you take Mike and Diane with you and I'll take Warren, Abigail, and Samantha with me. I want you guys to cover this area," I said, pointing to the map they would be using. "And we'll take the rest."

"When and where do we want to meet up again?" Shirley asked, as she folded her map in half.

Looking at my watch, I decided three hours would be enough time for both teams to get a sense of what the situation was in the area they were scouting, so that meant we'd have to pick a place to meet around noon.

"How about we meet back at animal control? Maybe Leann will be back by then."

"That'll work," Shirley said.

Now that I had established the teams and assigned the scouting areas, I needed to share some general instructions with everyone before we took off. "What I want you to do is find the people. Obviously, they've already evacuated, so we'll have to go by the Red Cross shelters, which Mike has marked on each map. And we should go to the roadblocks where people may still be exiting the flooded neighborhoods or just hanging around waiting for news. You can almost always find people there that need help with their animals."

"What if we see an animal in trouble?" Mike asked.

"Do what you can to get the animal somewhere safe, then page me," I said.

"Will do," Mike said, as he repositioned his red baseball cap on his head.

"And be safe out there!" I cautioned. No one had been injured during the flood in Bainbridge and I wanted to be sure all the volunteers in this disaster went home with nothing more than sore muscles and maybe a few minor bumps and bruises.

"I'll keep them in line," Mike said. "I've got my rope with me if they get out of hand."

"Good. We'll see you in three hours."

For the rest of the morning, both teams went about looking for animals to help. My team talked to lots of people, but they either didn't have any animals or had already tucked them away someplace safe, which we were happy to hear. In three hours, the only assistance we were able to provide was to a minnow stranded in a puddle left when the water receded in a neighborhood that bordered a creek. It wouldn't be but a few more hours before the puddle completely evaporated, so we scooped up the minnow in a paper cup and released him in the creek.

As we were waiting for Shirley's team to show up at animal control, I was beginning to think we might just be heading back home the next day. Shirley's team would have to return with lots of requests for help in order to justify keeping eight people in Texas.

It was 12:15 when the other van pulled into the parking lot.

"How'd you guys do?" I asked as Shirley, Mike, and Diane walked up to where we were sitting in the grass.

"There's a woman by the name of Jewell Wright who needs our help," Shirley said, reading from her notebook. "When she evacuated, she didn't have a way to get her six cats out, so she put them in her attic, thinking they'd be safe up there."

"And she has a 10-foot-high ceiling in her living room, so there's a good chance they were high enough above the water to survive," Mike added.

"How high is the water now?" I asked.

"It's gone down a lot," Shirley said. "Mike, how deep did the National Guardsmen say the water was back in there?"

"It varies, but anywhere from two to three feet."

"How high did it get?" I asked.

"Nine to ten feet," Diane replied. "Anything trapped below that didn't have a chance, I'm afraid."

"Wow, that's a big drop," I said in amazement. "Can we drive to the house?"

"No," Shirley said. "But there's a National Guard truck assigned to drive the residents in and out of the neighborhood. I already asked if we could get a ride with them and they said no problem."

"Okay then. Let's go find Jewell's cats," I said, getting up and brushing the grass off the seat of my pants. "Shirley, we'll follow you."

The narrow residential street leading into Jewell's subdivision was a hub of activity as people maneuvered small boats and four-wheel-drive trucks through the receding water.

Everyone was determined to get back home for the first time to see what damage the water had done. The National Guard truck that was shuttling people back and forth was parked at the water's edge, waiting to make its next trip.

"Diane and Abigail, why don't you stay here with the cars while the rest of us go see what we can find?" I said, as I was pulling on my waders. "While we're gone, you can talk with more people and see if anyone else needs any help."

"Can do," Diane said. "Terri, why don't you give me your keys in case we need to move the van."

"Good thinking." I handed them to her.

"That's Jewell over there," Shirley said, pointing out a petite woman, who I guessed to be in her early thirties, walking toward us. "She asked us earlier if she could go with us. I said yes. I hope that's alright with you?"

"Sure," I said, lowering my voice as Jewell got closer. "We'll just have to be sensitive to what she may or may not be ready to see."

"Hi, I'm Terri, the director," I said, as Jewell joined us.

"I can't tell you what a relief it is to have you here," she said, tears welling up in her eyes. "I was frantic trying to figure out who to call."

This is why we go to where the people are instead of waiting for them to find us. If we waited for them, in many instances it would be too late for the animals.

When we were geared up, we climbed into the back of the truck. The truck moved at a snail's pace through the muddy water, stopping from time to time to let riders off in front of their homes. Jewell, seated on the bench next to me, remained silent. I could only imagine what it would feel like to be in her shoes right then. This had to be incredibly difficult. The anticipation alone would be unbearable. Not only was she going to see her flooded home for the first time, but she was also about to learn whether her six cats were still alive or dead. In just a few more minutes, she would know.

The outcome would either tear her apart or she would be filled with a sense of relief. I prayed it would be the latter.

The truck stopped again, and Jewell said, "This is where we get off."

Climbing down from the truck, we found ourselves standing in the middle of the street in water up to our knees. We didn't move until the truck started up again and disappeared around the next corner. What surrounded us was unbelievable: caved-in walls, toppled fences, uprooted trees, cars lying on their sides, and displaced belongings everywhere. The water had left nothing untouched. I felt for Jewell and her neighbors. They had a long struggle ahead of them.

"Is that your place?" Mike asked, as Jewell stared at the house that seemed to be the worst victim of the water. It had sat too close to the river that had overflowed into this neighborhood, leaving devastating scars to the structure. She could only nod.

"Shirley," I said softly, so Jewell couldn't hear, "why don't you stay here with Jewell, while the four of us go in and have a look around? If the cats didn't make it, I don't want her to be with us when we find them."

"I'd be happy to." Shirley returned to where Jewell was still standing. Not knowing what else to do, Shirley put her arm around Jewell's shoulder, hoping it would provide some comfort while they waited for us to come back.

"Mike, you want to take the lead?" I asked, knowing we couldn't delay any longer what we had to do.

"Yep. I can do that."

We got into the house through an unlocked side door. It took a couple of persuasive shoves from Mike's shoulder to get the door to budge. When it gave way, he peeked around it cautiously.

"Oh, man!"

"What?" I asked, afraid of what I'd hear.

"The water got all the way up to the ceiling in here."

"How high's the ceiling?" Warren asked.

"It looks like it was eight feet high, but when the drywall on the ceiling got wet, most of it fell down, along with the insulation," Mike said. "I can see straight up into the attic now."

This was not what I wanted to hear.

"You ready for us to come in?" Warren asked.

"Yeah, but be careful," Mike said. "The linoleum is going to be real slippery and in addition to all the dry-wall and insulation in the water, there's a whole bunch of other stuff floating around."

Staying within arm's reach of one another, we slowly made our way through the laundry room and into the kitchen. What we saw kept getting worse. Very little of what surrounded us could be salvaged. Jewell's home was a complete loss, which meant she'd have to start all over. She told Shirley earlier she had no flood insurance.

The next room we had to pass through was the dining room. As we stepped over and around the tipped over dining-room table, chairs, and china cabinet, we said nothing. There was only one more doorway to pass through and then we were certain we'd get our first peek at the living room with the high ceiling, and maybe the cats.

"It's as bad in here," was all Mike said, as he stepped aside to let the rest of us see what he had already discovered.

Floating on the surface of the water and stuck to every surface in the room were more jagged pieces of crumbling drywall and sopping-wet pink insulation. The 10-foot-high ceiling was gone. All that remained were the wooden beams and the roof above them. Nowhere did we see any cats peering down at us.

"We'll have to get up there somehow to look around," Mike said, turning to see what he could use to climb on. "It looks like there's some kind of crawl space up next to the chimney. They might just be hiding in there."

"Maybe if we call them, they'll meow back," Samantha suggested.

When we tried, we got no response.

"Mike," Warren yelled from the kitchen, "I think you're tall enough that if you stand on the kitchen counter, you can get up in the attic and then crawl across to the living room on the beams."

"It's worth a try," Mike hollered, as he backtracked into the other room.

"Terri, why don't I go back outside with Jewell? I think you're going to need Shirley," Samantha said.

"I think you're right. Thanks, Sam," I said, noticing the sadness in her eyes. This was all so new to her, even though in the course of working on my book she had heard some of the heartbreaking stories from other disasters I'd been to. Experiencing it yourself is another matter, and I could tell it was really hard for her. She now had a firsthand understanding of what I did.

The waiting was difficult as I listened to Mike crawling at a painstakingly slow rate through the attic overhead. He still had quite a ways to go, so I decided that instead of standing in the living room by myself, doing nothing, I would look around for any signs of the cats. Maybe they had found a way to get out of the house before the water rose to the ceiling. What I found I was not expecting.

In the entry hall, hanging by its front claws from the wooden mini-blinds was a bloated body. When I spotted the lifeless form, I immediately covered my eyes, hoping that when I moved my hands aside I would realize that I was mistaken, that what was really hanging there was a piece of clothing or a furry pillow or maybe just a stuffed animal. But when I looked again, I knew without a doubt it was a black-and-white cat. It was the one Jewell was most anxious to find.

When I moved closer, I could see the frozen expression on the young cat's face. It was one of absolute horror. Her large golden eyes were wide open and bulging and her tongue was hanging out of her partially opened mouth. She had to have been terrified as she had struggled to climb the blinds, clinging to them as the water got higher and higher.

This is what I had protected myself from for so many years. Before I began doing disaster work, I could not have looked at an animal in this condition. I would have done almost anything to hide from seeing something this horrible. But now, here I stood, about to unhook each claw, one by one, from the badly damaged blinds, while holding onto the stiff, wet body with my other hand so the cat wouldn't fall into the water that had taken her life. Then I'd have to hold open an ordinary black garbage bag and place her inside. What would be the hardest part would be holding the plastic-wrapped body in my arms and carrying her outside to where Jewell was nervously waiting. With each step, I felt as though I wanted to crawl into the bag with the cat and hide, but I couldn't.

When Jewell saw me and what I had cradled in my arms, she covered her mouth with both hands and began shaking her head like a defiant child. As I got closer, I could hear her muffled pleas: "No! No! Please, no! I prayed this wouldn't happen. Why did this happen?"

"I am so sorry, Jewell," I said, when I reached the spot in the middle of the street where she had been waiting for what she hoped would be good news. "I am truly sorry."

Time seemed to stand still at that moment. The weight of the cat in my arms and the pain in Jewell's eyes were the only two things I was aware of as I stood motionless in the water. I could think of no words that would have even begun to comfort the woman who stood in front of me, so I left it to my tear-filled eyes to convey what I felt.

"Which one?" Jewell asked, when she moved her hands away from her mouth.

"The black-and-white one, I'm afraid."

Jewell then reached for the bundle in my arms. She pulled the body tight to her chest and began rocking back and forth, her chin resting on the tiny head inside the bag.

When I thought I couldn't stand the hurt I felt inside for another second, I heard a joyous chorus from the house behind me. Shirley stuck her head out the door and said, "We've got ourselves three lives ones in here."

"Jewell, did you hear that? They found three of the cats alive," I said, placing my hands on her shoulders. "Three of them made it."

"I have to go to them," she said, stepping around me, still holding the dead cat to her chest.

While Mike and Warren remained in the attic with the frightened felines, using cushions from the couch to block their escape routes, Shirley and I worked to build a makeshift ladder out of chairs and tables, directly below the niche the cats had found right up against the chimney. Jewell sat on the only table we hadn't used, cradling her dead cat in her arms and calling each of the survivors by name in a reassuring way, based on descriptions Warren had provided.

Shirley and I had to rearrange the mountain of furniture twice before we felt the precarious ladder was reasonably safe to climb. When we got to that point, I said to the two guys crouched above me, "Here I come."

"Just let us know when you're ready for us to start handing down the cats."

Standing near in case I lost my balance, Shirley guided me up the wobbly ladder, telling me the best place to put my hands and feet before I positioned them higher. When I got within reach of the beam, I grabbed on and didn't let go until I saw the fuzzy face of an orange cat being handed down to me by Mike. While Shirley stood with the Evacsack open, I carefully lowered the cat I had by the scruff of the neck and deposited it, feet first, inside the rescue bag. When I let go, Shirley quickly closed the opening, securing the cat.

We successfully repeated the same process two more times.

Still clinging to the beam overhead, I looked across the room to where Jewell was seated, amidst her cats. As Shirley handed the survivors to her, she spoke quietly to them through the bags, saying to each one, over and over again, "I am so sorry. I am so sorry."

When she looked up and saw me watching her through tear-filled eyes, she said with a wide smile on her face, "Thank you. Thank you for what you've done."

That is the reason I no longer hide.

CHAPTER NINE

Not Knowing

W E NEVER found Jewell's other two cats. After searching the house further, we discovered a broken window in one of the bedrooms, with the glass completely gone. Most likely, they had escaped, or that's what we wanted to believe. It was our hope that once all the water receded and Jewell was able to return home permanently with the three cats who had survived, the last two would return, unharmed.

The afternoon was half over when we said good-bye to Jewell, wishing her well. Just before she got into her car, she said to me, "You know, I could never have gone in the house by myself." She looked down at the ground then and nudged a pebble with her shoe, delaying her next words. "I was so afraid I'd find all six cats drowned, and that's an image I could not have lived with."

"I know," I said, stepping forward to give her a last hug. "I'm glad we were here and that we found three of the cats alive."

"I am, too," Jewell said, as we stepped apart. "But I messed up this time by not having a way to get them to safety and I will *never* make that mistake again."

"I know you won't."

As all of us watched Jewell's car slowly make its way down the still-crowded street, her cats safely tucked away in the backseat in cardboard carriers we had given her, I knew I had a decision to make: whether or not we should stay in this disaster. Were we really needed enough? The only other rescue we had done that afternoon was to relocate an armadillo who had gotten wedged in a tree when the water receded. I knew having Abigail along would come in handy. She handled the lucky little guy like a real pro, releasing him in an area where he would be safe.

"Well, director lady, what's on the agenda now?" Mike asked.

"Lunch," I was quick to reply.

One of the Red Cross mobile feeding trucks was parked nearby, so we grabbed a stack of bologna and cheese sandwiches, my meat going to a Basset Hound named Clarence who walked past with his owner. We chose the curb for our picnic site, finding front-row seats to a parade of disaster victims. Many of them were on foot, others safely encased in vehicles, some with small boats in tow. Everyone moved by quickly, urged on by their need to know. Their faces were a collage of fear, uncertainty, bewilderment, and sadness. The hope that by some miracle they would be spared was gone. We had seen from the back of the National Guard truck what they were headed for and we already knew that Mother Nature had not been kind to them.

After we ate, it was time to rally the troops and move on. Still sitting on the curb, I said to the volunteers seated on either side of me, "First of all, I want to say to those of you who were at Jewell's place, you did good." Looking at Mike, Warren, Samantha, and Shirley, I felt so proud of them. "I wish we had found all six cats still alive, but it just wasn't meant to be. Finding three provided a much-needed high for all of us. And, all of you were incredible with Jewell. I know we helped her in more than one way."

It was an emotional rescue and, for a few brief moments, none of us said anything. I think the full impact of what we had done and seen was catching up with us.

"Okay, where do we go from here?" I asked with a burst of energy. "Diane and Abigail, did you talk to anyone else who asked for help?"

"No. It was more of what we heard this morning," Abigail said, shaking her head. "And now that people are able to return home, in spite of their houses being a total mess, they seem to feel that they can take care of their own animals."

"Well then, what I think we should do is go back to animal control and see if we can find Leann. I want to hear it from her that things are under control. If she says yes, then I suspect we'll probably pull out tomorrow."

The looks on everyone's faces hinted at what they were feeling. Of course, we were pleased that people, for the most part, had taken responsibility for their own animals. Not having anything to do was a good thing, but at the same time, everyone, especially the volunteers who were doing this for the first time, had geared up emotionally and physically to help animals and were disappointed to some degree.

⁓

THE RIDE back to animal control seemed to take longer. The adrenaline-driven excitement that had fueled us earlier was fading. I realized I was tired and hungry for a good meal. The dry cheese sandwich hadn't even begun to appease my empty stomach. If talking to Leann resulted in nothing more to do, I would take the volunteers out for a real dinner and return to the Lidells' house to make arrangements for all of us to fly home in the morning.

When I got to animal control, I would have to call Sharon and Marty. Earlier in the day, I talked to them, and to Shirley's husband, Mack, who was still waiting to hear if we needed the supplies from Georgia. I told all of them to hang tight until they heard back from me. It was now time to call and tell them to stay home.

For Sharon and Marty, there would be no problem canceling their plane reservations. We'd come up with a new, less expensive way to fly to and from disasters. These special tickets (issued to airline employees and then passed on to us by those individuals who love animals and want to help) cost a fraction of a full-fare ticket. We have to fly standby, but there is no penalty if you cancel at the last minute. We would just hold onto the tickets and use them to get volunteers to the next disaster.

Something that came over the car radio just then postponed my phone calls to Missouri and Georgia: "A levee has broken along the Trinity River causing the evacuation of residents in the town of Liberty. This town of 11,000 people is under a state of emergency." This sounded serious. I turned the radio up. "Two evacuation shelters have been opened and more will probably be needed if the floodwaters continue to spread across the flat landscape."

We were only a couple of blocks from animal control, so once we got there I would discuss this new development with the entire group. Leaving Mike in the car to monitor the radio, especially any information on roads that had been closed as a result of this new flooding, the rest of us looked at a map to determine how far away Liberty was. It was nearly four o'clock. If it were too far, it would be better to stay in Conroe for the night, since there wasn't much we could do in the dark anyway. At first light, we'd head out and see what we could find.

"Looks like it's about an hour and a half east of here," Warren estimated.

"And there are several ways to get there, so hopefully at least one of the roads will remain passable."

As we were huddled around the map watching Warren point out the possible travel routes, an animal control truck pulled into the parking lot and a minute later a woman got out. My guess was that Leann had returned.

"Hi, are you Leann Plyes?" I asked, catching up to the uniformed woman just before she entered the building where our day had begun.

"Yes, ma'am," she said, with a puzzled look on her face. "What can I do for you?"

I proceeded to explain to her who I was and our reason for being there, which seemed to change the expression on her face to one of relief.

"I can't believe you came all the way to Texas to help out. That's alright," she said, directing her comment to the entire group of volunteers who had joined us.

"So, is there anything we can do to help?" I asked.

"As a matter of fact, there is," she said, tossing her long brown ponytail over one shoulder. "There's a roadside zoo out of town that sits right next to the river. When the water started rising, the people who run the place left, leaving all the animals behind." Leann paused and cleared her throat before she continued. "As far as I can tell, because it's too flooded to get back in there right now, most, if not all of the animals in cages probably drowned."

"They just left them?" Abigail asked in disbelief.

"Uh huh, and it doesn't surprise me," Leann replied.

"What kinds of animals did they have?" Shirley and I asked at the same time.

"They had a lion and a bear and a hippo and a whole lot of smaller, less exotic animals. It's a small herd of hoofed animals, though, that I need help with."

"What do you mean by hoofed animals?" Mike asked.

"Deer and antelope," Leann explained. "They were kept on an island in the middle of the zoo. When the water rose, they had no fence to keep them in, so they escaped. Now they're in the woods adjacent to the zoo. What scares me is that they'll get spooked, run onto the highway, and get hit by a car."

"So you need help rounding them up," Mike interjected before Leann finished.

"That's right," she acknowledged. "I just left there, realizing there wasn't much I could do by myself, so your timing is perfect."

"Have you thought of darting them?" Warren asked.

"That's an option, but I'm afraid if we do that, the tranquilizer won't kick in fast enough and when they feel the dart hit, they'll take off running and end up in the road anyway."

"So what you want to do, I take it, is herd them back into the zoo?" Mike questioned.

"Yeah. There's an area where I think we can do some makeshift repairs on the fence that will hopefully keep them confined until something more permanent can be done," Leann said. "We've been trying to get this place closed down for a long time, and I think this might just be what it takes to finally make that happen."

"Thank goodness!" Abigail exclaimed.

"Yeah, to give you an idea of what kind of place it is, the people that work there allow the public to bring in bags of Oreo cookies to feed to the hippo, who has an addiction to the sweet things. Now tell me that's a real healthy diet for that animal."

"That's awful," Abigail said, shaking her head in disgust.

"Do you want help now?" I asked.

"Sure do," Leann said with relief. "I'd like to get them out of the woods before dark."

Warren and Abigail rode with Leann, while the rest of us followed in my van, continuing to monitor the situation in Liberty as we drove to the zoo. Things were getting progressively worse, so I called Sharon and Marty on my cell phone and told them to get on the last flight into Houston that evening and I would be at the airport to pick them up. Shirley called Mack to let him know we still weren't sure whether we'd need the supplies or not. He and Greg would wait for an update from me.

When we arrived at the zoo, we got out of the vehicles and stood by the side of the road. From what we could see, the place had been trashed. The water had not receded much, so it was still not possible to get back to where the animals had been kept, but it was pretty obvious that any caged animals were no longer alive.

Trying to beat the setting sun, we moved to the wooded area next to the zoo and formed a human wall between the road and the animals we needed to herd. It wasn't long after we penetrated the woods that we found the six escapees huddled together, their big eyes staring at us as we approached slowly. I had somewhat mixed feelings when I saw the gorgeous creatures. They were probably experiencing freedom for the first time in their lives and, in spite of being frightened, they had to be enjoying it. There was a part of me that just wanted to leave them where they were and not herd them back into a life of confinement. How long would they survive, though? Being this close to the highway, I suspected not for very long.

Weaving our way through the trees and the thick undergrowth with our arms extended to prevent the animals from slipping past us, we encountered a whole menagerie of disgusting bugs. The most plentiful ones were the annoying mosquitoes that feasted on our exposed skin. Being this close to the river, the woods were a breeding ground for the pests.

In an hour, we succeeded in getting the animals farther away from the highway, but not into the area where we wanted them. We were all beginning to feel frustrated, knowing we had little daylight left. We were talking about trying to lure them into the fenced area with food when three men arrived in a pickup truck. They told us they worked at the zoo and that they wanted us to leave, their demeanor anything but friendly. We tried to convince them to let us help, pointing out that with 11 people there was a greater chance of herding the animals back within the perimeter fence, but it was obvious they wanted us out of there. Since this property belonged to the zoo, there was nothing we could do but walk away, Leann included.

As I passed the men's pickup, I noticed a gun rack in the back window with two rifles displayed. I just hoped they didn't intend to use them on the frightened animals we had been trying so hard to help. *If only the animals had cooperated,* I thought to myself, as I returned to the car feeling defeated. I was now afraid that if a car didn't kill them, a bullet would.

We were all deep in thought on the drive back to animal control. It was hard for me to forget the animals we had just left in the woods, but I knew I had to focus on the animals in Liberty. I assumed they needed us just as much, and they were the ones that we could probably do the most good for now.

When my passengers got out of the van to use animal control's restrooms, I stayed behind and called the office in Sacramento to update Deanna on the situation in Liberty.

"It sounds like that's where you need to be," Deanna said, after I told her everything I heard on the radio. "I'd say head that way in the morning and see what you find. If it turns out people don't need any help, think about pulling out day after tomorrow."

"Will do," I said, and hung up.

Before I talked to the volunteers, I went to find Leann, who had gone inside to see if there were any other flood-related calls that had come in during the time we had been gone. When I found her, she was seated at the desk that had been occupied earlier by the man who had informed me that everything was under control. I was glad he was more right than wrong.

"So, do you need any more help?" I asked Leann, realizing she looked as tired as I felt. "If not, then I think we're going to head for Liberty in the morning."

"There aren't any new calls, so I think the worst is behind us," Leann said, as she shuffled through a stack of phone messages. "From what I heard on the radio, it sounds like Liberty is getting nailed, so I think that's were you guys need to be."

Sliding my business card across the counter, I said, "If anything changes here and you need something, page me. I'll be glad to send you some help."

"Appreciate it," Leann said, taking my card. "And thanks for what you did today. I just wish we could have done more for those poor animals from the zoo."

"Me, too."

We had been prepared to do a lot more than we did in Montgomery County. Finding three of Jewell's cats was reason enough to feel that our day in Conroe had been a success, though. As we prepared to move on to the adjacent county, we hoped our services would not be needed there, but we wouldn't know for sure until we could assess the situation ourselves. I had a hunch that we would find a whole lot more to do there than we had in Conroe—and, boy, did we.

CHAPTER TEN

Permission

NINE OF us drove to Liberty on Friday morning, Marty and Sharon having joined the group the night before. The enthusiasm of the previous day was not as evident among those of us who had been in Texas for three days. Our two newest recruits were the ones who were raring to go. Sharon told me while we were packing up the van that morning, "I didn't get any sleep last night. I was just too excited. All I wanted to do was go out and find an animal to help."

I laughed. It hadn't been that many disasters ago that I had stayed up all night, anxious for the next day to arrive. Now I understood the need for sleep during a disaster, and I had learned to get as much of it as I could while I had the chance.

I had taken everyone out for Mexican food the night before, and then we returned to the Lidells' home, settling in just after nine o'clock. We gave Mike and Pat a full account of what had gone on that day, detailing our rescue of Jewell's cats. There wasn't a dry eye in the living room as we remembered the cat hanging from the mangled mini-blinds.

"I don't know how you do it," Pat said, wiping away a tear. "I'm afraid I'm too emotional to see things like that."

"Unfortunately, it's part of what we do," I said, speaking for the rest of the group. "What helps is that we find more animals alive than dead. And it's the victories that keep you going, like the three survivors we found today."

With all the stories told and our energy fading fast, we spread our sleeping bags out on the floor again, and one by one fell asleep. I dreamt about Jewell's cats that night, only this time they all survived. If only that had been what had really happened.

THE DRIVE to Liberty took an hour and a half. Along the way, we saw lots of areas that had flooded, but the water was still a safe distance from the highway. It was 9:30 when we arrived in the town that had been besieged by the flood. We could tell right away that the normally slow-paced routine of a small town had been completely disrupted. Liberty had not only been invaded by water, but also by people coming to help, us being the latest arrivals.

Just after leaving Conroe, I got on my cell phone to see how much information I could gather about this community we were headed for. I hoped it would save us some time later. The clock was ticking for the animals and we would have to move quickly if we were going to find any survivors.

After several phone calls, I tracked down the number to the command center in Liberty. The line was busy the first time I tried and continued to be busy. After pushing redial 23 times, I finally reached a flustered woman who quickly passed me on to one of the public information officers, who was extremely helpful.

As I had guessed, Liberty didn't have a permanent emergency operations center. They were too small to afford one and, prior to this disaster, some people might have thought it wasn't even necessary. After all, when was the last time

Liberty had a disaster? The answer to that one, I learned, was "Never."

So, as it happens in many other small towns across the United States, the police station had been transformed into a temporary command center. In addition, the town had a motor home that had been converted into a mobile command center. It was now set up in the parking lot behind the police station. All the important decision-makers would be in there. Most likely, one of them would be the person I would have to talk with to get an idea if any animal problems had already been reported.

When I asked the public information officer if Liberty had an animal control agency, he told me they did. The small shelter was located next to the water treatment plant, which brought back memories of the pound in Bainbridge, Georgia. Once again, another animal shelter and water treatment plant made good neighbors.

"Right now the place is at least five feet underwater," the man told me.

"Do you know if they got all the animals out in time?" I was quick to ask.

"Don't know the answer to that one," the man said, apologetically. "But considering we only have one full-time and one part-time animal control officer, and they both report to the police department, I reckon they might not have had enough time to do anything for the animals. Everyone's pulling double duty right now, and we're barely keeping up with the havoc this flood has caused."

Sounds like we found a place that needs us, I thought to myself, before asking my next question. "Can you tell me who I need to speak with to find out if animal control needs any help?"

"That would be Police Chief Tidwell," the man answered.

"Do you know where I can find him?"

"That's easy," the man said. "When you come to the command center just look for the person with all the people standing around him. The chief's the one running this show."

"He's the incident commander?" I blurted out.

"Yep, and he's one very busy man right now."

Thanking the public information officer for all of his help, I hung up, and said to Warren, who was riding with me, "Looks like our first challenge is going to be getting to talk to the man in charge, and I suspect the last thing he has time to talk about is animals."

Finding a place to park close to the police station was no easy task. The parking lot and most of the adjacent side streets were packed with military jeeps and hummers, ambulances, boat trailers, Red Cross and Salvation Army mobile feeding trucks, law enforcement vehicles from different neighboring cities, and a whole assortment of other cars with government agency emblems on the doors that indicated they were officially recognized as emergency response vehicles.

"I'm sure this is a whole lot more company than this town is used to," I said to Warren, as we continued to search for a place to park.

We finally found a spot in front of a Methodist church. Taking advantage of the shade under one of their trees, I gathered the volunteers together to tell them what I had learned from the public information officer while we were en route to Liberty.

"So the person you need to talk to is the police chief?" Mike asked.

"Uh huh. Mr. Tidwell himself."

"Do you think he'll let us help?" Abigail asked.

"I don't think he knows that he needs our help," I replied. "But I'll do what I can to convince him he does."

I didn't tell the group, but I had yet to figure out exactly how I was going to accomplish this. More than likely, I'd be doing it by the seat of my pants. I hoped that the guardian angel who seemed to really like animals would pitch in and help some, too.

"What I'd like to do is have everyone but Warren stay here. I think if we approach the chief as a group, we'll more than overwhelm him."

"Would you like us to start talking to people?" Shirley asked. There had been quite a few people milling around the police station parking lot. We figured most of them were evacuees.

"Yeah," I said, "see what you can find out. And if you find out anything that you think I can use to convince the chief that the people in his community need us, come and find me. I think I'm going to need all the ammunition I can get."

"Will do," Shirley replied.

Warren and I walked the two blocks to the police station, discussing our strategy on the way. "What I want to do first is just stand back and see if we can pick out who the chief is, which should be easy according to the public information officer," I said. "We just have to look for the person with people lined up waiting to talk to him."

"So are we going to get at the end of that line?" Warren asked.

"Not quite yet. What I'd like to do is just watch him for a while to get a sense of what kind of person he is, so I'll have a better idea, hopefully, of how to approach him."

The Red Cross had a mobile feeding truck set up at the edge of the parking lot, so Warren and I got a cup of coffee and then tried to be as inconspicuous as possible, which was an easy thing to do. Everyone around us was busy with some important job or another, and they didn't show the least bit of interest in us.

"I suspect he's in there," I said, pointing to a 30-foot motor home that had the words "Command Center" stenciled in big letters on the side. "And since we don't have the magic password that gets you inside, we're just going to have to wait until he has a reason to come outside."

We didn't have to wait long. A man who looked to be in his early fifties stepped down from the motor home, followed by several people important enough to be admitted into the command center. They walked just a short distance, where they stopped to talk with a man wearing military fatigues. We couldn't hear what they were saying, but assumed it had something to do with the flood.

"Warren, I think the best thing to do is have you talk with him first, without me," I suggested. "I'm beginning to think I've got too many marks against me."

"And what marks are those?" Warren asked.

"One, I'm a woman. Two, I'm here to talk about animals. And once I tell him I'm from California, I think I'll really be in trouble," I said, raising my eyebrows.

"You've got a point there," Warren admitted. "So what do you want me to ask him?"

I spent the next five minutes prepping Warren, all the while keeping one eye on Mr. Tidwell. "And when you feel it's safe for me to step in, wave me over," I said, when I felt I had prepared Warren as well as I could.

"I hope I can do this," Warren said.

"I know you can." I gave him a pat on the shoulder.

I watched Warren cross the parking lot. Some of the men who had been with the chief had left to go speak with other people, so by the time Warren reached the chief, he was standing alone. He had a look on his face that seemed to say, "Isn't this over yet?"

I questioned whether the chief was in the mood to talk about animals, but since this might be our only chance, I was glad that Warren stepped forward and offered his hand as he began to introduce himself. Under my breath I said, "Okay, angel, this is when we need you."

Two minutes passed and Warren was still talking with the chief, his back to me. When he turned and looked at me, that was my signal to come forward. It was another minute before that happened. Even though I was less than 100 feet away, it seemed to take me forever to get to where the two men were standing. I quickly glanced at Warren's face to get a sense of where the conversation had gone, but it provided me with no clues.

"Chief Tidwell, this is Terri Crisp, the director of the Emergency Animal Rescue Service. She'll explain what we are prepared to do for your community."

"Glad to meet you, ma'am," he said, rushing through the words.

I figured I probably had, at the most, three minutes of this man's valuable time. I sort of knew what I needed to say in that short time, but it wasn't until I opened my mouth and the words came out that I realized I somehow managed to say all the right things. The whole time I was talking I kept my hands behind my back, so the man wouldn't see them shaking. I just hoped he wouldn't hear in my voice how nervous I was.

"First of all, I want to say how sorry I am about what's happening in Liberty. This is tough on everyone and I hope the town rebounds quickly. We'd like to do our part to help make that possible. I can only imagine how busy you must be, which is why I won't take much of your time. From talking with several people, I've learned that animal control is part of your department. Under normal circumstances, I imagine it's a big responsibility to keep up with all the animal concerns in Liberty. Now that it's flooding, certainly the demands are going to increase," I said, pausing for only a quick second to catch my breath.

"Apparently, the two officers you have are busy doing other things for the police department, which must mean that right now no one is dealing with the animals that need to be rescued. Well, that's where we might be able to help you out. We're trained to rescue animals. We can gather up those that have been left behind, and whose owners are now thinking it was the wrong thing to do, leaving their animals behind when they evacuated. Naturally, out of your concern for their well-being, you aren't going to let the people return to their homes to retrieve their pets. If we don't do it, there's a good chance those animals will drown. Then, in a few days or weeks, when everyone returns home, they are going to find the remains of animals, and we're not just talking dogs and cats. I suspect there's going to be a fair number of cattle, horses, sheep, goats, and pigs.

"If we could get all those animals to a safe place now and take care of them, in the long run we'll be saving your animal control officers a whole lot of time, because it'll be them that people will most likely call to ask to come get the animals, which are really going to be stinking by then. With only one full-time and one part-time employee, it's going to take a heck of a long time to gather up and dispose of all those carcasses. As people wait their turn, they are going to start to get impatient and mad, and I'm afraid some of that anger may be directed at you, which I would hate to see happen. But if we are able to get those animals to safety and take care of them until people can return home, they're going to look back on this flood and say, 'Yeah, Chief Tidwell even saw to it that the animals were taken care of.' If you want to tell the people in your town that you asked us to come here and do this job, it doesn't matter to me. I just want to do what we do and I don't care who takes the credit."

"And I should mention that our services are free. It won't cost the city a penny to have us help with the animals. Considering what you'll have to pay in overtime to clean up the mess of animals over the next few weeks, maybe even the next month, if we don't help, this is a bargain that might just be too hard to pass up." I reached into my vest pocket and handed the chief my business card. "My pager number is on this card. If you want to think about what I've just said and get back to me later today or tomorrow, that's fine. We're not going anywhere."

Quickly, I tried to remember what I had just said. Had I left out anything important? I looked to Warren for help and he just winked at me, which I took to mean, "You did good, kid."

"Where would you take these animals?" the chief asked, sounding not completely convinced that we were what he needed. "Our shelter flooded so you can't use it."

"I realize that, sir, and I want to mention that I can also help you get a grant from North Shore Animal League to help repair the shelter once the water is gone." The mention of money seemed to perk his interest.

"So where would you put the animals now?"

"We'd find a safe, enclosed field somewhere close to town that wouldn't be threatened by the flood. We've done this quite a few times in the past, so I know we could find a place again."

"And you say this won't cost?" he asked, eyeing Warren and me.

"Not a penny," I replied, with a tiny bit of growing confidence. It seemed I had finally gotten his attention.

"Okay, we'll take your help," he said, sounding almost reluctant to admit he needed it. "Go see the people in the command center and they'll lay down the rules for you. And you better make sure you don't create any headaches for us because we have so many that even a truckload of Excedrin couldn't get rid of them."

I wanted to give the man a hug, but I refrained, knowing that such an act would confirm for him that I was one of those bunny-hugging types, and all my hard work to convince him that we could be trusted would have been wasted.

All I said was, "Thank you, sir."

Warren and I both shook the chief's hand and walked toward the command trailer, just as two other men approached the chief with what I assumed would be more headache-causing problems.

"We did it," I said to Warren, in almost a whisper. "I can't believe he said yes."

"You really did a good job of getting his attention by saying all the right things. At first I wasn't sure you could pull it off, but you did. Congratulations."

We were in the command trailer receiving a briefing on the flood for almost a half-hour. There were still areas that were way too dangerous to enter. They circled those areas on the map they gave us, telling us to stay out until they let us know it was safe. Neither Warren nor I got the impression that the people who briefed us were pleased that we were there. It seemed they just wanted to give us the information that the chief wanted us to have, and then they could move on to far more important things.

When we left the trailer, we were armed with maps and the permission we needed from the powers that be to rescue and shelter animals. What more could we want? Well, an actual location to house the animals would have helped, but I was confident something would turn up—I just didn't know how soon.

CHAPTER ELEVEN

Just What We Needed

WHILE WARREN and I had been talking with Chief Tidwell, the volunteers had been mingling with the disaster victims, trying to determine whose animals might be in trouble. When a short gray-haired man approached Shirley, little did she know that he would do as much to help us as we would do to help him.

"Excuse me, ma'am," the man wearing the blue flannel shirt said, after clearing his throat. "Did I overhear you say that you are here to help the animals?"

"Why, yes," Shirley responded. "We're with Emergency Animal Rescue Service."

"Good," he said, obviously working at holding back his tears. "How does a person request your help?"

"All you have to do is just tell me what you need."

"I need to find my Siamese cat. His name is Boy."

"Is he still at your home?" Shirley asked, as she pulled a rescue request form out of her back pocket.

"Yes. When they came in a boat to evacuate me yesterday, I'd been hunting for him, but he was hiding too good," the man said, with a distant look in his eyes. "The National Guard kept saying, 'We've got to go, sir. We've got to go, sir.' I didn't want to leave him, but I ran out of time."

"Was the cat outdoors?" Shirley asked, waiting to put the information on the form she was starting to complete.

"Oh, no! Boy was never allowed out of the house. My wife was too afraid something would happen to him. He was her baby."

Hearing the man use the word "was" suggested to Shirley that he had either given up hope the cat was still alive or something had happened to his wife. Thinking it was most likely the first option, Shirley tried to offer encouragement. "We'll find Boy. Don't you worry. Cats are real resourceful and, since they can climb, I'm sure he's found a nice high dry spot to wait out the flood."

"I don't know. He's pretty old," the man said, not convinced that Boy would survive.

"I'm sure he's doing everything he can to make it through this, so he can be with you and your wife again," Shirley said with confidence.

"My wife is dead," the man said, tears forming in his eyes.

"Oh, I am so sorry," Shirley said.

"She died four years ago." The man removed his glasses and used his shirt cuff to wipe away his tears. "That's why I have to find Boy. He meant the world to her and she'd be so upset if she were here now. In fact, I don't think she would have left the house without him. She would have risked her own life to stay with him."

"Well, we'll just have to go and find him," Shirley said, her voice cracking. Not knowing whether we had gotten permission to go into the flooded areas to retrieve animals, Shirley told herself that one way or another she was going to get this man his cat. If she didn't, Shirley sensed that Boy might not be the only one who didn't survive the flood.

"If you could do that, I'd be so grateful," the man said with relief. "When I'm with Boy, I feel like I'm near my wife and I miss both of them something terrible right now."

Shirley was still talking to the man when Warren and I returned from our meeting with the chief. After all the ups and downs of the previous day, I was anxious to tell the group we were finally going to get to do what we came to Texas for in the first place. All the volunteers had been standing nearby listening to Shirley's conversation with Boy's owner, which explained why all of them had such serious looks on their face when Warren and I walked up. Before I shared my news, I asked Shirley if everything was alright.

"This gentleman needs help finding his cat Boy," Shirley explained. Then she turned to the man beside her and said, "And I'm sorry, I didn't get your name."

"Dr. Davidson."

Shirley continued to explain why this man needed our help. "Dr. Davidson was evacuated yesterday and, when it came time to leave, he couldn't find Boy. He'd like us to see if we can rescue him."

"We should be able to do that," I was quick to respond. "Chief Tidwell has given us permission to rescue animals."

"Terrific!" Shirley exclaimed.

"I know. Finally we'll be able to do something," I said to the group of volunteers who now had looks of excitement on their faces. "The only thing we still have to do is find a place where we can set up a temporary shelter. If we rescue animals, but have no place to keep them, then what's the point?"

"You can use my place," the doctor offered. "If you find Boy, he'll need someplace to go temporarily, since the family I'm staying with doesn't like cats."

"I appreciate the offer, but what place are you talking about?" I asked, confused that he might mean his house, but certainly that couldn't be it.

"My old medical practice. It's no more than a mile from here and there's no threat of it flooding."

Now the man had my attention, and the more he told me about the property he was offering us, the more interested I became. It sounded very workable.

"Can we go see the place?" I asked.

"Certainly," he said, reaching into his pocket and pulling out a wad of keys. Looking through them, he said a moment later, "And I even have the key. It's lucky they were in my pocket when I left home yesterday."

"Do you have a car?" I asked.

"Yes, but I'm afraid it's full of water," he explained with a laugh.

"I'm sorry," I said, realizing this was yet another loss in Dr. Davidson's life.

"Oh, don't be. It was time to get a new one anyway, and my insurance will take care of it."

"Well, then, why don't we give you a ride to your medical practice and we'll see if it'll work," I said enthusiastically. It was time to get this show on the road.

Dr. Davidson's medical practice was located at 705 Main Street, in the heart of downtown Liberty. Up until four years prior, the single-story brick building, which looked more like a home than a medical facility, had been where Dr. Davidson took care of the people in his town when they got sick. He had been in business at this location since the end of World War II. When the doctor gave us a tour of the building and the half-acre grassy, tree-shaded property that surrounded it, I knew immediately that it would perfectly suit our needs.

"Did you see the medical equipment in that place?" Shirley whispered, as Dr. Davidson locked the back door.

"I know, they look like props from a Frankenstein movie," I said with a shiver.

As we had gone from room to room, we felt as though we had traveled back in time. Everything was antiquated. The place could easily have been mistaken for a museum; the lobby furniture, the trays of medical instruments, the x-ray machine, the exam tables, the rotary telephone, and the Smith Corona manual typewriter, which sat on a desk next to a stack of well-used carbon paper that would probably have fetched more now as antiques than they had cost brand-new. It was hard to believe that Dr. Davidson had practiced as recently as four years prior using all these things. It was amazing.

"I know it's a little dusty in there, but it's nothing that a little elbow grease can't get rid of," Dr. Davidson said, joining Shirley and me. "I walked out of there the day my wife died, and this is the first time in four years I've been back."

"Wow," I replied. "Are you sure you want to let us use it?"

"Of course," was Dr. Davidson's immediate reply. "My wife would want me to do this for Boy and the other animals in our town."

"In that case, we'll put the place to good use. I think we'll use the building primarily for a place for volunteers to sleep. We'll put up some tents in the grassy area outside and put together some kennels, and keep the dogs there," I said, imaging the setup in my head.

"If you want to put some of the smaller animals inside, that would be fine with me," Dr. Davidson offered. "The back exam room would probably be the best spot. There's nice sun that comes in that west window in the afternoon. Boy loves to lay in the sun, so I suspect the cats you rescue will, too."

"I agree that room would be the best place, and we'll reserve the spot near the window just for Boy," I said, grinning at Dr. Davidson.

"Well, thank you," he said quietly. "I know he'd like that."

For the next half-hour, we worked out the details of our arrangements with Dr. Davidson, agreeing that as soon as we got the place set up, we would go in search of Boy. I promised him that would be before dark. I knew, if Boy was alive, he wasn't going anywhere—and he was high enough that the water was no longer dangerous.

"Dr. Davidson, do you have water, electricity, or phone service in the building?" I asked, as I made notes of jobs to assign to the volunteers.

"No," he said, rubbing his chin. "I don't think it would be any trouble getting them connected though."

"Good," I said, relieved. "Do you mind if I have one of the volunteers work on getting the phone connected today?" Using my cell phone as our primary source of communication would get extremely expensive.

"That would be okay," Dr. Davidson replied. "I'm sorry I don't know anyone at the telephone company anymore, but I'm sure there's someone there who would be happy to help."

"Good," I said. "How about the water and electricity?" Having both of these would definitely make our job a whole lot easier.

"The electricity is off, but I think we can get that turned on today, too, but the water is another matter," he said, adjusting the glasses that had slipped down his nose. "Some pipes broke just after I closed up the place and I've never gotten around to having them taken care of."

As Dr. Davidson was talking, I noticed an outdoor faucet on the building next door. A sign on the brick wall above it said "Today's Rental."

"Do you think your neighbors would mind letting us use their water if we paid for what we used?" I asked, remembering that we had gotten our water from the golf course next door when we were in Bainbridge.

"I'm sure it would be okay with them. I'll go over and have a talk with the owner."

"Then I think that'll do it," I said, glancing down my list. "While you take care of the water and electricity, I'll get the volunteers busy on some other things, including getting us a phone that works. Dr. Davidson, I can have one of them drive you to wherever you need to go."

"Good," he replied. "I'll be ready to go just as soon as I check on the water. Oh, and here's the key to the building. That'll open the front and side doors."

After Dr. Davidson returned, having gotten permission to use our neighbors' water, he drove off with Warren. The volunteers had been checking out the property. I yelled for them to gather round. Realistically, I thought we could get the facility open and functioning within four hours. In order to do this, all nine of us would have to take on multiple tasks.

Shirley's first job was to call Mack and tell him that it was a go for him and Greg to bring us the supplies from Georgia. I estimated that if they left that afternoon, we would probably see them late the next day. The supplies they were bringing were definitely going to be needed, but we had the basics to get started. Along with what I figured we could round up in Liberty, we'd do just fine until the reinforcements arrived.

"Okay, listen up," I said to the seven eager individuals who stood around me. "I've made a list of things that we need to do to get this place opened up this afternoon, and I've assigned each of you to certain jobs."

I could feel the energy that surrounded me as the volunteers waited for their assignments. After two days of spending more time looking for something to do as opposed to actually doing something, they were more than ready to be busy.

"Here we go," I said, finding the right page in my notebook. "Sharon, I want you to contact the telephone company and see if we can get the phone hooked up today. Explain to them what's going on and that United Animal Nations will be responsible for the installation cost and the calls we make."

"Do we want just one line?" Sharon asked.

"I think that'll be enough. I'm afraid if we start to make things too complicated we won't get the phone working today and that's what's most important. This is when people really need to reach us, and not having a phone will make that more difficult."

"Can I use your cell phone to call them?"

"Sure," I said, handing Sharon my phone. "And when you get finished with the phone company, find out if there is a printing place in town where we can get some flyers made up with the following information—who we are, where we are located, what services we can provide."

"Hold on," Sharon said. "I can't write that fast."

While I waited for Sharon to catch up, I looked at my watch. It was 12:15. We had made some real headway that morning and I was pleased.

"Okay, I'm ready," Sharon said, looking up from her pad.

"Include a line that says the services we are providing are free, indicate we are available 24 hours a day, and don't forget to include the phone number that the telephone company gives you."

"That it?" Sharon asked.

"I think so. Oh, to be safe, why don't you show me the flyer you make up before you have it printed," I added.

"Will do."

Sharon went to sit on the front porch to make her phone call while I continued assigning other, equally important jobs.

"Diane, I would like it if you and Abigail worked on locating us some tents and caging. See if you can tap into some of the same kind of resources we utilized in Bainbridge."

"How many animals do you think we'll get in?" she asked.

"I'd guess no more than 150 to 175. Plan on that for now. If we end up with more, we'll deal with it then."

"Can we take your van?"

"Sure," I said, tossing her my key. "Be sure you empty it out before you leave."

"Got ya," Diane acknowledged, as she and Abigail walked toward the van.

"Hey, guys," I yelled. "Something else. See if you can swing by one of the evacuation shelters and round us up at least 10 cots, so we don't have to sleep on the floor again."

Diane responded with a thumbs-up as she and Abigail prepared to unload the back of my van, which included the two totes with the essential items we would need to get started and the things that Pam had brought us from San Antonio.

"Okay. Next on my list," I said, scanning my notes. "Samantha, I'd like you to get hold of the local radio station and give them the same information I told Sharon to include on the flyer. She can share her notes with you, so you won't have to try and remember everything I told her. And tell them the sooner they can air the information, the better."

"Do you want me to check and see if there is a town paper, too?" Samantha asked.

"You can do that. I suspect that if they have one, it's a once-a-week paper and more than likely it comes out the middle of next week, but check anyway. If they do, give them the same information."

"Okay. I saw a phone booth over by the command center, so I'll go use that and let you know what I find out," Samantha said, stuffing her notepad in her back pocket as she went to find Sharon.

I had three volunteers left—Marty, Shirley, and Mike—to work with me. It would be our job to get the grounds and the building cleaned up and ready to receive animals. There was a carport on one side of the building that would be an ideal location for intake. Since Marty had done intake during the floods the previous summer, she was the logical person to set up this area.

"Marty, can you get intake set up?" I asked.

"Sure," she replied. "Do you have the forms, camera, film, and ID collars and tags in one of the totes?"

"Yeah," I replied. "And I saw a folded Ping-Pong table against the wall in one of the back exam rooms. You can use that to put everything on. Mike, you want to help her get it out here?"

"I can do that," he said, taking a last puff of his cigarette, dropping it on the ground, and putting it out with his boot. "What do you want me to do after that?"

"I'll have you help get the outside area cleaned up. There has to be a rake somewhere. Maybe check and see if the clinic has a broom closet."

Dr. Davidson had been more than generous by letting us use the place and anything we found inside. The only thing he asked in return was to have his cat rescued. I reminded myself that I'd have to keep track of the time to allow for getting to Dr. Davidson's home before it got too late. Finding Boy was our top priority of the day.

"Shirley, why don't you and I see if we can tackle the exam room where the cats are going to go. We've got the cages Pam brought us that we can set up, and as soon as Sharon is done with my phone, I'll give Pam a call in San Antonio to let her know to contact her friends in Dallas who have the 25 cages we can borrow."

"Sounds good to me," Shirley replied.

For the next hour, we all busily completed our assigned tasks. Samantha returned first to let me know that the local radio station had agreed to start making the public service announcements later that afternoon, and that a reporter from the *Vindicator* would be by as soon as possible to do an interview for the Wednesday edition of the paper. With both of those tasks completed, I asked Samantha to return to the command center to see whether the Red Cross would put us on their food delivery schedule. None of us had eaten since early that morning, so I knew everyone was getting hungry, even though they probably hadn't had the time to realize it yet.

Warren returned next to let me know we would have electricity within the hour. He had dropped Dr. Davidson off at the friend's house where he was staying. "He was starting to get real tired," Warren said. "So I suggested he try and get a nap and as soon as we knew anything about Boy, I'd come by and get him."

"I'm glad you did that Warren," I said, smiling.

"What do you want me to do now?"

"I'd like you to do some checking on the vet situation. See how many vets there are in town and if any of them are open. I suspect we won't need them today, but I'm sure we will over the weekend, so it's important to find out what their availability is on Saturday and Sunday. Somehow I don't think this town has an emergency clinic that's open all night."

"I'll go do that," Warren said, pulling the van keys out of his pocket.

I returned to where Shirley was working in the designated cat room. Walking back in, I could begin to see our progress. If we had to, we already had space set up for half a dozen cats. Hopefully, our first tenant would be Boy.

"Terri, can you take a look at this?" Sharon asked, walking up behind me and handing me the first draft of the flyer she'd been working on. "And, you'll notice there is a phone number near the bottom. It should be working by four o'clock."

"Good deal," I said, as I began to read the flyer.

Sharon had done a great job and the flyer was ready to be printed and distributed. If we were going to help people, we needed to let them know we existed. We would post the flyers at the command center, in all the evacuation shelters, at the banks, grocery stores, gas stations, post offices, feed stores, and, of course, at Wal-Mart. We'd blanket the town of Liberty with flyers. After all, we were it as far as any organized effort to help the animals in Liberty. We had a big job ahead of us, but I knew we could do it. Look what we had already made happen in less than five hours.

I continued to work with Shirley to get the cat room ready for our anticipated boarders. As I assembled the last crate, I thought, *Someone is surely watching over us because luck alone couldn't have made this happen.* All I could say was "Thank you."

CHAPTER TWELVE

Seeing Things Differently

"TERRI, WHERE are you?" Abigail shouted, after I heard the squeaky screen door slam shut. "Your number-one procurement team has returned."

"I'm in here," I called, anxious to find out how Abigail and Diane had done finding the supplies I'd sent them after.

"She sounds pretty excited," Shirley commented. She was bent over scooping litter into disposable litter boxes. "Do you remember how excited we'd get during Hurricane Andrew when we found something we desperately needed?"

"Do I ever. Remember the bathtubs we found that had blown out of mobile homes?" I said, as I finished lining the bottom of the last cat cage with a four-year-old section of Liberty's newspaper, the *Vindicator*.

"Yeah, they were a real find. We'd have been in trouble if we didn't have the water we collected in those bathtubs every afternoon when it rained."

"Wow, this looks great," Abigail interrupted, as she walked into the cat room where Shirley and I had been working for the last hour.

"Yeah, this will work just fine," I agreed, looking around the room that had taken on a whole new look. "So tell me, what did you guys find?"

"Diane and I got everything on our list," Abigail said, looking extremely pleased as she read from her notepad. "Sterling Funeral Home has agreed to loan us three tents, Cachere's Feed Store will let us use some of their chain-link panels, and Lee Tim's Home Center has a couple of large dog runs for us to use. And," Abigail paused for a moment to turn to the next page, "if we go back to the Red Cross and talk to the shelter manager later this evening, she said she'd have some cots put aside for us, too. Not bad, huh?"

"I'm very impressed," I said. This was a lot of good stuff that we definitely needed and couldn't afford to buy.

"Thanks," Abigail said, as she put her notepad in the back pocket of her jeans. "I was really surprised at how willing people were to help out. And everyone but the Red Cross is going to deliver the stuff this afternoon. Can you believe that?"

"I can. That's what people do during disasters," I explained.

"It's truly amazing."

"Well, be prepared to be even more amazed, Abigail, because this is just the beginning," Shirley said, as she placed litter boxes in the cages. "You'll see another whole side to people, and it's the really good one."

"Director lady," Mike called, peering in though the open window that was partially covered by a torn screen. "We've got ourselves a problem out here."

My first assumption was that a person was the cause of Mike's concern, but it turned out that our problem didn't involve a person or even an animal. Mike rested his elbows on the peeling window ledge of the cat room and explained that, while raking leaves along the west side of the property, he had uncovered a cluster of fire ant hills, home to thousands of the crawling insects.

"Ouch. Those are nasty buggers," I said, remembering my encounter with fire ants during Hurricane Andrew. I still had a couple of tiny round scars on my forearms from picking up a dog who had become covered with the insects after a volunteer placed him in an outdoor exercise pen where tall grass concealed the ant hill. The dog disturbed its occupants. When I reached for the panicked dog, I saw the ants clinging to his fur, but I assumed they were harmless. I quickly found that I was wrong as they proceeded to bite the squirming dog and me repeatedly.

"You want me to go and get some of those granules that you drop in the mound to kill them?" Mike asked. "I'm pretty sure I can even get the stuff at that grocery store down the block."

"Better do it, cause we definitely can't put any dogs out there until we get rid of the ants." I reached into my pocket and handed Mike some money through one of the tears in the screen. "You can take my van. I think Diane still has the key."

"Mike, do you need some help cleaning up outside?" Abigail asked, her energy level raised by her successful procurement trip.

"There's a big pile of leaves, tree branches, and other garbage along the back fence that still needs to be bagged," Mike explained. "You can take care of that while I'm gone if you want."

"Will do," Abigail said, pulling on her work gloves.

"Appreciate it," Mike said, as he backed away from the window to go look for Diane. "Terri, anything else you need from the store?"

"Can't think of anything," I replied.

"Is the toilet functional?" I heard Abigail ask, as she passed the bathroom on her way down the hall.

"Yes," I yelled. "But you have to get the bucket out of the bathroom and fill it with water from the faucet next door. Since we don't have running water, we have to flush the toilet by pouring water into the bowl, which is a hassle."

"Sure beats going behind a bush, though," Abigail was quick to point out. She was right. We really did have things pretty easy compared to our accommodations in Bainbridge. Dr. Davidson's place was going to work just fine for the animals and us.

Warren was the next volunteer to return to the shelter with information he had gathered about the veterinary situation in town. He had learned that there were only two veterinary clinics in Liberty, and one of those practices had already flooded. He hadn't talked to that veterinarian yet, but would try and track the doctor down later. "I'm going to suggest he gets in touch with the American Veterinary Medical Association to see if they might be able to provide him with some financial help, so he can get his practice opened up just as soon as possible after the water recedes."

"Good idea," I said to Warren. "I imagine it would be pretty hard for this town to do without a second vet for very long."

"Definitely. As of now, Dr. Myers is the only one. He's agreed to do everything he can to help us," Warren explained. "There's another vet in Dayton, which we passed through coming into town on Route 90, and Dr. Myers thought for sure they'd do what they could, too. I can do some minor things myself, but I'll be limited since I'm not licensed to practice in Texas."

"What if we need help over the weekend or at night?" I asked, as I swept the dingy gray linoleum floor in the cat room.

"Dr. Myers gave me his home number and said to call if there was a real emergency."

"Perfect. I just hope we won't need that kind of help."

"Me, too," Warren agreed. He picked up a black metal dustpan and positioned it in front of the four-year accumulation of dirt that I'd ushered into a pile with the broom. "So, any idea when we might go look for Boy?"

Looking at my watch, I was surprised to see it was already 2:30. "Oh, it's getting late, isn't it?"

"I'm sure Dr. Davidson is worried out of his mind," Warren remarked. "I hope he got some rest because all this stress can't be good for him."

"I know," I said, leaning on the broom. "Warren, I think everyone is back, so why don't you gather people together outside and I'll join you in a minute. We'll do an update on where we are with getting this place ready to open and decide what else needs to be done in addition to finding Boy."

"Okay," Warren said. He deposited the contents of the dustpan in an already half-filled garbage bag slumped near the doorway, then he left to round up the other volunteers.

"Shirley, do you still have Dr. Davidson's rescue request form?" I asked, laying the broom against the wall.

"It's in the van," she replied.

"I think I'll have you and Warren go and get Boy," I said, pulling my hair up into a ponytail and holding it in place with one hand while I fanned my sweaty neck with my other. "How far away is his house?"

"Not far. Maybe two or three miles is all."

"And we know for sure that we need a boat to get there?" I asked.

"I think so."

"Okay. Then why don't you and Warren first stop at the command center and see if they might be able to get somebody to take you guys out there by boat."

"You want us to leave right now?"

"Yeah, it's getting late and I'd hate to think of Boy being stranded in that flooded house another night," I said, letting go of my ponytail. "Why don't you take Mike with you. While you're out there, you can do some assessing, too. I'd like to start doing rescues tomorrow and I'm curious whether we're going to be searching for just dogs and cats, or if there are horses and cattle that need help, too."

"What time do you want us back?" Shirley asked, as she bent down in the doorway to tie her shoe.

"We were told at the command center that we had to be off the water by 4:30. No exceptions."

"Gotcha," Shirley said, standing up. "If we don't run into any hassles getting a boat, we should have plenty of time."

"I hope so. Be safe out there, and bring back that Siamese—alive."

After our first rescue team had left, I talked with the remaining volunteers. Samantha had returned from the command center with news that one of the Red Cross mobile feeding trucks would be stopping by three times a day to feed us. Our first meal was scheduled to arrive sometime that evening.

"I wonder if they have any green beans and grits left over from Georgia?" Diane asked. The possibility of surviving on two of my least favorite foods again made me think of the mud pie we'd all had at Joe's Crab House just two nights earlier. Another slice sure would hit the spot about now, but I didn't dare dwell on the impossible.

"Considering we're in Texas, they'll probably be passing out lots of beef," I concluded. "So for us vegetarians, it's back to a diet of processed cheese slapped between two pieces of stale Wonder Bread, minus any condiments."

"Yummy," Abigail said. "I'm glad I listened to you during the workshop and brought some edible provisions with me."

"Sharon," I said, after acknowledging Abigail for being so well prepared, "what's the word on the flyers?"

"They'll be ready by four o'clock."

"Could they run off a thousand?" I asked.

"They're giving us a thousand, but only charging us for five hundred," Sharon responded, with a triumphant smile. She, too, was learning the skills of procurement.

"Very good. What I'd like you, Abigail, and Diane to do this evening is start getting them distributed, and be sure you take lots of rescue request forms with you. Without a doubt, you're going to come across people who have information about animals that need rescuing."

"We'll be ready," Sharon said. Diane and Abigail nodded in agreement.

Just then a delivery truck slowed down on the street in front of the shelter. The sign on the driver's door said "Cachere's Feed Store." It appeared our chain-link panels had arrived.

"Abigail, is the ant situation under control?" I asked, as we watched the truck back slowly into the driveway.

"Yes, they've moved on to insect heaven."

"That's good to know," I said. "I really didn't want to take home any more scars from this disaster."

All of us spent the next hour lining up chain-link panels to create dog runs, careful to make sure the pesky fire ants had indeed departed. Since the late October days were still warm, we shaded the runs with tarps and placed an airline crate, minus the door, inside each run. These would give the dogs a place to get out of the rain should another storm system move through the area after the weekend of predicted sunshine.

The funeral home tents arrived just before four o'clock. The two young kids who unloaded them stayed to help us put them up, intrigued by our mission. When the cages arrived on the U-Haul from Georgia the next day, we would stack them in a line under the three 20-foot-square tents, as a place to keep the smaller dogs. Later on, Lee Tim's Home Center dropped off the two dog runs they had promised us. We set them up next to the rest of the enclosures. When we were finished assembling and placing everything, I figured we would have room to house maybe 30 to 40 dogs, depending on their sizes, and plenty of room to expand.

The first canine to arrive was a shaggy Poodle. We were hammering the last tent stake into the ground when her owner arrived on foot, carrying the badly matted dog in her arms. Marty had the intake area set up, so she was ready to welcome our first evacuee.

"Is this the place that takes care of the animals?" the middle-aged woman asked, putting the dog down on the asphalt driveway next to her. "The cop at the roadblock said he thought you all might be doing something to help out dogs and cats."

"Yes, that's what we're here for," Marty replied, as she came around the side of the Ping-Pong table to where the barefooted woman was standing with her four-legged companion.

"What does it cost?" she asked. "'Cause if it costs any-thing, I don't got no money."

"It's free," Marty informed the woman. She bent down to pet the dog who stood quietly next to her owner, both eyes partially hidden behind strands of dirty, matted fur.

"Can I leave my dog here now? I got nowhere else to take her."

"Of course," Marty said. "Let me just get some informa-tion from you." She reached for a clipboard with an intake form attached to it and began to get from the woman the in-formation we needed about how to reach her to ensure that when it came time for the dog to go back home, she would be returned to the right person.

As Marty was starting to complete the animal description section of the form, she noticed that the dog had still not moved from the spot where the woman had set her down. She just stood there, her head pointed straight ahead. The only thing that moved was her black nose, working to sort out the smells of this new place.

"What's your dog's name?" Marty asked, returning her attention to the form.

"Maggie," the woman said. The Poodle wagged her tail in response to her name, but still did not move from the spot she seemed to be glued to.

"How old is Maggie?" Marty asked, glancing at the dog again.

"Six," the woman answered. "No wait, I think she's seven." This time Maggie tilted her head slightly when she heard her owner's voice.

"Is she spayed?"

"No," the woman replied. "We just got rid of her last lit-ter of puppies, which is good. It was hard enough just getting the National Guard to let me bring her on the boat when they evacuated me and my son."

"Did you find homes for all the puppies?" Marty asked out of curiosity.

"Oh no, we took them to animal control two weeks ago. That's what we do with most of her puppies. Once in a while, we can find someone to take one, but that doesn't happen very often."

"Have you ever thought about getting her spayed?" Marty inquired, trying hard to conceal her disapproval.

"Yeah, every time we find out she's pregnant, but we never seem to have the time or the money to get her fixed before she gets knocked up again," the woman explained, running her fingers through her short blonde hair.

"Would you like us to get her spayed while she's here? We can set it up with the local vet and we'll pay for it," Marty said, hoping the woman would take her up on her offer. She'd already decided she would pay for it herself if EARS didn't have the money.

"You can do that?" she asked.

"Yes," Marty said empathetically.

"That would be awfully nice of you," the woman said, bending down to give Maggie a pat on the head. "I think she's had her fill of motherhood."

Before the woman changed her mind, Marty had her sign the intake form and the line giving permission for Maggie to be spayed. *This flood is going to be the best thing that's ever happened to this dog,* Marty thought, as she watched the woman signing her name.

"Is that all I need to do?" the woman asked, handing the completed form back to Marty.

"That's it," Marty said, reaching for a leash to hook on to the dog's well-worn nylon collar. "We'll take good care of Maggie, so don't you worry."

"Bye, Maggie," the woman said, as she bent down to give the dog a kiss on the top of her dirty head. "You behave yourself." Maggie's stubby tail started to wag again, but she still did not move from the spot where she'd been standing since she first arrived.

"You can come by and visit her if you want," Marty explained, as the woman backed away from the table.

"I don't know," she said, looking at her dog one last time. "My house is in pretty bad shape, so I'm going to be awfully busy, I reckon."

"Well, we'll be here, so stop by if you can. I'm sure Maggie would like to see you."

"I will," the woman said, as she started toward the road.

"Well, Miss Maggie," Marty said, bending down to talk to the dog. "I think the first thing we need to do is get you a haircut and a bath. It looks like it's been a very long time since you've had either."

Scratching Maggie behind the ears, Marty wondered why the dog was still standing in the same place, showing no concern that she was being left behind. Most dogs would be pulling at their leash to leave, too.

"Excuse me, ma'am." It was the dog's owner, calling from the end of the driveway. "I forgot to tell you something."

"What's that?" Marty asked, knowing she had asked her all the questions she needed to.

"Maggie's blind."

CHAPTER THIRTEEN

Saving Lives

F RIDAY WAS a long day. After getting the tents put up, I made a call to United Animal Nations before they went home for the weekend. I was anxious to tell Deanna how our first day in Liberty had gone. The last time I'd talked to her was the afternoon before, and a lot had happened since then.

"So that's it," I said, concluding with the story about Maggie. "This disaster is the best thing that could have happened to her. We already have an appointment for her to get spayed on Monday."

"Good," Deanna said. "It sounds like she's brought way too many puppies into this world."

"So any volunteers calling in, offering to help?" I asked, I rubbing my eyes and thinking about how good it would feel to go take a nap. *Fat chance of that, though.*

"As a matter of fact, there are. Two trained volunteers from Chicago just happen to be in Houston right now and they wanted to know if you needed any help this weekend," Deanna explained.

"Yeah, we could use them," I replied, thinking how nice it was to finally have trained people contacting us. Doing the EARS workshops was starting to pay off. (The two

Chicagoans, Melinda Nelson and Bruce Axton, ended up joining us on Saturday.)

"There's also a volunteer from California, named Shirley Bollinger, who is willing to pay her own way to Texas if you can use her," Deanna added. "She says she has extensive dog-handling experience. She also mentioned that she lost her home during the Oakland Hills firestorm in October 1991. I guess she could relate to what the people in Liberty are going through."

"How long can she stay?" I asked.

"She can be there by tomorrow afternoon and stay as long as you need her."

"Great. Tell her to come on down," I said, pleased to be adding another member to our team.

After I got off the phone, I decided I would attempt to give Maggie a badly needed haircut, which Marty had started before she got sidetracked by another project. I borrowed a pair of scissors from the intake area and went to retrieve the shaggy dog. When I called her name, she greeted me with a wagging tail.

"Okay, Maggie. I have to warn you, I've never done this before," I said, as I carried her to the carport. "But then I guess you won't be able to see if I do a good job or not, will you?"

Seated on the now-empty supply tote I had brought from California, I began clipping away the ringlets of matted fur, some twice as thick as my thumb. Carefully, I pulled the fur away from her eyes and trimmed four to five inches off, getting a good look at her clouded eyes for the first time. *Even if you could see, with all this fur in the way, you'd still be blind,* I thought.

Maggie stood perfectly still for all of this, seemingly relieved to be getting rid of the nasty fur that had covered her body for way too long. As I continued to trim, attempting to even out her haircut, which kept getting shorter and shorter, I decided Maggie's bath would have to wait until the next day. It was already starting to cool off as the sun got lower in the sky. Since we had no way to warm water, Maggie would have to take a cold bath, which wouldn't feel good this late in the day.

My first stab at being a dog groomer was interrupted when I saw the van that Shirley had taken to the command center several hours earlier pull into the driveway. The glare on the front windshield kept me from seeing inside, so I couldn't see the faces of the passengers to tell whether their rescue had been a success or not. It was only when Shirley stepped out of the back door with a lumpy, orange Evacsack held tight against her chest that I knew the answer.

"We found him!" Shirley said in a jubilant voice, trying to control her excitement so she wouldn't frighten the cat in her arms.

"Where was he?" I asked, walking toward the returning rescue team, with a partially coifed Maggie tagging along beside me on her leash.

"He was upstairs behind a couch," Warren explained. "And he didn't have a drop of water on him."

"Does Dr. Davidson know yet?" I asked, peering to see the cat through the orange mesh rescue bag.

"No, we thought we'd bring Boy back here first, and then go get the doctor," Shirley said, adjusting the weight of the bundle in her arms. "We figured this was a reunion everyone wanted to see."

"You better believe it." I felt choked up just thinking of how thrilled the doctor would be.

While we got Boy acquainted with his temporary home, Warren went to get Dr. Davidson. We offered the rescued feline some food and water, but he wasn't the least bit interested in either. He had been without both for at least 24 hours, but what he wanted instead was our attention. Speaking to us in true Siamese style, he seemed to be telling us how glad he was to be out of his flooded house and someplace dry, with lots of people around to spoil him. He had come to the right place for that.

We were still taking turns holding Boy when we heard the screen door squeak open, followed by, "Boy! Where are you? Here, Boy."

The response to the familiar voice from down the hallway was the loudest meow we had heard from Boy thus far. He had definitely recognized his dad. Dr. Davidson hurried toward Boy with outstretched arms. At the doorway of the cat room, Shirley handed the very vocal Siamese to him. Leaning his head against Boy's, the doctor hugged the cat, exclaiming over and over again above the equally excited meows, "Thank God! Thank God! Thank God!"

After the excitement of the reunion had simmered down, we put a very happy and relaxed Boy in the cage by the west window, the spot we had reserved just for him. Knowing now that he was safe and Dr. Davidson was nearby, Boy went to his food bowl and ate all the food we had offered him earlier. Watching the contented cat eat his dinner reminded me that we hadn't seen the Red Cross yet. I knew it had to be close to six, so I hoped it wouldn't be much longer before our "meals on wheels" arrived.

Not long after, a honking horn distracted me from my continued attempts to make Maggie look more like a dog and less like a mop that had cleaned one too many floors. Leaning far enough forward to look around the corner of the building, I saw one of the familiar red-and-white mobile feeding trucks parked at the curb out front. Dinner had arrived.

Putting Maggie back in her cage with the promise to return after I ate, probably with a doggie bag, I found a bucket of fairly clean water to dunk my hands in. As I continued toward the curb, I wiped my wet hands on my dirty jeans in an attempt to dry them. Not quite Mom's definition of washing your hands before dinner, but it would have to do.

When I could see the people who were serving dinner through the opened side window of the truck, I stopped and said, "I can't believe it."

The two people who had brought us our dinner were Bill and Billie Smart, our vegetable soup friends from Georgia.

"When we heard you guys were here, we asked if we could have you all as one of our stops," Billie said, after stepping out of the truck so that I could give her a hug. "After all, who else would know how to feed you finicky eaters?"

"It's so good to see you guys," I said. "Did you bring us some of your good Veg•all soup?"

"Nope," Billie said with a giggle. "Tonight's menu was supposed to be 'mystery meat,' canned peaches, and lima beans, but I rounded you guys up some macaroni and cheese, three loaves of bread, and a gallon of extra-chunky peanut butter."

"Great," Diane hollered. "No green beans and grits."

"Ditto," I said.

Bill and Billie stayed while we ate our picnic dinner in Dr. Davidson's front yard. There was more talking than eating, as we reminisced about our long, hot days in Georgia. This was the beginning of what I had hoped would happen; that is, seeing familiar faces as I responded to one disaster after another. Prior to the flood at Bainbridge, each disaster brought a whole new collection of people who wanted to help; their only experience was what they had seen from a safe distance on television. It was my dream that, with each disaster, EARS would bring together more of the people who had been through it before; it would be their firsthand experience that would allow EARS to do even more for an ever-growing number of animals. The dream was becoming a reality.

~⸻◦

AFTER OUR personal caterers left, with a promise to deliver breakfast by eight o'clock, we all went back to work. Shirley, Mike, and Warren went to the Red Cross to pick up our cots, which would feel so good after sleeping on the floor for the two previous nights. The flyer distribution team had taken the other van and a thousand flyers, and headed for a long list of destinations.

That left Samantha and me alone at the shelter. She decided she would head home the next day so that she could get back to work on the book. "It's been good being here and seeing what you do. I think it will make a difference in the book."

I agreed.

I could faintly hear Samantha on the phone inside the clinic making flight arrangements, as I sat in the carport with Maggie, combing and trimming her fur. She was actually starting to look pretty good, which was amazing considering my inexperience.

Seated under a single lightbulb overhead, which illuminated the carport, I enjoyed the solitude and the quiet of the evening. I felt tired, but content. It had been a good day, and I expected the remaining ones we had in Liberty, however many there would be, to be equally gratifying. These were good people I was working with, and I knew there wasn't much we couldn't handle as a team. There would definitely be the expected ups and downs, but when it was time to pack it up and head home, I didn't doubt that we would all feel proud of what we'd done for the animals.

"Good evening." It was Dr. Davidson who interrupted my thoughts.

"Well, hello," I said smiling. "Did you have a good dinner?"

"The best," he replied. "Knowing that Boy was safe, I could finally eat something. I'd been worried sick before."

"Did you come to say good-night to him?"

"Yes. And I brought him some chicken," the doctor said, holding up a crumpled, brown paper bag. "He loves chicken. My wife used to give him a bowl full every night about this time. She sure spoiled him."

"Well, it looks like you're continuing to do the same," I said with approval.

"He's all I've got. I don't know what I would have done if I'd lost him."

"Well," I said, standing up, "let me put this little girl back and we'll go give Boy his treat."

When I put Maggie into her cage, she turned to face me. With the door still open, I got down on my knees, placed my hands on either side of her head, and gently tilted it upward. Looking into her eyes that couldn't see me, I whispered, "You and Boy are the reasons I came to Texas. I now understand it was just as important to be here for the people who care about both of you, too. We saved a cat today, but I believe we also saved a man."

JUST AFTER we finally crawled into bed, Diane alerted us, upon returning from brushing her teeth, that we were not alone in the clinic. When she had turned the light on in the tiny bathroom, half a dozen cockroaches had scurried into the crevices along the baseboard. We knew they would remain there only until they felt it was safe to once again prowl the building, which, after all, they'd had free run of for the last four years.

"Are you sure they were cockroaches?" Abigail asked in a disgusted voice, as she pulled her sleeping bag tighter around her neck.

"No doubt about it," Diane said, sitting down on her cot and pulling off her socks, which had collected a fair amount of dirt on the trip to and from the bathroom. "And they weren't babies. They were some big ol' suckers."

"I'm sleeping in the van," Sharon announced, jumping up from her cot and grabbing her sleeping bag and pillow. "I'm not sharing my bed with no cockroaches."

"I'm going with you," Marty declared, as she, too, grabbed everything off her cot.

Undoubtedly, the cockroaches were not just residing in the bathroom. To check, Diane turned off the overhead fluorescent light in our converted bedroom for several minutes. When she flipped the switch back on, we counted at least 50 panicked cockroaches running for cover. We decided to sleep with the lights on.

CHAPTER FOURTEEN

Not a Chance

THE EXISTENCE of our shelter was widespread public information by Saturday morning. Sharon, Abigail, and Diane, as well as Marty, had been thorough in distributing flyers throughout Liberty the evening before. The result was more people showing up to leave us their animals. The first weekend arrival was at our back door just after 6:30 A.M.

"Is anyone here?"

I was sound asleep when the faint voice from outside woke me up. I fumbled to unzip my sleeping bag, slowly pulled my legs out, and felt for the floor. The linoleum was cold on my bare feet.

"It sounds like we have company," Shirley said in a sleepy voice from her cot in the far corner of what had once been Dr. Davidson's waiting room. "You want me to go out and check?"

"No, I can." I reached for my boots. Before I put them on, I pounded each of the heels against the floor, turned the boots over, and shook them, in hopes of dislodging any creepy crawlers that may have taken up residence while I was asleep.

Finding no cockroaches in my boots, I slid them on and tucked the shoelaces in the tops; it was easier than messing with trying to tie them. Only half awake, I thumped past sleeping volunteers toward the hallway that led to the side door where our early morning visitor was waiting. As I went around the corner, misjudging the turn and running into the doorjamb, I heard the person knocking repeatedly on the screen door. *This is way too much noise for this time of the day,* I thought to myself, as I reached for the brass doorknob.

"Good morning," I said, trying to sound like I meant it. "What can I do for you?"

"I saw a flyer at the Red Cross shelter that said you take care of animals that don't have a place to go during the flood," the young woman said.

"That's right," I answered, opening the screen door to step outside. The cool morning air helped me wake up a little more, but it would really take a cup of coffee to do the trick.

"I have some kittens and a mama cat that I don't know what to do with," she said. "Can you take them?"

"Sure. Do you have them with you?" I looked past her. There was no car in the driveway.

"No, I have to go get them," she explained. "Before I dragged them all down here, I just wanted to be sure it was alright."

"By all means," I said. "Do you need any help getting them here?"

"No, I can do it. I'll bring them by just as soon as I can."

"Then we'll see you later," I said, as the woman turned to leave.

"I think the kittens are sick," the woman said, almost as an afterthought. "Will you still take them?"

"Of course," I said, with growing concern for the kittens. "If they are, the sooner you bring them to us, the sooner we can have a veterinarian look at them."

"I'll try to get back by here this afternoon," the woman said. "Thanks for your help."

After the woman left, I sat down on the doorstep to survey what we had accomplished the day before. Our collection of tents, with the name Sterling Funeral Home printed in white letters on each one, along with the dog runs, chain-link panels, and cages set up under and next to them, was an interesting sight indeed. Passersby on Main Street, especially former patients of Dr. Davidson's, couldn't help but wonder what had moved into the neighborhood. Maybe curiosity would prompt them to stop, and that just might lead to us helping another animal. In this case, it could be a good thing to be a little out of the ordinary.

Maggie and Boy were the first of many success stories during Liberty's flood. There was a rescue that first Saturday that will always be remembered as our most unique from the Liberty disaster. The call for help came from an unexpected source early in the morning. Since I was one of the few people up, I answered the phone.

"Is this the animal place?" a man with a heavy Texan drawl asked before I could even finish the word hello.

"Yes, this is the Emergency Animal Rescue Service," I said, putting my socks on, now that I was more awake.

"I'm calling from the command center and I was supposed to ask you all if you rescue wildlife?"

"Well, yes," I said hesitantly. "If there's a wild animal that really needs our help, we'll do something, but most of the time we find they do better on their own."

"Do you all do skunks?" he asked next.

I paused before answering, beginning to question whether I should take this man seriously. Just in case there was a skunk that needed help, I continued to respond professionally. I was pretty certain that the majority of the people who worked at the command center, most of whom were members of the good ol' boy's club, thought we were a bunch of "bunny huggers." I didn't want to do anything to give them more reason not to take us seriously.

"Sir, if there's a skunk who *really* needs help," I said, "then we would most definitely do something to help it."

"This skunk doesn't need help. It's the people at the place where he's trapped," the man explained. "He's gotten himself into a predicament that's causing problems for those people."

"Where's the skunk?" I asked, curious what his answer would be. If this was a joke, I suspected I was about to hear the punch line.

"He's in one of the port-a-johns at the Red Cross shelter."

Oh yeah, right, I thought to myself. This had to be a joke. I fully expected at any minute to have someone yell out, "Smile you're on Candid Camera."

"Ma'am, did you hear me?" the man asked.

"Yeah, but let me see if I heard you right. You're telling me there's a skunk trapped in one of the port-a-johns at the Red Cross shelter."

"Yes, ma'am," he said. "And they really need it out of there because they don't have enough port-a-johns as it is. There's a shortage, so this skunk has got to find some other place to relieve himself." The man half laughed at this point, which made me want to ask, "Are you for real?"

"If you all can't do something about him, I reckon our only alternative is to shoot the varmint," the man announced. "The marshal would have done that already, but some folks got all upset when they heard that's what he was thinking of doing."

"There's no need to shoot him," I said, reaching for a rescue request form from the stack on the desk in front of me. "Tell me which shelter he's at and we'll go over there right now and get him out of the john."

While writing down the address of the shelter and the name of the woman I was supposed to ask for, I kept thinking, *How are we going to get a skunk out of a port-a-john and not get sprayed?* There was no manual to turn to for this one.

"Okay, I think I've got all the information. I appreciate you calling us," I said, looking out the window in hopes of catching a glimpse of Abigail. Maybe our wildlife person would know what to do, because I sure as heck didn't.

"Uh huh," the man replied. "Call and let us know if we have to end up going over there and shooting that skunk."

"I assure you that won't be necessary," I said, feeling an urgency to get over to the shelter before someone got trigger-happy.

"Whatever," the man replied, and then said good-bye.

After hanging up the phone, I sat on the stool for a minute, too dumbfounded to move. I wondered if when we got to the shelter, there would be a stuffed animal sitting on the toilet with a sign around his neck reading, "Fooled You." Or maybe this would turn out to be nothing more than a wild goose chase.

"Abigail!" I yelled, when I spotted her walk past the open door with a dog she was taking for its morning walk. "Got a minute?'

"Sure," she replied, coming up the steps and in the backdoor with the Dachshund who barked at everything. "What can I do for ya?"

"Have you ever rescued a skunk?"

"A skunk?" she repeated in disbelief.

"Yes, a skunk," I said. "You know, one of those black-and-white creatures who you don't want to be too close to when he decides to lift his tail?"

"Do you know of a skunk in trouble somewhere?" Abigail asked, realizing that I was serious.

"Yep. I'm afraid so." I told her of my conversation with the man from the command center, adding that at first I had thought the call was a joke, and I still wasn't 100 percent sure that it wouldn't turn out to be one. "You up for checking it out?"

"Sure, why not? And if it turns out to be a joke, no big deal. I can handle it."

"I wish I could go with you, but the truck from Georgia should be pulling up sometime this morning and I want to be here when it arrives," I explained, as I handed Abigail the rescue form. "Why don't you grab Mike and take him with you?"

"Okay," she said, rolling up the form and sticking it in her back pocket. "Do you want us to go right now?"

"Why don't you finish walking the dogs and wait until breakfast arrives. They've assured me they won't do anything until we've arrived. Who knows, by then the skunk may have decided to move on his own."

"If there is a skunk, I assume you want us just to shoo it out of the john and get it headed toward a less-populated area?"

"Sounds like a plan to me, because you sure as heck aren't bringing it back here," I said with a laugh. "That's where we draw the line."

"Okay, we'll go see if this little guy exists and, if so, try and figure out a way to convince him he doesn't want to hang out in the port-a-john any longer. Wonder why he even went in there in the first place?" Abigail said, shaking her head.

"Who knows?" I reached down to pet the Dachshund who had been surprisingly quiet. "Anyway, I appreciate you doing this. You might want to consider going by the grocery store to buy some big cans of tomato juice—I hear it helps get rid of the skunk scent," I joked. "If you and Mike get sprayed, you're sleeping with the dogs, if they'll have you."

"Ha, ha!" Abigail said. She pushed the screen door open and let the dog out ahead of her. "You have so little faith in my skunk removal skills."

"So, you never said if you've done this before?"

"Nope," was all Abigail said, as she disappeared out the door.

⌒⌒

IT WAS mid-morning when the 25-foot U-Haul pulled up in front, with a pickup close behind. Our cache of supplies had arrived. A stiff Mack stepped down from the front seat as I walked over to greet him. Greg got out of his pickup (it would get them back to Georgia).

"Welcome to Liberty," I said, extending my hand to the two men in turn. "Can't tell you how much I appreciate you bringing us all this stuff. We're filling up fast, so we sure can use what you've brought us."

"Glad we could help," Mack said, taking off his sunglasses. "Is Shirley around?"

"She's out with some of the volunteers doing some rescues, but she should be back before too long." I looked at my watch. It was already 11 o'clock. "So how long can you guys stay?"

"We've got to head back tonight," Greg said, stretching his arms above his head. "I have to be back to work on Monday, but I sure wish I could stay."

"Me, too," I replied. "You were such a big help in Bainbridge, and I know we could use you again here."

"Oh well, I'll just have to catch you the next time a disaster brings you to Georgia."

"I'll hold you to that," I said, as I watched Mack open the back of the packed U-Haul.

It took nearly an hour to unload the truck and put everything where it belonged. We had already taken in 59 animals, so we were glad to have the additional cages that Mack and Greg had brought. The 25 cages from the Dallas Cat Club were due to arrive sometime late that afternoon, which would give us even more space for animals. Pam had given me this news upon her arrival from San Antonio that morning, just as we were enjoying our breakfast (cold scrambled eggs, canned peaches, and more extra-crunchy peanut butter, which we spread on stale saltine crackers).

When we had less than a dozen totes to take off the U-Haul, Shirley returned with the volunteers and 11 more rescued animals.

"You guys were busy," I commented when Shirley walked up carrying three Evacsacks with a cat in each one. "Yeah. These troublemakers really made us work hard. They were not about to be caught, but we didn't give up."

"Hi, stranger," Mack said, as he joined us in the intake area.

"I saw the truck, so I figured you and Greg must have made it." Shirley put the cats down, so she could give her husband a hug.

"Yep. We hit some pretty nasty weather passing through Mississippi, but other than that, it was a pretty easy trip."

"Shirley, why don't you and Mack go and get yourselves some lunch, and take Greg, too," I said, handing Shirley some money. "We've got things under control here."

"Are you sure?" Shirley asked.

"Get," I said, pointing toward the street. "And if the place you go to has mud pie, bring me back a couple of pieces."

"Only a couple of pieces and not the whole pie?" Shirley questioned.

"That's right. I don't want to be too greedy."

The second truck to arrive came from the SPCA of Texas, located in Dallas. Along with the truck and the supplies inside, we got Bobby French and Lawrence Hopkins, two of the organization's experienced field staff.

"Thought you all could use some help," Bobby said, after introducing himself. "Don't know for sure what we can do since this is our first disaster, but we're willing to do anything and we learn quick."

"We don't do windows, though," Lawrence explained in his British accent.

"You're in luck, we did the windows yesterday," I said, laughing.

While I was showing the guys around, the woman who had appeared at our backdoor early that morning returned. Marty came and got me, and said, "You've got to come see these kittens."

The woman was standing next to the Ping-Pong table with a three-foot-high pink laundry basket on the ground beside her. Next to the basket was a tan airline crate, its door facing toward the street so I couldn't see what was inside. As I approached, she said, "Sorry I couldn't get here sooner, but I had to wait for a ride."

"I'm glad to see you again," I said, remembering that I had offered to transport the kittens when I'd talked to her earlier. I wish she had taken me up on that offer. "How are the kittens doing?"

"Not very good I'm afraid," the woman replied softly.

Moving to where I could see into the basket, I saw staring up at me a cluster of kittens; two grays and six black ones. I guessed they were no more than two and a half weeks old. Each tiny body was soaking wet and three of them had really gunky eyes, which wasn't a good sign.

"Where are the mothers?" I asked.

"The five that I found on a roof are orphans. The other three belong to the mama cat that I have in here," she said, turning the small crate around so that I could see the gray Tabby inside. "I was afraid that if I put the three kittens in with her she might squish them."

"Are you planning on keeping the five orphans?" I asked.

"Normally, I'd say yes, but our house is in such bad shape I just don't think I could take good enough care of them right now. So, I just want the mama and three kittens back."

"Okay," I said, relieved that the woman didn't want the other five kittens back. "We'll have you sign them over to us. When they're old enough to adopt, we'll find them good homes," I explained. "Marty, why don't you go ahead and start the paperwork, and I'll have Pam get these guys taken care of."

"Thank you, ma'am," the woman said. "Can I pay you for your troubles?"

"It's nice of you to offer, but our help is free," I said, reaching for a kitten who had managed to scale the side of the laundry basket. "Hey, little one, where do you think you're going?"

"They're all wet because I gave them a bath," the woman explained when she saw me take the bottom of my shirt and begin rubbing the kitten's wet fur. "The five that came off the roof were covered in poop and it got on the other ones. I would have dried them off, but my hair-dryer is back at my house under water."

"Well, we'll get them taken care of," I said, putting the kitten back in with the rest.

I left the woman with Marty so I could go look for Pam and Warren. When I explained to them what was going on, they stopped what they were doing and went to see what needed to be done for the eight newest arrivals and the gray Tabby, who didn't look to be in the best of health either.

I returned to giving Bobby and Lawrence a tour of the facility. Just as we were returning to the intake area, Abigail called my name.

"You're back," I said, as she approached. "And you don't stink."

"Of course not," she smiled.

"Where's Mike?" I asked suspiciously. "He's not off somewhere soaking in tomato juice, is he?"

"Nope, he ran to get some smokes, no tomato juice," Abigail responded with confidence.

"So, was there a skunk?"

"Sure was, and he was in the port-a-john, just like the man said," Abigail explained. "Not exactly the place I would have chosen to sleep, but then I'm not a skunk."

"How'd you get him out?" I asked. "But wait, before you tell me, I need to introduce you to our two newest recruits, Bobby French and Lawrence Hopkins from the SPCA of Texas."

"Glad to meet you," Abigail said, shaking hands with both men.

"Same here," they replied.

"This story about the skunk sounds real interesting, so go on," Bobby said to Abigail, as she took a sip from her bottle of water.

"Okay, so Mike and I first surveyed the situation, which I might add was being observed by a crowd of at least 30 people, all watching from a safe distance," Abigail said.

"What we determined was that the little guy, and he was a very young skunk, must have gotten into the space surrounding the toilet through a small, round opening on the back side. What probably kept him from immediately turning around and getting out of there, was that the port-a-john had been delivered late last night, so it hadn't been used yet."

"Do you think he got in there and then couldn't figure out how to get back out?" I wondered.

"Possibly, but it's more likely he wandered in there before dawn and decided it was a nice, dark place to sleep away the day. If he'd been left alone, he probably would've moved on tonight, but those people at the shelter were real anxious to get rid of him," Abigail said, laughing. "I've never seen so many people scared of such a little thing."

"So how'd you convince him to leave sooner?" Bobby asked.

"Mike went inside the john and banged on the plastic wall that encases the toilet. There was no way that the skunk could spray him, and if he sprayed the inside of the port-a-john, we figured it probably wouldn't smell much worse than it normally did," Abigail said, matter-of-factly.

"So how long did it take before he came out?" I asked.

"It wasn't but a few minutes before the little guy's head appeared at the entrance to the opening at the back. He blinked a couple of times, looked around, sniffed the air, and then decided he'd go look for a quieter place to sleep," Abigail said, as if that was what she expected him to do all along.

"And that was it?" I exclaimed. "No near misses or anything?"

"Nope. It was a real easy rescue, and while we were there we got a whole slew of rescue requests from the people staying at the shelter, so it was lucky we went there," Abigail said, handing me the stack of forms. "Quite a few of the people didn't speak English, so it was a good thing I knew Spanish. We really need to remember next time to have the flyers printed in Spanish, too."

"Good idea," I said, remembering that we had a banner printed in Spanish during Hurricane Andrew that enabled us to reach a whole other segment of the community who had animal needs, too. "Well, all I can say is that I'm real glad you came to Texas, Abigail," I said with a smile. "To reward you for all your hard work, I'll let you call the command center and give them the good news about the skunk."

"I don't know if they'll think it's good news. I think they were hoping they'd get to use the skunk for target practice," Abigail said, sliding her hands into her front pockets. "I'm just glad we didn't give them the chance."

CHAPTER FIFTEEN

The Accident Victims

SATURDAY HAD been a predictably hectic day, so when Sunday morning rolled around, we welcomed the brief respite from the constant phone calls, the arrival of more animals, and the line of people seeking our help. Once again the community was in church, grateful to be alive, and momentarily unconcerned about their animals.

The dogs didn't know the difference between a Sunday and a Wednesday, though; they still insisted on being walked at the first sign of daylight. The barking began at 6:45, instigated by none other than the noisy Dachshund. Still clad in our nightwear, we moved slowly outdoors, mumbling good morning to one another as we grabbed a leash off the row of nails in the carport. There were 110 animals on the property that morning, half of them dogs, pleased that their persistent barking had roused us from our sleep.

"Okay, okay. Hold on," I said to the Pug, on whose collar I was trying to hook a leash. Her owners had dropped off the energetic dog the afternoon before. When we put her on a chain under one of the tents, she jumped on top of the green airline crate within her reach and sat down. We expected to see her use the crate as a doghouse, which was our intent, but she obviously had other plans for it. When she

189

was still in the same spot later that evening, Diane said to me, "I think she's learned from this flood that you always seek out higher ground. If it floods under her tent, she'll be the one that survives."

The Pug who took planning for a disaster seriously was sniffing the grass in Dr. Davidson's front yard, looking for that perfect spot to squat, when a white pickup truck with "City of Liberty Animal Control" printed in brown letters on the side pulled up at the curb.

"Howdy," said the uniformed man who got out of the truck, as he crossed the grass to where the Pug and I were standing. "My name's Steve Bautsch. I'm one of the animal control officers."

"Glad to meet you, Steve. My name's Terri Crisp and I'm the director of the Emergency Animal Rescue Service," I said, shaking his hand, realizing I was still dressed in the sweats and oversized sweatshirt that I had worn to bed. *Boy, am I making a great first impression,* I thought. *And I haven't even brushed my teeth.*

"Heard you all are doing a great job, so I just wanted to stop by and say how much we appreciate it," the young man said, reaching down to pet the Pug who was trying very hard to get his attention.

"We're happy to help out," I said, using the leash to pull the Pug back when I realized she was getting muddy paw prints on the officer's jeans.

"Yeah, we would have been up a creek without a paddle, no pun intended," he said with a laugh, "if you all hadn't shown up. The city has us doing everything and anything but helping the animals." He brushed the paw prints off his pants. "In fact, I'm headed to the command center now to pick up some FEMA official who needs to be driven around to all the evacuation shelters. I wanted to be sure I made time to stop by and see you all first."

"I'm glad you came by," I said, wishing he had shown up when I was more presentable. "Some of us were wondering what happened to the animals that were in your shelter. Did you get them out in time?"

"Oh, yeah. There weren't more than seven dogs and we relocated them to different people's homes. They're all getting along just fine, I'm told. In fact, we're thinking some of the people might end up keeping the dogs, which would be terrific. We don't find homes for many of the animals once they come to the shelter."

"Glad to hear you got the seven dogs out and that some of them may not go back when this is over," I said with relief. "If any of those homes don't work out, though, we've got room for them here, and I bet we could eventually adopt them out."

"I appreciate the offer, and I'll definitely keep that in mind."

"Isn't there a humane society or SPCA in Liberty?" I asked, certain that if there were, we would already have heard about it, but I wanted to be sure.

"Nope, we're all the animals have," Steve said, shaking his head. "And it ain't enough, the way this town's growing. They need something besides animal control, but there's too few people around here who seem to agree."

"That's too bad," I said. I had observed in the short time I had been in Liberty, that animals were not a high priority for most of the people, unless they were functional animals such as horses or cattle.

"Terri, Shirley needs you inside," Sharon yelled from the driveway. I could sense urgency in her voice, so I decided I'd better go see what was going on.

"Well, I hate to cut this short, but I guess I'm needed," I said. "Thanks again for coming by, Steve. If there is anything else that we can do for you, please let me know."

"I better get going, too," he said, walking toward his truck. "How long do you all expect to be in town?"

"My guess is probably a week, but we'll keep you posted."

"If you need to reach me or the other animal control officer, whose name is Mark Bartell, you can always get us through the police department dispatch," Steve said.

"Thanks," I said, waving good-bye to the officer just before he drove off to provide chauffeur services.

Sharon met me as I came around the corner of the building. "Here, give me the leash. I'll put the dog away cause Shirley really needs to talk to you."

"Where is she?" I asked, handing the Pug over to Sharon.

"She's in the room where the eight kittens are. I warn you, she's got some bad news."

Rubbing my neck as I walked quickly to where Shirley was waiting, I tried to think of what it could be that she had to tell me. When I came through the doorway of the room where we had isolated the kittens from the rest of the cat population, I immediately saw what it was that Shirley had to tell me. Two of the kittens were lying on the counter, dead.

"What happened?" I asked Shirley, who was holding a third kitten who was crying loudly as Shirley paced back and forth like a frightened mother trying to calm a very sick child. The sound coming from the squirming kitten was unlike anything I had ever heard before. I wouldn't describe it as a meow. It sounded more like a painful cry.

"I'm not sure," Shirley said, her voice muted by her tears. "I came in to check how they were doing and found the two dead ones in the cage, and the third one lying next to them screaming."

We had put all eight of the kittens who had arrived together the afternoon before in a large cage with the gray Tabby so they could all nurse from her. We had been supplementing the mother's milk with kitten formula, taking turns feeding them every two hours, even through the night. In addition, we were giving the three sickest ones subcutaneous fluids, which seemed to be perking them up. We thought that all the tender loving care was making a difference, so what went wrong?

"When Pam fed them last, she said all eight of them, even the three that hadn't been doing so good, were looking better," Shirley explained, as the kitten in her hands screamed louder. "I don't understand how they could have gone down-hill so fast."

"Has Warren seen them?" I asked, taking the kitten from Shirley. The little guy was no happier in my hands, showing his objection with more dreadful crying.

"No, he's out on a rescue," Shirley said, going over to where the other two kittens were. She stood there, silently stroking the dead kittens lying side by side on the Formica counter. I could imagine the questions running through her head. They were probably identical to my own.

"Where's Pam?" I asked, knowing that we had to do something for this kitten immediately.

"She went to find Jody."

Jody Garrison and Ana Sadler had arrived the day before from Dallas, bringing with them the 25 cat cages and a vast amount of cat experience, all of which was being put to good use.

"We've got to get this kitten some help," I said, as all four of his tiny legs stiffened in my hands. "I wrote down Dr. Myers' home number in my notepad. Here, Shirley, hold the kitten and I'll go give him a call."

"I'll take him." It was Jody who came up behind me and carefully removed the kitten from my hands.

As I stood in the doorway watching Jody and Shirley give the kitten a quick once-over, I wiped away a tear. This was so hard to watch. Hopefully, they would figure out what was wrong and be able to relieve some of the pain until Dr. Myers arrived. Grabbing a Kleenex from a box on the counter, I was about to blow my nose before I went to make the call, but I noticed that my hands smelled like bleach. I had not done any of the cleaning that morning. It had been my job to walk dogs, so how did I get bleach on my hands? Then it came to me.

"Pam, smell the kitten," I said.

"What?" she asked, puzzled.

"Smell him and tell me what you smell."

Bringing the kitten close to her nose, Pam breathed in and immediately pulled the kitten back from her face. "Bleach."

On top of the kitten's cage was a bottle of Clorox behind a stack of newspapers we used to line the bottom of the cages. The bottle was lying on its side, which is why we had not seen it sooner. Grabbing the container, I checked the top. It was loose.

"We've got to get the rest of the kittens and the mother out of the cage," I instructed, setting the bottle of bleach on the floor so I could help.

"Here, put them in here," Shirley said, opening the door of a cage on the other side of the room.

"When you pick them up, smell each one of them," Pam said, still holding the sick kitten.

"This one smells okay," Jody said.

"So do these two," Shirley said, with relief.

The remaining two smelled like kitten formula, not bleach—thank goodness.

"How about the mother?" I asked Jody, as she pulled the Tabby from the cage.

"There's a little bit of a bleach smell on her belly, but it's not bad," Jody said, after sniffing the cat.

"To be safe, let's give her a bath," I said. "Shirley, can you and Pam do that?"

"We'll take care of her," Shirley said, as she headed out the door to round up a bucket, towels, and a bottle of cat shampoo.

"And Shirley," I yelled, before she got too far, "ask Sharon and Marty if they can come in here and feed the other five kittens because they're about due for another feeding."

"Will do," Shirley replied.

When I turned back from the door, I spotted the bleach bottle on the floor where I had set it down, and all I could do was ask, "Why?"

The third kitten was euthanized. I asked Mike to bury the three kittens along the back fence under the shade of a poplar tree. I'd found a small cardboard box to put them in, wrapping the tiny bodies in a bright yellow towel, before placing them inside and closing the lid. It was our greatest loss during this disaster and, undoubtedly, those of us who were there will always feel some degree of responsibility for what happened.

Sadness shadowed each of us for the rest of the day. No matter what we were doing, the three kittens remained on our minds. It was a loss that was hard to understand, and everyone was having a difficult time dealing with it.

"Losing those kittens was so unfair," Sharon said, while I was helping her feed the cats later in the afternoon. "For the first time in three years, I smoked a cigarette. I had to do something to ease the pain."

When everyone was still not themselves later that night, I knew we had to talk about what had happened, and I had to figure out what to say to them. I just hoped I picked the right words.

"I know all of you are hurting inside," I said, looking at the solemn faces surrounding me under the carport. "What happened this morning was tragic. I don't doubt that if there was anything that could have been done to prevent it, there is not a one of you that wouldn't have done it. But it was an accident. I've seen how hard each of you have been working to comfort and care for the animals who have been brought to us. There is no way that anyone could ever convince me that one of you would do something to harm an animal. It's just not possible."

"But this shouldn't have happened. It was human carelessness that killed those kittens," Sharon said, her eyes filling with tears. "If they had drowned in the flood, I could make better sense of the loss."

"All of us have learned a tough lesson today and it kills me that the kittens had to pay with their lives for the mistake.

I wish to God there were something I could do to bring them back, but there isn't. They're gone." I paused for a moment to take a deep breath, then I continued, my voice quivering. "What we can do from this moment forward is to promise ourselves that we will do everything we can to prevent this kind of accident from ever happening again."

"Terri's right," Shirley said, sensing I needed some help. "This is a disaster. A lot of unfair things happen to people and animals. Each time you think about the kittens, look around at the animals who are still alive. If we weren't here, probably a good number of them would be gone, too. We do the best we can and, when all is said and done, we hope that we've saved far more animals than we lost. So far we have."

There was nothing else to say. We would each have to cope with the loss in our own way. Time would undoubtedly lessen the intense pain we carried with us that Sunday, but time could never erase the memory of the three accident victims who came so close to surviving.

CHAPTER SIXTEEN

The Obstacle

The VOLUNTEERS were still unusually quiet as we went through our walking, cleaning, and feeding routine on Monday morning. A decent night's sleep had done little to lift the sadness of the day before. I knew what they needed was a distraction. Something that would grab hold of them and make them forget, at least for a little while. I was trying to figure out what would work, when the perfect distraction arrived.

I was on my way into the clinic to call United Animal Nations and to tell Deanna about our weekend, especially about the loss of the kittens, when I heard a voice say, "I just don't know what to do. The bitch won't have anything to do with him. I've tried everything, but she just ignores him."

I couldn't help but hear the very short, frustrated woman talking to Marty in the intake area. Before going inside, I decided to hang around for a minute to listen to where this conversation was headed.

"How long has she refused to take care of him?" Marty barely slid the question in before the woman continued talking.

"It's been since about 10 last night. Just before the news," the woman said, still talking, as she began rummaging through the bulging purse slung over her shoulder, a black, imitation-leather "catch all," large enough to hold a basketball. Her efforts produced a crumpled pack of Salems and a book of matches. "I would have come by then, but I didn't think you'd be open and I wanted to see if they'd show my house on the news."

Lighting the cigarette, the woman inhaled and a couple of seconds later blew out a cloud of smoke. "My in-laws were all bent out of shape because the damn thing kept them awake all night. I can't wait until this flood is over, so I can move back into my own house. I'd live on the roof if I could. Even that would be better than spending another night in the same house with those complainers. They're going to drive me crazy before this thing is over."

"Ma'am," Marty said, her words totally ignored by the woman who went on to say, "This is the fifth litter the bitch has had. She's always done good by her puppies. Why she decided to become a neglectful mother now, I don't know. She's given me just one more thing to have to worry about."

"Ma'am . . ." Marty tried again to get the woman to stop talking so she could ask her some questions, but it didn't work.

"I wanted to take the puppy to our vet this morning, but I couldn't get there. The street was flooded, so I reckon his place is underwater, too," the woman said, putting the cigarette between her lips and inhaling again. "I was thinking the reason the bitch maybe doesn't want to have anything to do with the puppy is on account it's sick or something. You know, animals can sense when there's something wrong with their young. Who knows, maybe its mind is messed up or something."

"Do you want us to take care of the puppy?" Marty was finally able to ask, when the woman blew out more smoke, which was followed by a hacking spell.

"I was hoping you could," the woman said, after she stopped coughing and dropped her cigarette on the asphalt driveway, putting it out with the toe of her rubber boot. "If it stayed at my in-laws, I'd be afraid they'd try and drown it or something. There's something wrong with people who don't like animals."

The woman began rummaging through her purse again, seemingly ignoring what Marty was asking her.

"Is there only one puppy?"

"Uh huh. The other one was dead when the bitch pushed it out," she replied, as she pulled a pack of Juicy Fruit gum out of her purse. Unwrapping two pieces, she stuck them both in her mouth, wadded up the wrappers, and dropped them on the ground.

Smacking her gum, she asked Marty, "Are you sure you want to take care of the little squirt all day and all night? It'll wear you out."

"That's what we're here for," Marty assured her. "We were doing that . . ."

Marty didn't finish her sentence. I knew she had caught herself about to tell the woman about the kittens who had died, but she stopped.

"We can take care of the puppy," Marty said, the woman not even aware of the abrupt change in the conversation. "I need to ask you some questions, though."

I really had to get inside to make my call, but I was curious about where the puppy was. I assumed from what had been said that the woman hadn't brought him with her.

"So what color is the puppy?" Marty asked, as she started to fill out the part of the intake form that asked for the animal's description.

Without saying a word, the woman reached into her purse and pulled out a man's sock. Reaching inside she pulled out a three-week-old Chihuahua. "What do you need to know?" the woman asked, holding the puppy up so Marty could get a good look.

That was when I realized the perfect diversion had been delivered to us. It would have been better if we'd had a dozen three-week-old puppies to feed, hold, and spoil, but one would do the trick. As it turned out, the little guy was always in someone's hands being tended to whether he needed it or not. He created a lot of good feelings and that was exactly what we all needed.

⁓

BY EVENING, the mood at the shelter had improved. Bill and Billie brought us dinner, which consisted of vegetarian lasagna, green salad, garlic bread, and chocolate cake. Our caterers had detoured to the grocery store that afternoon, knowing that we couldn't survive another meal with macaroni and cheese as the main course. We were some happy campers as we started to talk about calling it a day around 10 o'clock, all our chores completed and our bellies filled with some good food. But bedtime wouldn't come until much later for some of us.

"Who's calling us at this time?" Shirley asked, as we sat under the carport, swatting annoying bugs, and eating the last of the chocolate cake left over from dinner. "I hope it's a wrong number because I want to go to bed."

"It might be Ken," I said, getting up. "I left him a message to call me tonight. Since I haven't talked to him or the girls in five days, I figured he'd want to know I haven't run off with a Texas cowboy."

"You're so bad," Sharon said. "I don't know how that man puts up with you."

"Me neither, but I'm sure glad he does," I said, climbing the stairs into the clinic.

I picked up the phone on the fourth ring, and said, "Emergency Animal Rescue Service. May I help you?"

"I'm calling from the command center," the man said abruptly. "We need your help."

Oh, please don't tell me the skunk is in the port-a-john again, I said to myself. I didn't think we could be lucky enough to get him out of there a second time without getting sprayed.

"Can you bring no more than four of your people down here?" he asked. "Say in 10 minutes."

"Sure," I said. "Can I ask what you need us for?"

"There's a cow on the railroad tracks," he said, as if it were no big deal. "If you all can't get her to move, we'll have to shoot her."

Boy, these guys sure are anxious to shoot things around here, I thought.

"The train's scheduled to start running again in the morning, now that the tracks have been inspected and they found no flood damage. That means the cow's got to be gone before then. Understand?"

"Yes, sir," I replied. "We'll be there in 10 minutes."

I knew I had no time to waste. As I came out the screen door, I yelled, "Mike, Warren, Abigail, grab your gear and be in the van in five minutes; we've got a rescue to do."

"Where?" Abigail asked, as she finished chewing her last bite of cake. "We can't go out on the boats at night."

"Can't explain now," I said, walking past her to make sure I had what I needed in my van. Thank goodness we had put the rescue supplies and gear back in the vehicles, so we would be ready for any rescues the next day. The requests for help had slowed down considerably, but you never knew when that next call for help might come. The call from the command center was a good example of how quickly things can change during a disaster.

"Where are we going?" Mike asked, as he came up beside me to throw his gear bag in the back of the van.

"To the command center."

"There's no skunk in the port-a-john is there?" Mike asked with some apprehension in his voice. "If so, I'm bowing out on this one. I think someone else should have the thrill of convincing a skunk to take up residence elsewhere."

"Well, you're in luck; there's no skunk. What we're going to do is help a cow on the railroad tracks. It sounds like it's right up your alley, cowboy. You bring your ropes?"

"I don't go nowhere without them," Mike assured me, as he got in the backseat.

"Warren! Abigail! Let's go," I yelled, as I opened the driver's door. "Shirley, if something comes up and you need me, I've got my cell phone. And you all better save me a slice of that cake."

We made it to the command center in nine and a half minutes. There was considerably less activity compared to the day we had arrived in town. The neighborhoods that had been evacuated were still deserted. In some places, the water was beginning to recede, but it was taking its merry ol' time doing it. For those who had been living in shelters, it had been a long five days.

"You guys wait here a minute," I said, as we got out of the van. "I'll go over to the command trailer and find out what's going on."

As I knocked on the door of the trailer, I could see four men inside, two of them leaning back in their chairs with their hands laced behind their heads, giving me the impression they weren't too busy.

"Ma'am," the man closest to the door said when he opened it. "What can I do for ya?"

"I'm with the Emergency Animal Rescue Service. We got a call about a cow on some railroad tracks. The man who called said to come to the command center, so here we are."

"How many are there of you?"

"Four, which is how many people the man said to bring."

"Wait here," he said, closing the door. Standing outside, I was unable to hear anything being said in the trailer.

It was almost five minutes before he opened the door again and told me, "We radioed the deputy sheriff who called in the report. He'll be here shortly to show you where to go."

"Should I wait right here?" I asked.

"That'd be fine," he said. "If you want some coffee, there's some over there in the fire station."

"Thanks," I said, surprised by the offer.

The four of us had just finished filling Styrofoam cups with coffee when a sheriff's car pulled into the parking lot. "Looks like our escort has arrived," I said, after taking a sip of coffee that tasted like it had been made with floodwater. I dropped it in the garbage can as we left the fire station.

As we passed the command trailer, the man I had talked to earlier stuck his head out the door and pointed toward the deputy sheriff walking our way. "That's who you need to talk to," he said.

"Thanks," I replied. The four of us walked toward the man who looked to be about 50. "Officer, we're with the Emergency Animal Rescue Service," I said. "I understand you're going to take us to where the cow is."

"That's right," he said. "But actually I can only take you partway. We'll go as far as we can in a car, then a special truck the railroad has that can ride along the rails or on the road will have to take you the rest of the way, 'cause the cow's three miles out of town and the roads out that way are still flooded. The truck's waiting for you, so we'd better get going."

"We're in that white van," I said, pointing to our vehicle.

"Okay. You all follow me."

When the sheriff's car pulled out of the driveway, we were right behind it.

"So have you ever done a rescue like this one?" Abigail asked.

"No," I replied as I turned the corner, a car length away from the cruiser. "Mike, you ever done one like this before?"

"Nope, can't say that I have, but I've gotten cows out of lots worse situations. This one should be a piece of cake," he said with confidence, which made me grateful we had Mike along. The cowboy was finally going to get to show us his stuff. Hopefully, we'd be a help to him.

There was still a curfew in effect, so we had the streets of Liberty to ourselves as we headed out of town. We had gone about a mile west on Route 90 when we turned right onto a two-lane country road. Ahead of us in the distance, we saw what looked like a big truck blocking the road, its shape outlined with amber lights and reflective tape.

"I bet that's the railroad truck the officer told us about," Mike commented, leaning forward from the backseat to get a better look.

"That would be my guess," I said, as the car in front of me started to slow down. I pulled the car over to the side of the road behind the cruiser and turned off the motor.

"Mike, why don't you and Abigail grab what you think we'll need, and Warren and I'll go have a talk with the officer and those two guys standing by the truck," I said, before opening my door.

"Will do," Mike replied.

Warren and I walked over to the truck where the officer was now standing, too.

"Hi," I said, extending my hand to the man closest to me. "I'm Terri and I understand you all have an ornery cow problem."

"Yep," the man said, as he shook my hand, "a real stubborn one."

"Well, we're here to see if we can help." I shook hands with the other man. "Oh, and this is Warren. He's a veterinarian."

When Mike and Abigail joined us, I finished the introductions, getting the formalities out of the way, so we could get down to business, something I sensed these guys were anxious to do, too.

"So tell us what we need to know," I said, looking at the two men.

The younger of the two started to explain how they had crossed paths with the cow. "We were asked this afternoon to come out here and inspect the tracks for any damage caused by the flood. We had to walk the tracks so we could get a good look. When we came to one of the trestle bridges, we spotted something bobbing up and down underneath. A lot of stuff from people's houses had passed through there and at first we thought it was just more of that, but when we looked closer, we realized it was a cow."

"Yeah, and it was actually pretty amazing we even saw the thing 'cause there was only enough space between the bottom of the bridge and the surface of the water for her to keep half her head above water," the other guy commented.

"Sounds like she's one very lucky cow," Abigail said in amazement.

"So I take it she's no longer under the bridge?" I asked, after agreeing with Abigail.

"Right," the first man said. "We were able to use a shovel and move some of the debris out of her way so that she could get out from under the bridge. There was so much junk surrounding her that she was trapped, which was why she was still under there."

"It's amazing she didn't drown, 'cause she was getting awful tired," the other guy added.

"So what happened after you freed her?" Mike asked.

"There was hardly any current, so she didn't get swept downstream. When she was free of the bridge, she swam parallel to the tracks and got up on the levee that the tracks sit on. The water is still so high out there right now there's only about a four-foot dry slope on either side of the tracks, but it was enough ground for her to get up on and out of the water."

"Yeah, as far as you can see in all directions, all you see is water," the second man said. "And cutting right through the middle of it are these elevated railroad tracks. They were underwater on Sunday, but the water dropped enough so the train can run again."

"That is, if we get the cow off the tracks," the first man said, taking his Dallas Cowboys cap off to scratch his head.

"Does she appear to be hurt at all?" Warren asked.

"Nope. She sure was hungry, though," the man with the cap said. "I called a buddy of mine and he brought out some alfalfa. She about knocked me over trying to get to it when I walked up to her."

"How long ago did you feed her, and did she eat a lot?" Warren asked.

Looking at his watch, the guy said, "It had to have been about three, maybe four hours ago, and she had a bucketful."

"Do you have any more alfalfa?" Mike inquired.

"Yeah, it's in the truck. She'd obviously gone several days without eating, so I didn't want to give her too much at once."

"That's good," Mike concluded. "She'll still be hungry, which we can use to our advantage."

"So if the tracks between here and where she is are dry, why can't a couple of us just get behind her and start herding her along the tracks toward town? Then Mike, you can be waiting on this end with your rope ready to lasso her," I suggested.

"We tried that," the second man said. "We thought we could get her walking along the tracks and get her to where there was some dry pastureland. We figured it probably wouldn't be where she came from, but at least she'd be safe and dry until her owner tracked her down."

"Is she branded?" Mike asked.

"Yep, but we couldn't make out the brand."

"So why didn't that work?" I asked.

"There are two trestle bridges between here and where she is. When we got to the first one, she wouldn't go any farther. The open space between the railroad ties and being able to see the water passing underneath spooked her. She just dug in her heels, like she was saying, 'I ain't moving.'"

"I can see why," Abigail commented.

"I take it there are more bridges in the opposite direction?" Mike asked.

"Yes, sir."

"So she's trapped between trestle bridges on two sides and floodwater on the other two," I said, rubbing my forehead as if that would help me think better. We had to come up with a way to move the cow, because the train was coming through there, no matter what.

"That's the problem," the man without the cap said. "But we have half a solution that might work if you all can come up with the other half."

"What's that?" Mike asked.

"We have a crane on the back of the truck, similar to what you see on the back of a tow truck. We've also got some five-inch-wide leather slings that can hook to the crane. If we could get her in the sling and hoist her up, then we could move her that way."

"So I take it our part of the job is to figure out how to get her in the sling," I said with a laugh.

"Right," the man with half a solution answered.

"Mike, what do you think?" I looked at our cowboy.

"Let's give it a try 'cause we ain't getting anything accomplished standing around," he replied.

"Can we leave our van here?" I asked the officer, as Mike and Warren started throwing our gear on the flatbed truck.

"That would be fine. I'm going to wait here until you all get back. If there's any problems, the guys can radio me and I'll radio the command center. So holler if you need anything. And be safe."

"We will," I promised, walking toward the monstrous truck.

"And don't get into that water," he yelled over the noise of the truck, which had just started up. "It's crawling with hungry water moccasins."

"Really?" I said, frowning.

"Really," he replied.

Oh, boy, and three days ago I was worried about getting bitten by fire ants, I thought, as I climbed up on the truck with the rest of the team.

The bed of the truck was about 25 feet long and 10 feet wide. It had no railings or tailgate. Like the U-Haul trucks we had used, you had to step on a six-inch flat bumper to climb up on the back of the truck. The four of us sat on the edge of the bed, our feet resting on the bumper. There wasn't much in the back with us; just a couple of toolboxes under the cab window and, in the middle of the bed, was the crane, which extended about six feet beyond the truck's bumper. Looking at this extended arm, as the truck backed down the tracks, I asked Mike, "Do you think this is going to work?"

"Time will tell," was all Mike said.

The three-mile drive in reverse reminded me of the Jungle Boat ride at Disneyland. There were no alligators or hippopotami poking their heads out of the water, but there were all kinds of other animals, which we could see with the help of the truck's spotlight. Instead of threatening to come out of the water to get us, they were scrambling to get into the water, out of our way. The cow had not been the only four-legged creature to seek refuge on the levee. We saw, spread out along the three miles of track, deer, raccoons, field mice, possums, jackrabbits, coyotes, and even a skunk, at the sight of which Abigail was quick to comment, "Wonder if he's the one from the port-a-john."

Looking back in the direction we had come, I could see the wet animals cautiously pulling themselves out of the water and standing on the levee, eyeing the truck to make sure we weren't coming back.

I hoped the water would recede quickly because these animals had to be getting hungry. I suspected the food chain had sustained some of them, but how long would it be before the supply of smaller, more vulnerable creatures ran out? There was part of me that wanted to save all the animals on the tracks, not just the cow, but I had to remind myself that the fate of the wildlife was best left up to natural selection.

"There she is," Mike said, pointing to the cinnamon-colored cow standing smack dab in the middle of the tracks about 500 feet ahead.

When the truck came to a stop, we were still a good hundred feet from the cow, who seemed too frightened to move, or maybe she was just too exhausted.

"She looks so scared," Abigail whispered.

"I would be, too, if this truck was coming toward me and I was beginning to think my only option for getting out of its way would be to get back into that nasty water," I said, looking at the cow, who stood staring at us with her big black eyes.

"Why don't we all just stay here on the truck for a few minutes, so I can figure out what to do, now that I've seen her and where she's located," Mike said, resting his chin between his thumb and index finger. The two men in the truck were watching us through the cab's back window, waiting for our signal to get out.

"She's real thin," Warren said softly. "But I don't see any cuts or scrapes, and she's standing on all four legs, which is a good sign."

"Uh huh," Mike said, remaining silent for a minute before he continued. "The way I see it, if we walk toward her, she has three choices. One, she can turn around and run farther down the tracks. Two, she can jump back into the water. Or three, she can stand still."

"Somehow I don't think she'll pick the third one," I said, hoping she would prove me wrong.

"Me neither," Abigail injected. "She'll probably turn and run."

"I agree," was Warren's guess.

"So, given that she'll most likely choose to turn and run, or probably walk in her case, I need to have someone standing on the other side to serve as a roadblock," Mike said. He looked at Warren. "You want that job?"

"How do I get past her?" Warren asked.

"You walk as far to the right of her as you can, moving very slowly, and don't look at her," Mike explained. "If she starts to move, you stop until she settles back down."

"I'll give it a try," Warren offered.

"Once we get Warren on the other side, I'm going to tie one end of my rope to the truck's bumper and I'll have the other end in my hands. Then Terri and Abigail, I want you to stand on either side of me with about three feet between us. If she comes toward you I want you to stop her from getting past the truck. When I start walking toward the cow, I want both of you to do the same. Got it?" Mike asked. "And put on your gloves in case any of you need to grab the rope."

We all nodded, reached into our gear bags, and pulled out gloves.

"Then let's do it."

It took Warren close to a half-hour to make his way past the cow. She moved several times, but Warren did as Mike said and stopped, standing perfectly still without making eye contact with the cow. When she settled down, he took a few more tiny steps forward.

When Warren was in position, Mike, Abigail, and I slowly lowered ourselves to the ground and lined up, side by side. As I waited for Mike to take that first step, I could feel my heart pounding. I was definitely scared, but it wasn't so much a fear of the cow charging me and pushing me into water-moccasin-infested water, as it was that Mike's plan would fail. I wanted so badly for this rescue to be a success. This cow had fought too hard to survive to end up being shot.

I raised my eyes toward the dark sky overhead, where I hoped the guardian angel planned to help us again, because I really suspected we were going to need some extra assistance on this one.

We were about ten steps from the cow when Mike stopped. Abigail and I stood still, too, as Mike began to slowly raise his end of the rope, getting ready to throw the loop around the cow's neck. It seemed as though the world suddenly kicked into slow motion. I knew I shouldn't move even my head, so out of the corner of my eye, I tried to see what the cow was doing.

All of a sudden, the world snapped back into full motion and the flurry of activity around me became a blur of people and sounds, the one most distinguishable was splashing water. When things settled down enough so I could figure out what had just happened, I spotted the cow to the left of the tracks, standing chest deep in water, with no rope around her neck. The end that was intended to snare her lay on the ground. Mike, Warren, and Abigail were fine, but all of us were disappointed that our first attempt at plan A had not succeeded.

"Okay, that didn't work," Mike said, as we gathered on the other side of the truck so the cow couldn't see us.

"Do you have a plan B?" I asked, still feeling the effects of the adrenaline rush brought on by plan A.

"I think so," Mike said with a slight degree of uncertainty in his voice. "But let me give it a little more thought."

As we all stood in silence, we watched the partially soaked cow walk ever so carefully back to almost the same spot where she had been standing before she bolted into the water. She had to be so confused by all this. I wished there were some way that we could have just left her where she was and brought her food and fresh water until the floodwater receded. Then we could have brought out a temporary corral and lured her into it with the best food we could have found. It would be a whole lot less stressful on her and us, but this was not an option. We had to deal with the present reality and the shrinking time before the train would be on the move again. I looked at my watch; it was already 10 minutes past midnight.

"Okay, I think I've got it," Mike said with renewed enthusiasm. "First thing we need to do is move this truck back down the tracks in the direction we came from. We need to give this cow some time to calm down, and she's not going to do that with us here."

So we relocated 500 feet down the tracks, where Mike explained plan B to the drivers and us.

"Those slings you guys have, can we attach two of them to the crane at the same time?"

"Sure, that's no problem," the Dallas Cowboys fan said.

"Okay, then, what I'm thinking we'll do, and tell me if you think this will work, is drape two of the slings about three feet apart across the railroad tracks, and not attach them to the crane yet. Then we'll take two ropes, tie a slipknot in each one, make about a two-foot-wide circle with each rope, and put them on the tracks on the outer side of each sling. Let me show you," Mike said, looking around for a stick. He drew a diagram in the dirt with the stick. "You'll end up with a circle, a sling, a three-foot space, a sling, and a circle. Understand?"

The consensus seemed to be that we were following along, at least to this point.

"Then we get the alfalfa you guys have and put it on the ground next to the circle closest to the truck. What I'm hoping is that the cow is hungry enough to wander over and eat. Then this is the tricky part," Mike said, referring to his diagram in the dirt again. "When her front feet are inside the circle closest to the truck and her back feet are in the other circle at the same time, we yank the ropes and they'll tighten around her legs."

"You mean hog-tie her?" Warren asked.

"Exactly. Then we'll have to get her down on her side. Once we do that, we wiggle the slings back and forth under her until we get one right up behind her front legs and the other one in front of her back legs. The final step is to attach the slings to the crane, hoist her off the ground, rotate her so she's parallel to the back of the truck, and haul her into town."

We all stood and looked at Mike for a minute, trying to decide if he was serious. When we realized he was, we didn't know what to say.

"Anyone have any questions?"

"What about her head?" Warren asked with obvious concern. "It seems like all the support will be around her midsection."

"After we get her on the ground, I'll make a rope halter and hold on to the other end of the rope to keep her head pulled up," Mike suggested. "I know she's not going to be real comfortable, but I don't see that we have a whole lot of other choices."

"What if she starts thrashing around?" Abigail asked, the frown on her face an obvious expression of her concern, too.

"We'll use bandannas and blindfold her, which should keep her somewhat calm, and we're just going to have to take it slow. This will probably be the longest three miles any of us have ever traveled."

"Especially the cow," I said, not convinced this plan would work either, but I agreed with Mike. "What other choice do we have?"

"What happens if we get to one of the trestle bridges, lose her, and she goes into the water with ropes tied around her legs?" Abigail asked.

It was a terrifying thought, but we were getting too close to what we were trying to prevent from happening, which was the deputy sheriff coming out and shooting her because we couldn't get the cow moved and had run out of time.

"It's up to fate," Mike said quietly.

"Let's give it a go. If it looks like it's getting too risky, we try plan A again," I suggested.

The group agreed to try the new plan.

When we returned to where we had left the cow, she looked at us suspiciously as we moved slowly to get the slings and ropes in place on the ground in between the rails. Before we moved the truck back into position, we practiced what we were each supposed to do, which built a little more confidence in the plan.

When Mike felt everything was ready to go, he gave the Dallas Cowboys fan a thumbs-up, which meant, "Get the alfalfa." When the cow saw the food, she moved quickly to where Mike had dropped it. He had guessed right; she was desperate enough to risk coming closer to us. Knowing how hungry she was, we gave her a few minutes to eat before we once again frightened her.

With the ends of the two strategically placed ropes each in the grasp of Mike and Warren, we waited nervously for that right moment. The tension was unbearable, but we had to remain calm for the cow's sake. We watched her move her feet, forward and backward, as she chewed the alfalfa.

"Just a little to the left," I wanted to say. "Oh, no, don't back up."

It became incredibly frustrating watching the cow. Just when she only needed to take one more step forward, she would back up half a step. She had eaten about half the alfalfa, so if we were going to follow through with plan B, a move would have to be made soon.

All of our eyes suddenly switched to Mike when the cow finally had her feet exactly where we wanted them. I took a deep breath. I wanted to cover my eyes, but I had to see. The ruckus that followed was once again a blur, as Mike and Warren held on tight to their ropes, with the two railroad guys jumping in behind each one of them to provide backup.

I moved to see past the tangle of men and there was the mooing cow, down on her knees, struggling to get up. I had to remind myself that we were doing this for her own good, but it was still hard to see, knowing she didn't understand that all we were trying to do was help her.

"Lean into her," Mike yelled to Warren, the sweat pouring off his forehead. "We've got to get her down."

It took all four men to get the cow on her side. She lay there, her head against the rail as the guys wrapped the ropes around her legs. I looked into her eyes. They seemed to say, "I have no more fight left in me."

"Quick, wrap that back rope around one more time, and be careful she doesn't kick you while you're doing it," Mike warned. "Those hooves can do some serious damage, and I suspect about now this cow would like to give the four of us a swift kick you know where."

When the ropes were exactly the way they wanted them, the guys bent down on one knee, their heads lowered, trying to catch their breath.

"Phew, a beer sure would taste mighty good about now," Mike said, wiping his forehead with his shirtsleeve.

"I owe you one," I said to Mike, patting him on the shoulder. "You did real good, cowboy. All of you were amazing."

"Yeah, that was some pretty decent wrangling," Abigail acknowledged.

"Wasn't nothing," Warren said with a shrug.

"Yeah, right," Abigail said, giving Warren a light slap on the back.

"Well, we aren't done yet," Mike reminded us. "Here, would one of you guys grab this rope so that I can get a halter on the cow?"

It didn't take Mike long to get the halter on. Then he told the other railroad guy to hook the slings to the crane. While he did this, Abigail and I removed our bandannas and tied them together. Then, very gently, to keep from scaring her more, I covered the cow's eyes and tied the bandanna in a knot behind her ears. While I was doing so, I whispered to the cow, "Just hold on, girl. You'll be fine. I promise you."

That was a promise I hoped I could keep.

"Okay, I think she's secure," Mike said, inspecting the slings.

"Warren and Terri, jump up on the back of the truck, one on each side." We did as we were told.

"Warren, you've got the rope that controls her front feet. Terri, you take the one that controls her back ones." As Mike said this, the guy who had been holding the rope for him handed it to me.

Give me strength, I said silently, as I glanced back up into the sky. *'Cause I'm going to need it.*

"I'll control the cow's head," Mike explained. "And remember, you can't let her legs touch the ground when we're moving or they'll get caught between the railroad ties and we'll end up breaking this cow's legs."

"What do you want me to do?" Abigail asked.

"You sit up near the cab window and if I yell 'stop,' pound on the cab roof, so the guys know not to go any farther," Mike said.

"Oh, give me the hard job," Abigail joked.

"How fast do you think we should go?" the driver of the truck asked.

"I'd say no faster than 10 miles per hour, but we'll have to see once we get going."

"Okay, you're the boss," he replied. "You ready for us to hoist the crane?"

"I think we're as ready as we'll ever be. Both of you ready?" Mike asked, looking at Warren and me.

"I believe we are. Let's go for it."

"When you lift her, try and do it as slowly and steadily as you can," Mike instructed the guy controlling the crane.

Mike stood near the cow's head with the halter rope in his hand. When he said "go," I grasped onto my rope so tightly that my arms began to shake. The adrenaline was kicking in again; I would need all of it I could get.

Slowly, the cow rose off the ground. When she got to about three feet, Mike signaled for the crane operator to stop.

"Let me just check the slings one more time to make sure they didn't slip," Mike said, bending down so that he could see under the cow.

"Looks good," he said. "I think it's time to take this cow for a ride."

Mike climbed up on the truck and sat next to Warren, while the two men went around to get into the cab. The three of us held on tight to the ropes as the truck began to move. We had gone about 10 yards when the sling began to swing back and forth, so Mike told Abigail to pound on the cab roof. When the guy in the passenger seat stuck his head out the window, Mike yelled, "Slow it down."

When we started to move again, we couldn't have been going any faster than five miles per hour. It was going to be a long trip.

"How are your arms?" Warren asked.

"Okay right now, but I think we're going to pay for this in a day or two," I said, not taking my eyes off the cow.

"I think you're right," Warren said, as he slid his hands, one at a time, down the rope so he could get a tighter hold.

"We're coming up on the first trestle bridge," Abigail hollered. "Hold on tight."

Just as we were about to cross the bridge, the cow started wriggling in the sling, which prompted Mike to tell Abigail to get the driver to stop the truck again.

"She can hear the water running under the bridge," Mike said, jumping down from the truck to try and comfort the cow who was getting more nervous.

"Abigail, ask the guys if this truck has a radio," Mike said, still talking in a soft voice to the cow, as a mother would to an upset child, revealing his soft side.

"It does," Abigail yelled back a second later.

"Tell them to find the loudest music they can and crank that radio up as high as it will go."

The next thing we heard was a song I did not recognize, and would definitely never have an interest in listening to again. It was a horrible excuse for music, but if it drowned out the sound of the water, I wasn't about to complain.

"Okay, tell them to start it up again, but go *real* slow," Mike said, as he jumped back up on the truck.

As we inched ahead, the cow swayed slightly, but besides that, she didn't move.

"I think the music is working," I whispered to Warren.

"It sure looks like it."

We made it across the bridge and the cow seemed to be doing just fine. "Thank you! Thank you!" I said, realizing the guardian angel was back.

We were almost to the second bridge when I could feel something on my back. Since both hands were busy, I tried to ignore whatever it was, but it wouldn't go away. Finally, when I could stand it no longer, I called to Abigail, "Can you see what's on my back?"

"Is this in my job description?" she asked.

"Please," I pleaded.

"Okay, okay." Abigail crawled to where I was seated.

When she got right behind me, I heard her say, "Uh oh."

"What?" I asked, not liking the sound of that.

"Hold still," Abigail cautioned. "You've got fire ants on your back."

The first thing that came into my mind was, *Get a grip.* I'm not sure if that was intended to remind me to hold on to the rope tighter or to persuade me not to let the rope drop so I could jump up and down in what would probably be a futile attempt to get the ants off my back.

I continued to hold on to the rope, as I said in a very precise voice, "Abigail, how many are there?"

"Not a lot, but I suspect there will be more before long," she said. "The end of your rope is dragging on the ground, and each time we stopped, the fire ants must have decided to hitch a ride."

"I bet they're related to the ones that you had me kill," Mike said, trying to get me to laugh.

"Ha, ha, very funny. You can joke because you're not playing piggyback with a bunch of biting ants."

"Should we stop?" Warren asked.

"No," I said immediately. "The cow is doing great, so let's keep on going. Abigail, will you pull the end of my rope up off the ground and knock as many of those buggers off my back as you can?"

"Are you sure you don't want to stop?" Mike asked.

"I'm sure. Let's keep going. The sooner we get into town the better for the cow and me. It'll be the ants that won't be pleased that the ride's over."

We crossed the second trestle bridge with no problem. Abigail continued to guard my back against stowaways and I held on tight to the rope, wondering how many fire ant scars I'd end up taking home from this disaster after all.

"I can see the deputy sheriff's car and our van," Abigail let us know, in hopes it would give us the encouragement we needed to go the last distance.

"Good," I heard Warren say. "My arms feel like I carried this cow the three miles."

Mine felt pretty much the same.

As the driver used levers to switch the truck tires from metal to rubber ones so we could drive on the road, we held on tight to our ropes. When we got to where the deputy sheriff was standing, the driver stopped and both men got out of the cab to come back to see how we were doing.

"Congratulations. Quite a job, which I have to say I didn't think you'd be able to pull off," the officer said to all of us.

"Where do we take her from here?" I asked, not having the energy left in my arms for unnecessary talk.

"I radioed sheriff dispatch when you called to say you were on your way," the officer explained. "You're going to drop the cow at the corner of Austin and Sam Houston Streets. There's a fella who the sheriff's department calls when people call in about stray cows, so he's going to meet you there and take the cow off your hands."

"Is he on his way now?" I hoped.

"I believe so," the officer informed me.

"Good, then let's get going," Mike said, as anxious as I was to be able to finally let go of the rope.

The ride into town took longer than it had earlier that evening. Turning my left wrist slightly so I could see my watch, I saw that it was 2:35. We had left the shelter almost four and a half hours ago.

When the truck turned left onto Route 90, I knew we didn't have far to go, but the cow had no idea when this horrible ordeal would end for her. One more turn and then we'd be at the end of the line. We slowed to cross the section of the railroad tracks that passed through downtown Liberty, the driver knowing that the bumps would cause the sling to start swaying again. We sure as heck didn't want to lose the cow after bringing her this far. I could feel the tension in my neck, as I tilted my head back and then to each side. *Oh, what I wouldn't give for a neck massage*, I thought.

Abigail squinted to read the street sign. "It's Sam Houston Street," she said. "Hang in there, just a few more blocks."

"You haven't forgotten that you owe me a beer, have you, Terri?" Mike asked.

"Excuse me, I think you mean a case," I teased. "A beer is not enough thanks for what you did tonight. All of you were truly amazing, and I thank you for what you've done for this cow."

We felt the truck slow down as it pulled over toward the curb. "We made it!" Abigail shouted.

Those were the exact words I'd wanted to hear.

"Okay, cowboy, what do we do next?" I asked Mike, as I still hung on to the rope.

"We got to get this cow down on the ground first," Mike said, as the two railroad guys came around to the back of the truck. "We'll have to let her down real easy, and be sure you keep the ropes taut. When she touches the ground she's going to want to try to stand up again and I don't want her to do that until the guy gets here to transport her."

Once again, we worked as a team, the three rope holders hanging on just a little longer, while the crane operator slowly lowered the cow to the street. She let out a loud moo.

"What do you think she's saying?" Abigail asked.

"Please let this be over, would be my guess," I said.

When the cow reached the ground, she struggled slightly, but gave up quickly. It was a good thing, because I didn't have much strength left in my arms to fight her.

"I remember reading somewhere during vet school that you can control a cow by putting your thumb and index finger in each nostril and pinching the skin in between," Warren said.

"Yeah, you get the same effect from a nose ring," Mike said.

"Why don't you see if it works, Warren?" I suggested.

"I'll just do that," Warren said, handing his rope to Abigail.

"I was just kidding, Warren," I said, as his fingers got closer to the cow's nose. "You really don't need to do that."

"No, I want to see if it works," Warren said, as he eased his fingers into position.

When he pinched the skin separating the two nostrils, the cow squirmed a little, but then lay there in the street, perfectly still.

"Amazing!" Abigail exclaimed.

"Nowhere else but in Texas would you see a cow lying on a downtown street with someone's fingers stuck up her nose," I said, shaking my head.

Just then we heard a rattling sound coming from around the corner. "That must be the cow's ride," Abigail concluded.

Sure enough, a brown early-model Ford pickup with a blue horse trailer came into sight. Inside the trailer was a horse, and in the truck was a real honest-to-goodness Texas cowboy. When he pulled up next to our truck, he turned off the engine and worked his way out of the front seat, which took some doing as there wasn't a whole lot of room between his belly and the steering wheel.

"Howdy," he said, after spitting a wad of chew into the street.

"We sure are glad to see you," I said, as he came up behind the truck and stood where he could see the cow.

"Uh huh," was all he said in response to my greeting.

The next thing he did, without saying a word, was walk to the back of the horse trailer, unlatch the door, and open the side where the horse was. With no instruction from the cowboy, the horse backed out of the trailer, came over, and stood next to the man.

"Now that's impressive," I whispered to Abigail.

"Yeah. I don't know much about getting horses out of trailers, but I suspect it's not usually that easy," she responded.

The horse was already saddled, with a rope looped around the saddle horn. The man took the rope, made a halter, and slipped it over the cow's head, replacing the one Mike had made. Then, still silent, he got on his horse and wrapped the other end of the rope around the saddle horn.

"You all can untie those ropes around her legs now," he said, spitting some more chew into the street.

Mike undid the ropes as Warren kept his fingers in the cow's nose. He let go when Mike told Abigail and me to pull on the ropes. We yanked the ropes toward us. The cow had a hard time getting up at first, but with the help of the four men, she was soon standing. I knew it had to feel good. We thought we'd had an uncomfortable time of it, but the cow had to be feeling worse.

The cowboy quickly pulled up the slack in the rope as the horse moved closer to the cow. When he was beside the cow, who was being amazingly cooperative, he used the rope to lead her to the back of the trailer. With the help of Warren, Mike, and the two railroad guys, they were able to coax her into the trailer.

When the latch came down on the trailer door, we all yelled in unison, "We did it!"

We learned the next day from the sheriff's office that the cow had come from a herd of 62. So far, she was the only one the rancher had found alive. The Obstacle was a true survivor.

CHAPTER SEVENTEEN

Surprises

Our days in Liberty following the late-night cow rescue were less dramatic. Our bovine friend ended up being the last rescue we did during that disaster. Most of the evacuated people were able to return home on Tuesday, to see for the first time what they had only been able to imagine. Overwhelmed by the destruction, people could only stare at what had been their homes, and ask, "Where do we begin?"

Knowing how much those people had to do, we remained in Liberty through Saturday. By continuing to care for their animals, we gave them one less thing to have to worry about as they began the arduous task of reconstructing their lives. We would leave only after returning the owned animals (75 percent of the 128 animals we cared for) to a safe home or placing them in a local foster home, and finding new homes for every one of the remaining animals who had no owner or were unclaimed. On Wednesday, with the permission of animal control, we began working on locating new homes for the 32 animals with no place to go.

In every disaster, there are always animals that no one comes to claim. They are the ones, in many cases, left behind by owners who did not value them. With their lives complicated by the flood, the last thing these people wanted was something else to have to bother about. For these animals, the disaster was a blessing in disguise. Before we left Liberty, they would have new homes and they would not be left behind again. One of the fortunate ones was a Rhodesian Ridgeback mix.

Sharon and I took a ride out to the animal control shelter on Wednesday morning. I had learned from Mark Bartell, the animal control officer, that the water had gone down enough in the area around the city shelter that we could finally get to it by car. Before the week was over, I wanted to see what the place looked like, and so did Sharon.

During the Midwest floods the year before, Sharon had not gone on a rescue the entire time she volunteered. She was so good at intake that I kept her at that post during that disaster and again during this one. When she heard I was going to animal control, she asked shyly, "Do you think I could go along?"

"Of course," I replied. "I think it's about time you got a firsthand look at Mother Nature's handiwork. Wendy, you want to go, too?"

Wendy Borowsky had come in from St. Louis on Tuesday, taking Marty's place. She, too, had never gone on a rescue. When I asked if she wanted to go on this excursion, she replied, "I don't think I'm ready to see it yet."

"That's fine, just let me know when you think it's the right time," I offered. "I don't want to push you."

On our ride to the shelter, Sharon saw her first disaster: one house after another, ruined beyond repair by days of being submerged in water, sitting on property that had been altered by the moving water; old trees uprooted and dying; caved-in sections of black asphalt; tilting telephone poles; cars turned on their sides. Seeing snippets of a disaster on television doesn't come close to preparing you for seeing beyond what the camera can show. Television doesn't prepare you for the smell either. Seeing and smelling are the sickening realities. The immensity of it all is overwhelming.

"How do animals survive this?" Sharon asked in disbelief. "I've seen them come into intake, but now that I've seen where they've come from, I'm absolutely amazed any of them are left alive for us to rescue."

"I know." It was all I could say.

The shelter was a tiny, well-built, cinder-block facility with a corrugated tin roof. The water had risen to five feet high inside the office and kennel area. But from what we could see peeking in the mud-tinted windows, it was a mess that could be cleaned up with some good ol' elbow grease and a few days of sunshine to dry things out. As soon as I got back to Dr. Davidson's clinic, I would call Chief Tidwell and offer our help in tackling the cleaning job. I would also remind him that North Shore Animal League might be able to give the shelter a grant to replace some of the furnishings and equipment that were too badly damaged to salvage. That call was delayed when Sharon and I stopped on our return trip to pick up a passenger.

The young dog was wandering slowly alongside the road, her nose sniffing the muddy ground, which only the day before had been underwater. We watched her from inside the car for a few minutes to see where she was headed, but she didn't appear to have any particular destination in mind. It seemed unlikely that she was headed home because there weren't any houses nearby, just some old dilapidated house trailers, which we were pretty certain were worn before the floodwater even touched them.

This was the section of town referred to as the Oil Fields. When you came out here, you were on the wrong side of the tracks. We had gotten this impression from talking to some of the locals. "That's where people dump their animals when they don't want them no more," one of the volunteers told us when we were talking about this area. "And don't many of them live long after that."

Now that I had seen the place, I could see why.

"What do you think we should do?" Sharon asked, as we continued to watch the dog wander back and forth aimlessly across the deserted two-lane road. "The poor thing's so skinny, and she looks totally worn-out."

"Let's take her back into town with us and we'll let animal control know that we have her," I said, grabbing a slip leash from the backseat. "She'll be your first rescue."

It didn't take any effort to catch the dog. When she saw us coming, she lay down in a shallow mud puddle, her head resting on her front paws. "Hi, you," I said, as Sharon and I approached cautiously. "You want to go for a ride?"

I didn't get any response. She just lay there. When I got a little closer, I asked her again if she wanted to go with us. She didn't wag her tail, growl, lift her head, or get up to come greet us. She remained in the mud puddle, seemingly too frightened to move even a whisker.

"Okay," I said, as I edged closer to her. "We're not going to hurt you. We just want to help."

As Sharon and I continued to reassure her, I formed a loop in the leash I had in my hands, getting it ready to slip over the dog's head. So far, she had given me no indication that she was unwilling to let me do this.

When I got within arm's reach of her, I slowly lowered my hand, my fingers pointed down, so that I could pet her with the back of my hand. She still just lay there, looking up at me with her big brown eyes.

"Nice puppy," I said, when I was finally able to touch the top of her head and stroke her muddy fur. "That's a good girl."

When I felt she knew I wasn't going to hurt her, I gently slid the loop around her neck, giving her an extra minute just to lie there before I tried to coax her to stand up. That was when I learned she had never been on a leash before. She didn't fight it, but she wasn't about to follow alongside of me while I led her back to the van. I ended up carrying her, doing a great job of covering my clothes with mud. She went limp in my arms as we walked the short distance, seemingly relieved not to have to take another step.

For the next three days, the timid dog spent most of her time under the Ping-Pong table in the intake area, sleeping. She would only move to eat, drink, and relieve herself. At night, she slept in one of the vans with Shirley Bollinger, the volunteer from California. During the day, Shirley spent as much time as she could with the Ridgeback mix, trying to convince her that she was safe and didn't have to be afraid any more. As I watched the two of them together, I knew what was going to happen.

With Mark Bartell's permission, Shirley took the eight-month-old dog back to California with her, with the promise that if anyone showed up at animal control and identified the dog from the picture we left with them, she would return the dog to Texas. That call never came.

"Libby" now lives outside Jackson, California, on 40 acres that she shares with an assortment of other very spoiled animals. The second summer that Shirley had Libby, she took her and her other three dogs and drove across country with them to a camp in Vermont, called Camp Gone to the Dogs. How many canines get to go to summer camp? Definitely not the ones who live in the Oil Fields.

Libby's life got even better when Shirley opened Three Dog Bakery, a store just for dogs with a sweet tooth. She goes to work with Shirley and has become the official taste tester, sampling all the wonderfully delicious creations.

"For the first few months after I brought Libby home, she would walk along, her nose to the ground, looking for bugs to eat, which is probably what she had been surviving on before she was rescued," Shirley said, when we were reminiscing about our time in Liberty.

For the dog who would probably not have survived for long in the Oil Fields, the flood was the best thing that could have happened to her. It gave her life—and Shirley.

By Thursday, we had less than 30 animals still in our care, a sign that it was getting closer to the time to go home. I had talked to Ken finally, and told him to expect me back before Halloween, so I could take Amy, Megan, and Jennifer trick-or-treating. That gave us three days to take apart what it had taken us six days to create.

I had already made arrangements with Connie King, the EARS volunteer who worked for Burlington Air Freight, to have them haul our supplies to California for free. It was time that EARS had a storage unit to keep our growing inventory of equipment, as my garage could no longer hold everything. The truck would arrive on Saturday afternoon, so we had to have everything packed up and ready to go by then.

As I was working with Lawrence from the Dallas SPCA, taking down some of the now vacant dog runs, he told me, "You know, tomorrow is Bobby's thirtieth birthday."

"Really? You mean we have an excuse to have a party?"

"Yep, I think it's as good a reason as any," Lawrence said, as he continued to unscrew the bolts that held the dog runs together. "But he'll kill me when he finds out I told you."

"Oh, we'll make it a surprise party. Bobby will be having fun, so he'll forget about how we found out. We'll do it to-morrow night and have streamers, balloons, noisemakers, cake, and ice cream," I said, already making a mental shop-ping list. "It'll be a good way to wrap up this disaster and give everyone a chance to relax before we finish packing on Saturday morning."

"Sounds good to me, but how are we going to get him away from here?" Lawrence asked.

I thought for a moment, and then said, "We'll send you and Bobby out on a pretend rescue, only he'll think it's a real one. I'll have someone call in, we'll do a rescue request form, and send you somewhere, so that you will be gone for about an hour. That should give us plenty of time to get everything set up."

"Sounds like a plan to me," Lawrence said, handing me pliers to use on a stubborn bolt.

As I continued to disassemble dog runs, I thought about the birthday party we'd had in Bainbridge for EARS volunteer Cindy Foster. At the time, Barney, the purple dinosaur, was the theme of most four- and five-year-old's birthday parties, so when I went to get decorations, plates, napkins, and cups, I decided we'd do as the kids did. Even the cake I ordered from the bakery had the purple fella on it. It ended up being a fabulous party. We gathered under the Levy Funeral Home tent at 10 o'clock at night, the entire group of adults wearing Barney birthday hats, while we sang, accompanied by a chorus of howling dogs, "I love you, you love me, we're a happy family, with a great big hug and kiss from me to you, won't you say you love me, too."

I could hardly wait for Friday night.

⌒

"I'LL GET it," Shirley yelled, running for the phone. "Hello, Emergency Animal Rescue Service. Can I help you?"

"It's me," I said. I was calling from my cell phone, having used the pretend excuse that I had to go get some gas in the van.

"So you want to report an animal who needs to be rescued?" Shirley said, playing right along with the charade. "Yes, we can do that, but I'll need to ask you a few questions first."

"You're good," I said to Shirley, as she started to ask me the questions we asked for a real rescue.

When she got to the description part and asked me what kind of animal it was, I hesitated for a moment, then asked, "What should we make up? Wait, I know. How about a German Shepherd?"

"So, it's a German Shepherd," Shirley said, trying to sound serious as she filled in the space on the form.

The next thing Shirley needed to know was where the dog was located. We had already looked at a map earlier and decided on the corner of North Travis Street and Willow Street. It looked just far enough away to give us the hour we needed.

"Okay, we'll have someone out there shortly," Shirley assured me before saying good-bye.

Arriving back at the shelter five minutes after Lawrence and Bobby had left, I grabbed Wendy so we could pick up the birthday cake and the Chinese food we had ordered for dinner. I had picked up the balloons, streamers, and "Older than Dirt" paper goods earlier in the day and stashed them in a closet at the clinic. While Wendy and I were gone, the rest of the crew decorated.

When we got back, the intake area looked terrific. The group had cleared the Ping-Pong table of all the paperwork and replaced it with all the makings of a birthday party. The two dozen "Over the Hill" balloons and black streamers moved gently in the early evening breeze, as we all sat anxiously awaiting the return of the birthday boy and our coconspirator.

"They should be here any minute," Shirley said, looking at her watch. "They've been gone exactly one hour."

A half-hour later, they were still not back.

"Maybe Bobby found out what we were planning, kidnapped Lawrence, and they're headed back to Dallas," Pam said, as we all sat wondering where they were.

"Or maybe Bobby decided he'd take Lawrence out for pizza and beer and celebrate his thirtieth birthday, just the two of them?" I suggested. "I heard him say earlier today that he was craving pizza."

It was 7:10 when the two-man rescue team returned. They had been gone since five o'clock.

Following the chorus of "Surprise! Surprise! Surprise!" I asked Lawrence, "What did you guys do, drive to the other side of town through Houston? We were almost ready to send out a rescue team to look for both of you."

"You're never going to believe what happened," Lawrence began. "When we got out to North Travis and Willow, sitting on the corner was a German Shepherd."

"No way!" I blurted out.

"I'm not kidding you," Lawrence replied. "I couldn't believe it when I saw him. At first I thought, *These guys are really good, they even put the dog out here to make the rescue look real.*"

"No, we aren't *that* good," I said.

"So where's the dog?" Shirley asked.

"What was equally amazing was that he had tags on him, so we took him home," Lawrence explained. "That's why it took us so long to get back. We actually had a rescue to do."

Bobby's birthday turned out to be a surprise for all of us.

CHAPTER EIGHTEEN

The Truth

I CAME CLOSE to needing a dousing of ice-cold water to get me out of bed on Saturday morning. If Mike hadn't already gone back home to California, I suspect that's what I would have gotten as I tried to motivate myself to get up. Staying in bed seemed like a great idea.

I wasn't the only one who was dragging as we walked, fed, and cleaned the cages of the few remaining animals we had to take care of that last morning. The weather had turned cooler, so what I really wanted to do was find a warm spot to sit down and have a hot cup of coffee. Instead, I was in Dr. Davidson's front yard again, shivering, as the dog I was walking took her merry ol' time looking for the perfect spot to pee.

After the slowpoke finally found that spot, I walked her back to one of the dog runs that was still standing. When I saw how few people and animals were at the shelter that morning and I saw the blue Rubbermaid supply totes lined up, already partially filled for their trip to California, I knew there was another reason for my reluctance to start my day. Saying good-bye was never easy.

In eight days, I met animals and people I would never forget, and I knew I would probably never see most of them again. The bonding that goes on when you share an experience as intense as a disaster makes for some very special friendships. Leaving behind these new friends is something I dread as each disaster comes to an end.

"Well, we're about ready to pull out," Bobby said, as I walked up to the SPCA truck. "Thanks for letting us be a part of this, Terri. Lawrence and I got a lot out of it and we're going to take what we've learned back to Dallas, so when we get hit with a disaster, we'll know better what to do and what not to do."

"I'm glad you came," I said, hugging Bobby. "You guys were great."

"And thanks for the birthday party. It'll be one I never forget," the 30-year-old said.

"Maybe we'll get to celebrate another one with you," I said. "But next time we'll do it in a restaurant with pizza and beer."

"Hey, that wouldn't be as much fun," Bobby was quick to point out.

"You're right," I acknowledged, as Lawrence joined us.

"So, we ready to hit the road?" Lawrence asked.

"Yeah, we've got everything loaded," Bobby said, as he pulled down the roll-up door on the back of the truck.

"Where's the dog you're taking?"

"She'll be riding up front with us," Lawrence assured me.

"Don't forget her socks," I reminded the guys. The dog they were taking back to the SPCA for adoption had cut her foot during the flood. When Dr. Myers examined her, he suggested that we wrap something around her foot to protect it while it healed. On one of my Wal-Mart runs, I had bought infant booties, picking out a package of bright purple ones.

"I already got them, along with her new collar, leash, food dish, toys, and bed," Lawrence said, counting the items off on his fingers. "You guys really know how to spoil an animal."

"We try hard," I said, hugging Lawrence. "Now get out of here, you two, before I find another German Shepherd for you to rescue."

There were only five of us left to wave good-bye as Bobby and Lawrence backed out of the driveway. In total, we'd had 31 volunteers. This included local residents Shirley Le Blanc, Joanne and Mike Bryant, Charles Adams, Roland Taylor, Courtney Rank, plus Traci and Sherry Hampton. They had been invaluable at the shelter and in helping us learn our way around town. We were especially grateful when the Bryants showed up. When they realized our bathroom had no running water or a shower, they offered us the use of their bathroom at home. After four days of sponge baths, we were more than ready to shed some lingering layers of dirt and wash our hair. And, they did our laundry, which we actually got back this time.

"So, you're not taking any animals home this time, Terri?" Shirley asked, as we went back to packing more totes after Bobby and Lawrence left.

"No, Ken would kill me," I said. "Besides, you guys didn't leave me any."

Shirley was taking a kitten and a puppy back to Macon with her. Then, of course, Libby was going to California. One of Sharon's friends who lived in Houston had adopted a Pit Bull with mange the day before, and Sharon was taking a puppy with a broken leg back to the St. Charles Humane Society for adoption after her leg healed. The last unclaimed animal was a very sick kitten who was going back to San Antonio with Pam. We had succeeded in placing all 32 of the unclaimed animals. It was now okay to go home. We had done our job and, once again, had made a difference—this time for 128 animals, and a generous man named Dr. Davidson who gave us a place to keep all those animals safe.

In the afternoon, we were just about finished loading the Burlington Air Freight truck, thanks to the help of some of our local volunteers, when a police car pulled up in front of the clinic. Shirley spotted it first and came back to the truck to tell me, "Terri, I think you've got company."

Stepping out of the patrol car was Chief Tidwell.

Realizing I looked like someone who had just spent all day packing, I quickly searched for my vest and put it on over my dirty clothes. Beyond that, there wasn't much I could do to look more presentable.

"Chief," I said as I walked toward the man, "good to see you again."

I hadn't seen him since the day we arrived in town. He continued to be a very busy man and I suspected he'd given us about as much of his time as he could spare that first day. I had called him and left a message after Sharon and I had returned from seeing the city shelter, but I'd never heard if he wanted our help getting the city shelter ready to open again. *Maybe that's why he's come by?* I thought. If that was the case, I was going to have to call Ken and say, "Guess what, honey, I'm going to be a little late getting home."

"Ma'am," he said, tipping his cowboy hat. "Looks like you all are fixing to leave."

"Trying to," I replied.

"I bet you're ready to get back to your family in California," he said, as he watched the volunteers continuing to load the truck.

"It'll be nice." I wondered if this was leading up to the question, "Any chance you can stay maybe another day?"

"Well, I just wanted to come by and say thank you," he said, rubbing his chin with his hand. "You all were a big help."

I realized it took a lot for him to tell me this.

"Thanks, Chief, we were glad to help out," I said with a smile.

"You know, when you all came up to me that first day and explained what you wanted to do, I'll tell you, I wasn't too keen on the idea. I fully expected you all to be another one of my many problems." He paused for a moment as he slid his hands into his front pocket and fiddled with some loose change. "You turned out to be anything but that, though. In fact, I know you prevented a lot of problems that probably would have caused me some real headaches for some time to come."

I pulled in my bottom lip to keep it from quivering. I just hoped he wouldn't ask me a question, because I knew I wouldn't be able to answer it. It was taking everything I had just to hold back the tears.

"You know how you said that if I wanted to, I could tell the people in this town that I called and asked you to come here to help the animals," he reminded me.

I nodded my head, remembering our conversation. I was still amazed that anything I had said to him had made any sense, because I had been scared to death he was going to tell us he didn't need our help, when I knew he sure as heck did.

"Well, I'm not going to tell them that," he said, looking me straight in the eye for the first time since I'd met him eight days earlier. "Instead, I'm going to tell people the truth. We were plum lucky this time that you all showed up. Your business card will be in my desk and, if this ever happens again, I *will* call you."

CHAPTER NINETEEN

Planting Seeds

MOTHER NATURE must have been worn out after the floods in Texas. The remaining two months of 1994 were quiet, giving me time to complete my first book and get it to my publisher just after the holidays. The following year, EARS responded to six disasters, including our first one outside of the United States.

On January 21, Shirley Minshew and I flew from San Francisco to Japan, our final destination the coastal city of Kobe, which had been devastated by a 6.9 earthquake four days before. Our help had been requested, and the trip paid for, by the Franz Weber Foundation in Montreux, Switzerland.

War has never directly touched my life. These life-extinguishing conflicts have always happened far away to other people, in other countries. Experiencing the aftermath of the catastrophic earthquake in Kobe made me wonder if I was getting a glimpse of what it was like to view a countryside ripped apart by war.

The experience of being two American women immersed in a foreign country where the government and the people were struggling to rise from total chaos and suffering was at times frightening, and often exciting. It was like one of those real-life adventures you read about in *Reader's Digest,* only this time Shirley and I lived it.

Our daily commute to and from the worst-hit area of Kobe took us at least six hours, and gave us a face-to-face look at the survival of people and their animals in a culture very unlike our own. Getting to Kobe from our hotel in Osaka required a 4 A.M. wake-up call from the front desk, which we assumed translated as "good morning" each time we picked up the phone and heard the voice on the other end.

In order to travel the normally short distance of 15 miles between the neighboring cities, we first walked two miles through a maze of alleys and narrow streets, moving en masse, shoulder to shoulder, with Japanese civilians rushing to their own particular destinations. When we reached the congested Umeda train station, Shirley and I wove our way through the crowd, trying very hard not to lose one another. By some miracle, we had figured out how to purchase tickets for the Hankyu line from automated dispensers with instructions only in Japanese. Then, we rushed to board, hopefully, the commuter train that would take us five miles closer to the epicenter. We disembarked in a city called Nishinomiya, where the tracks suddenly ended. They were too badly damaged for the train to continue beyond that point, the steel guides broken and scattered like a handful of Pickup Sticks.

Back on foot, we hiked four blocks to our next destination, alternating between the sidewalk and the street, depending on which provided the safest path. Moving with us were crowds of people, bicycles, motor scooters, and an occasional compact car, badly dented by falling objects. Our walk ended when we reached a temporary bus stop.

The earthquake had spared few of the cars in Kobe and most of the roads were too damaged or cluttered with debris to allow anything larger than a bike to pass. For this reason, buses normally used to show tourists the local sites were now being used to transport disaster victims in and out of the devastated area.

The wait for the bus was always a minimum of an hour. When we finally made it to the front of the three-block-long line, we stepped aboard to stand in the aisle, crammed up against people who stood in complete silence. The quiet seemed unnatural, as we were accustomed to American disaster victims who want to tell their stories to anyone who will listen. The Japanese people on the bus just stared straight ahead, their faces absent of any emotion that we could read. Their gauze bandages were what told of the personal scars the earthquake had etched on their weary bodies and minds.

Our five-mile-plus bus ride never followed the same course. We zigzagged and backtracked, and sometimes went in circles, as the driver searched for a cleared path through the city. As we traveled deeper into the worst-hit areas, there were very few blocks that didn't have houses that had slid off their foundations, coming to rest in the middle of the street.

Frequently, the bus got stuck in one place for a very long time, while we waited for cleanup crews to remove the roadblocks that the earthquake had placed in our way. As the bus inched ahead, we stood in the claustrophobic space, our eyes searching the bizarre landscape for animals. It was hard for me to comprehend the surroundings as real. I would have found it easier to believe that I was on a tour bus at Universal Studios, passing the cleverly crafted and realistic sets of a new earthquake movie. The blaring sound of police and fire sirens jolted me back to reality, though, reminding me that this was indeed a real city in deadly turmoil.

One of our detours took us across a concrete bridge that the earthquake had split into two sections, one side at least a foot lower than it had been before the fierce shaking. As we crossed the unstable structure, we closed our eyes and crossed our fingers, hoping there wouldn't be an aftershock strong enough to break the bridge in two at last and send it crashing into the river below.

When the bus could no longer maneuver the narrow streets, now littered with crumbled bricks, twisted metal, splintered lumber, fragments of roof tiles, smashed cars, and personal belongings, we got off the bus in single file, so the bus could turn around and go back for its next load.

We walked the remaining portion of our journey. The one- to two-mile walk got us to the Mominoki Animal Clinic, which had opened within hours after the earthquake. This closet-sized veterinary clinic became our base of operation for the five days we spent trying to do what we could for the animals.

We learned from the clinic's veterinarian, Dr. Murata, that most people had rescued and were determined to take care of their animals themselves. The human shelters that we visited did allow pets, but we never saw Rottweilers, Pit Bulls, and Chows, which are breeds we so commonly see in disasters in the United States. Homes in Japan are compact and most do not have a yard, so people do not have the larger breed dogs. Most of the dogs we saw were small enough to fit in a woman's purse, and many of them were wearing sweaters to keep them warm.

It was impossible to determine how many animals were hurt as a result of the earthquake. Just over 25,000 people were reported injured, so the animals had to have suffered terribly, too. During the time we were at the clinic, however, the most severe injury we saw was a dog with a broken leg. There were also three cats treated for earthquake-related injuries, but they were not serious. We asked Dr. Murata if he'd heard of any veterinarians in the city treating an unusually high number of injured animals. He said he hadn't heard of anything out of the ordinary.

There was a continual flow of people through the clinic during the time we were there, though. A few were routine appointments, but the majority of the people brought their pets in to be seen for severe cases of diarrhea, loss of appetite, changes in sleeping behavior, and nervousness—all common postdisaster symptoms seen in people, too.

One of my concerns was that the longer animals were forced to live among the debris, which consisted of mounds

A dog, chained to a tree and left behind by his owners, barely escaping the fires in Alaska.

Crisp family members (clockwise, left to right: Amy, Ken, me, and Megan).

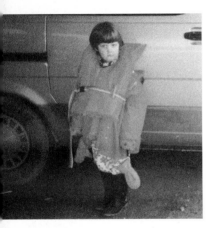

Megan Crisp in Roseville, California, making sure to wear her life jacket for the floods.

Derrold Daly (background), T. J. (right), and Tar Baby with other volunteers in Roseville, California.

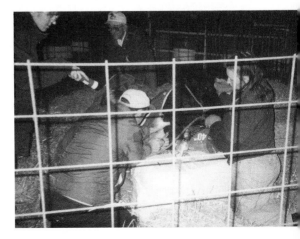

A CNN cameraman catches an update for EARS volunteers in Roseville, California.

Spoiled puppies in Roseville, California.

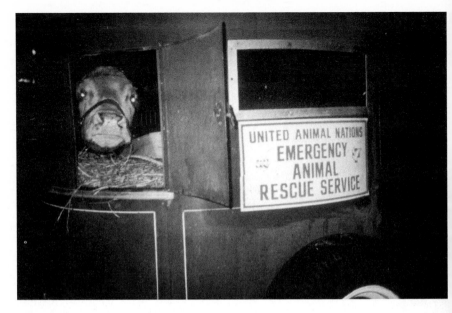

A lucky cow—one survivor of at least 35,000 who died in the Northern California floods.

Only one third of the donated pet food in Roseville, California.

EARS saying "thanks" to the volunteers and community for all their hard work during the Northern California floods.

Me and the National Guard's two-and-a-half-ton flatbed heroic truck in Grand Forks, North Dakota.

The only surviving bird in the senior apartment complex in Grand Forks, North Dakota.

Flood damage in Grand Forks, North Dakota.

A heroic rescue in Grand Forks, North Dakota.

Wendy Borowsky, with a variety of pets rescued from one house in Grand Forks, North Dakota.

Me and Arlette Moen, director of Grand Forks Humane Society, during a rescue.

The devoted, potty-trained dogs who "crossed their legs" until they got in the boat with the rescuers in Grand Forks, North Dakota.

of sharp metal and broken glass, the more the animals would suffer postdisaster injuries. After Hurricane Andrew, Shirley and I saw repeated incidents of eye injuries, deep punctures, severed limbs, and serious cuts among the animals.

Another thing we talked about was what would happen to the animals that people were trying to keep with them. The news reported approximately 290,000 people displaced as a result of the earthquake, which meant there were a lot of animals who were homeless, too. We were encouraged to see the human shelters allowing pets to stay there, but that wasn't a long-term solution. Eventually, owners would have to make other arrangements for their housing. As we had seen in previous disasters, it was likely that a percentage of the animals would be surrendered to local shelters with a slim chance of being adopted.

In the affected area, there were four animal shelters, comparable to American animal control facilities. Dr. Murata told us that none of them had sustained any major damage, so they were able to remain open to receive animals. Initially, the number of incoming animals had not been much higher than normal, but this was bound to change as the weeks went on.

We chose not to set up a temporary shelter in Kobe for several reasons. If we had, we would only have been able to supervise it for a short period of time and the need would have continued for weeks or even months after we left. If there had been an agency or a group of people that we could have trusted to continue operating a temporary shelter, we may have considered opening one. It was too risky, though, and we couldn't just abandon the animals when our time ran out. Once EARS takes on the responsibility of caring for animals during a disaster, we remain involved until the end, but we couldn't do that this time since the Franz Weber Foundation would only fund us to be in Japan for 10 days.

Another consideration was the cost involved. Even with donated supplies, it still takes a great deal of money to run a temporary shelter; these funds were not readily available to us.

Another obstacle was space. With so many buildings destroyed or unsafe throughout Kobe, useable buildings were at a premium. Any open space, which is rare in most Japanese cities, had already been designated for tent cities for the people.

Unlike what we were accustomed to in the United States, there was not a large outpouring of people who wanted to help the animals. When we wondered about the shortage of volunteers, Dr. Murata explained that volunteering to help animals was not a common practice. Even if it had been, everyone in Kobe was just struggling to survive, allowing them no extra time to volunteer. Another deterrent was the length of time it took to travel to the area, making it difficult to draw people from surrounding cities. A volunteer program could have been cultivated over time, but obviously not soon enough to help the animals in this disaster.

We eventually had a small team of volunteers recruited for us by the Cat Fanciers' Association and the Companion Animal Partnership Program, but it was in no way a large enough group to begin to make a difference. It was really frustrating to be in such an overwhelming situation without access to the network of EARS volunteers and the resources of supplies and equipment that we had become accustomed to having at our disposal. I felt as if I had returned to some of my earliest disasters, and it felt awful to be so unprepared.

We worked with two veterinarians besides Dr. Murata. All of them were eager to learn from us, but they weren't prepared to pick up where we left off. We determined that they were not quite sure how to implement in their community and culture the types of services we felt they needed to get the animals through this tough time. It was difficult to get them to commit to doing things, mainly because the concept of helping animals in a disaster was so new to them and must have been overwhelming. We were very careful to respect their way of doing things, yet continued to drop subtle hints as to what we felt needed to be done to address the immediate problems and the long-term ones.

What helped us deal with the inadequacies of the situation was observing the people in the affected area and the responsibility they felt toward their animals. Most of the dogs and cats we saw were with their owners, and provisions had been made to shelter and feed them. We learned through our translator that some of the people had even sent their animals out of the area to live with family and friends temporarily.

We did encounter stray animals in the neighborhoods where we were working, but not as many as we had anticipated, which helped our morale. The majority of these animals were cats. At one location alone, we counted 21. None of the cats were overly skinny nor did they look sick, which was encouraging. We tried to determine to whom they belonged, but we were unsuccessful. The cats were being taken care of, though, because there was fresh food and water at the location when we arrived. Some of the cats even had collars, which is something we rarely see when we respond to disasters in the United States. Wherever we spotted animals, we left food and water and made note of the location, so volunteers could continue to feed them once we left and until the free food ran out.

We never received a single request to rescue an animal trapped in rubble. I'm sure it had a lot to do with the absence of a central location where people could report that an animal needed to be rescued. Even if we had received a request, I doubt Shirley and I could have done much. We had brought very little with us to Japan, so finding the equipment we would have needed to extract an animal safely from a collapsed building would have been difficult. Throughout the time we were there, search and rescue teams were looking for missing people, and all the resources were being directed toward those efforts.

After I'd returned home, I read in my local newspaper that a six-month-old Golden Retriever named Dick had been pulled from the rubble, still alive, 18 days after the quake in Japan. The article reported that it took 34 firefighters and police four hours to free the dog, who had survived on the food and rainwater he could scrounge in the tiny portion of the dilapidated house where he was trapped. These kinds of resources were definitely not available to us while we were in Japan.

We knew there were more animals who needed help than those we were seeing, but it was hard to find them. We were pleased to learn over time that people who had found animals were quietly taking care of them. Some of the lost animals had belonged to people who had died during the earthquake, and neighbors had already agreed to keep them.

In our experience of disasters, it was unusual not to learn of missing animals during the time we worked the disaster. If there had been a central location advertised to collect this information, there might have been some calls, but any information pertaining to animals seemed to be something people did not feel comfortable discussing. It wasn't until we had been helping at the clinic for three days that we found out why.

A young man came to the clinic in the afternoon to pick up some cat food. When Shirley asked the interpreter to ask him how many cats he had, the reply was that he had four, but could only find three. "Ask him if he's seen the cat since the earthquake," I requested while the young man listened intently.

"He says he found bloody paw prints inside his house the morning after the quake," the interpreter told us. "His other cats are not hurt, so he thinks the one he can't find is injured."

"Does he want us to help him look for the cat?" Shirley instructed the interpreter to ask.

The young man looked shocked when he heard what Shirley's question was. An offer of help did not seem to be something he expected, and he didn't seem sure that he should accept it, which confused us. If I were missing my cat, I would be thrilled to have help finding her.

"Tell him this is what we do," I explained to our interpreter, hoping it would persuade the man to let us help.

The young man looked at Shirley and me with a puzzled look on his face. He seemed to consider our offer for a minute, then nodded his head. The interpreter said, "Yes, he will take your help."

When we arrived in the man's neighborhood, he remained at the curb, while Shirley and I searched the property for the cat. We thought it unusual that he didn't help us, but we figured he was afraid of what we would find. Our hour-long search was not a success. There were no fresh bloody paw prints to lead us to the cat.

When we returned to where the man was waiting, I asked the interpreter to find out if the man had talked to any of his neighbors. Maybe they had seen his cat since the quake.

The response I got was not what I had expected. The young man immediately began shaking his head when he was asked the question. The interpreter explained the reason for his negative response. "He says if he asked his neighbors about his missing cat, they would think he is a horrible person."

"Why?" I asked in disbelief.

"They would think how insensitive he is to be worrying about a cat when there are families still searching for missing relatives."

It was an aggravating situation, but we had no choice but to work within the limits of what was culturally acceptable, which meant we couldn't even put up lost-cat posters. The cat, who we assumed was injured, was never found. We know it broke the young man's heart because the interpreter had told us it was his favorite one.

It is impossible to determine how many animals died during this disaster. The final count of human deaths was 5,502. There had to have been a large number of animals who perished as well. People frequently ask me what the animal death count of a particular disaster was. There has never been an accurate system to tabulate this information, so I have to answer, "I really don't know, but my guess is too many."

The Japanese government asked the people in Kobe to bring any dead animals to the public health centers, so they could be properly disposed of, which people did. Again, without a backyard, there was no place to bury an animal, and placing him at the curb for collection was not acceptable (this practice is common in the United States).

We learned that the Japanese are almost fanatical when it comes to order and cleanliness. When we walked through the neighborhoods, we were amazed at how they were dealing with the accumulation of debris that came out of every home. In the disasters we had been to at home, the piles of debris in front of people's houses are a mess. We've seen people stand on their front porch and just pitch those things they no longer want. If the item makes it to the pile, fine; but if not, they don't care. In Kobe, the piles of garbage were neatly organized and stacked, taking up very little space.

———

WITH NO shelter to run, rescues to do, or lost animals to track down, we spent the majority of our time at the Mominoki Clinic distributing dog and cat food. Pedigree, Kal Kan, and IAMS had Japanese distribution centers, and they kept us supplied, thanks to the coordination of Bess Higuchi and Kayoko Koizumi, members of a cat fancier's group in Tokyo, who we connected with through Pam De La Bar. The food was brought by truck to the veterinary clinic, but the deliveries were sporadic, delayed by traffic problems.

Between the hours of 10 A.M. and 4 P.M., a steady flow of people stopped to pick up food. We also took food to the human shelters to ensure that owners would be able to feed their animals. Not having a car to use made the distribution very difficult, though. Our solution ended up being shopping carts. We looked like a couple of bag ladies, pushing our overloaded caravan of carts through the streets of Kobe. We wouldn't get far before we ran out of food and had to return to the clinic for more. It was a routine we repeated too many times.

Shirley and I were thrilled to learn that John Walsh and Wim de Kok, representatives of the World Society for the

Protection of Animals (WSPA), had arrived from Boston, Massachusetts, the day before we did. We met with them at their hotel in Osaka on January 27. During our meeting, they told us they had been struggling with the Japanese government, trying to convince them to open a temporary shelter for the animals.

Prior to the January 17 earthquake, John had been in contact with the government officials to encourage them to include animals in their disaster plan. He had sent a letter to them on January 5, indicating that WSPA would be happy to work with them to put together such a plan, since this is what WSPA does internationally under the umbrella of the United Nations. After the Kobe earthquake, the Japanese government definitely recognized the need to include animals in their disaster plan, but it came too late for the animals who lost their lives in Kobe.

In our time in Kobe, we also checked on the situation at the city's zoo and aquarium. The zoo animals were fine, except for one giraffe who had died. He had been sick prior to the earthquake, so it was unlikely that he would have survived much longer anyway. The aquarium lost many of their fish when the glass tanks broke, but all the sea mammals, including dolphins, whales, and sea otters, survived. We know that a lot of pet fish had to have perished, too, because it was a frequent sight to see broken aquariums in the neat piles of curbside debris.

Shirley and I left Japan on January 29. We had a lot to think about on our 16-hour flight across the Pacific Ocean. For me, the time in Japan was a reminder of the first disasters to which I had responded—the ones I went to by myself. EARS didn't exist then, there were no trained volunteers, and no one seemed to care much about the animals. I felt as overwhelmed then as I had in dealing with the seemingly impassable obstacles in Kobe. But I had to remind myself how far EARS had come since 1988. This gave me hope for the animals in Japan.

Shirley and I didn't have as many hands-on animal experiences as we would have liked during the 10 days in Kobe, but I think we planted some seeds of awareness, which, when you look at the bigger picture, will end up doing more good. Hopefully, the animals in Japan will one day have a program similar to EARS, so they can count on the help they need and deserve during the frequent natural disasters that tear this country apart.

CHAPTER TWENTY

The Fantastic, Fearless, Fireproof Feline

ARS HAD grown to 839 trained volunteers by the end of 1995. That number increased significantly after *Out of Harm's Way* arrived on bookshelves in March 1996. I traveled to 13 cities on my book tour, spending my days doing radio and television interviews and talking to bookstore audiences about EARS and the importance of being prepared to care for animals during disasters. It was a wonderful few weeks. When I shared my stories with people, they wanted to become volunteers.

Once someone has gone through the daylong EARS workshop, they understand their obligation to animals during disasters and, with lots of encouragement from me, they take this new information and share it with everyone they can. This growing force of individuals has made a difference for animals. As their numbers continue to grow, even more animals will benefit. The fact that my first book helped animals in this way is what made it such a success in my eyes, and I expect it to be the same with this book.

Spreading the word about disaster preparedness, not only for animals but also for people, is what saves lives. EARS has become a very loud voice, advocating the rights of animals to be moved to a safe location and protected during disasters.

That is what we do, so when I learned on June 6, 1996, of a major wild land fire near Wasilla, Alaska, EARS coordinators Wendy Borowsky, Sharon Maag, and I went into action.

The Miller Reach Fire, as this one came to be known, began on June 5 with a firecracker. Within one week, 37,336 acres of Alaska wilderness had burned, destroying lives and property.

We worked with John Scott, the director of Mat-Su Borough Animal Control, and a dedicated team of veterinarians and veterinary technicians, who had set up an emergency clinic in Wasilla. Our base of operation became the fire command center, established at the high school in Houston, about 60 miles northeast of Anchorage. Our assistance was accepted immediately. The emergency managers provided us with radio communication, gave us access into areas that had restricted entry, and invited us to attend the daily briefings.

Just after the morning briefing on our second day in town, we met a firefighter from Idaho who loved animals.

"I saw the back of your vests," the man said, stopping us in the hallway. "What is the Emergency Animal Rescue Service?"

As I explained to him what we did and what our role was in this disaster, he listened intently.

"This is great," he said, enthusiastically. "I've been fighting these kinds of fires for 14 years, and it's about time someone remembered that animals get caught up in the mess and die, too."

"Thanks," I said, glad to hear him voice this truth. "So, have you seen any animals in this fire that need help?"

"Not yet, but if I do, I'll sure as heck track you down," he said.

"Here's my business card," I said, handing it to him. "My cell phone number is on the back, so call if you come across anything we need to know about. Or you can probably catch one of us here at the EOC."

"Will do," he said, sticking the card in his wallet. "There are a lot of animals, especially dogs, in the areas where the fire is burning. Most of them are sled dogs, I think, since we're so close to Wasilla where the Iditarod Sled Dog Race starts every year. I'd hope those people care enough about their dogs to get them out in time, though."

"I hope so, too," I said, not confident that this would be the case for all of them.

"Well, I've got to run," he said, shaking my hand. "Good talking with you."

"Same here," I said, as he turned and blended into the crowd moving through the hallway.

After speaking with the man, Wendy, Sharon, and I responded to our first request for help of the day. During the morning briefing, we had learned of a man who had remained behind when everyone evacuated because he had too many animals to try and move. When the fire passed through the area where he lived, it split and, amazingly, burned a path on either side of his property, sparing him and his animals. The firefighter who told us about him said, "The fella was desperate for food to feed his dogs when we were out there yesterday afternoon watching for flare-ups. I know he'd appreciate getting some food if you have some to spare."

We had more than enough to spare, so that was where we headed. When we got to the man's house, which looked like an oasis in the middle of the burned wilderness, we could understand why he had decided not to leave. Everywhere we looked there were animals running loose. It was a real menagerie. All I could think of was how fortunate he was that none of them had died. As we talked to him, it was obvious he cared a great deal about his animals. But when you live in a place where the fire danger is so high, having more animals than you can evacuate is not a good thing. The man came very close to finding that out—the hard way.

"I really appreciate the food," he said, as we were walking back to our van, with dogs, cats, chickens, and even a goat tagging along with us. "The fireman told me yesterday that we're not out of danger yet. I guess the fire could turn around and backtrack, destroying what it didn't burn the first time. That's why I was afraid to run into town to get some food. You guys were a real lifesaver."

We were not the ones who deserved the thanks. It was Mother Nature he should have been checking in with. The outcome could have been so different. I don't know if this man realized how close he came to losing all his animals. Hopefully, he had learned a lesson this time around, and wouldn't be passive during the next fire. It seemed improbable that he could be so lucky twice. I was grateful that the man still had animals who could be fed. I told him, "I'm glad we found out you needed some food, and if there is anything else we can do to help, you can reach us at the number on the back of the business card I gave you."

"There is something else you could do," he said, with a serious look on his face. "You want to shoot somebody for me?"

Having lived in Alaska for six months during the Exxon *Valdez* oil spill, when I served as the staff coordinator at the otter rehab center, I knew this man was probably not kidding. Alaska is known as the last frontier, and I learned during the time I lived in this rugged state that guns were frequently used to settle disputes the farther out into the wilderness you got.

"So, who do you want dead?" I asked, in a tone that would indicate I thought he was joking.

"The man who lives down the road," he said, pointing in the direction we came from.

"What did he do to make you so mad?" I asked, again trying to make light of the situation.

"He killed his dog."

The story the man then told us is one of those memories that stays pinned to my mental bulletin board to this day. I will never forget that dog.

"He decided he was going to stay behind, too, and save his house," the man said, petting the head of a Labrador mix who had come up and nudged his nose against the man's hand. "Hell, I didn't care for a second if the fire took my house. It was the animals I was worried about."

"Did he save his house?" I asked.

"Sure as heck did. You should see how close it came, though. Hell, I thought it got close to my place, but the fire had to have been breathing down his neck. It circled him on three sides, burning within 200 feet of the place. If he hadn't cleared the brush and gotten some backup at the last minute from the firefighters, he'd have been a goner."

"So tell me about the dog." I really didn't want to hear what he was about to tell us, but I had to know.

"The dog was big, looked to be a Shepherd-Collie mix. He kept the dog tied up in back 'cause he used to run off all the time. I'd see the dog when I drove by, and I felt so sorry for him. I don't believe in keeping animals confined."

That was the truth, I thought, as I was looking at the ones who were wandering freely all around us.

"The guy had put up two metal poles about eight feet apart. Between them, he strung a cable, which he'd hook this dog's chain to. The dog could run back and forth between the poles, but he didn't get near enough exercise," the man explained. "Lately, the dog just lay there. I honestly think he was depressed. I know I would be if I lived my life on the end of a chain."

"Did the dog ever get to go inside?" I asked.

"Don't think so," the man replied. "He did have a dog-house he could go in when it snowed and rained."

"You wonder why he even had a dog," I said, shaking my head in disgust.

"I reckon to bark and let him know when something was prowling around his place."

"Where was the dog during the fire?" It was a question I hated to ask.

"Tied up," the man said, stopping then to cough, which I think was his way of getting out of saying another word at that moment. His eyes were a dead giveaway that he was about to cry.

"He didn't at least turn the dog loose?" I questioned.

The man just shook his head.

"How did you find out what happened?" I said, after I waited long enough for the man to regain his composure.

"I walked down there yesterday afternoon," he said, rubbing his eyes. "I was afraid of what might have happened to the dog. I felt I owed it to him to see if he was alright or not."

"And he wasn't?"

"Nope," the man muttered. "He wasn't."

"You don't have to tell us what you found, if you don't want to," I said, placing a hand on the man's shoulder. "I know this must be hard."

"I have to tell someone," he said, the tears welling up in his eyes. "I can't keep this inside any longer."

"Then go ahead," I whispered.

"He'd already gotten rid of the dog by the time I got there. I don't know what he did with him, 'cause he wasn't around. My guess is he probably dumped him out in the woods. When I walked behind the house, I could see the metal poles, the cable, the chain, and the burned doghouse." The man stopped. No longer able to control his tears, he looked me straight in the eyes and said, each word an effort to get out, "Between the poles I could see distinct black impressions of the dog's body on the brown grass as he thrashed around on the ground, trying to put out the fire, as his fur burned."

What could I say? Nothing. Absolutely nothing. So I just cried.

WE DIDN'T get a whole lot accomplished the rest of the day. The sadness was just too overpowering to muster up the energy to do much. Around three o'clock, we returned to the command center. We hadn't been in the building ten minutes when the firefighter we had talked to earlier that morning came running down the hall toward us.

"Boy, am I glad I found you guys," he said out of breath. "My crew is waiting in the parking lot, so I've got to hurry, but I convinced them to give me five minutes to come in here and look for you."

"What's going on?" I asked.

"Here," he said, handing me a piece of cardboard with a crudely drawn map on it. "There's a cat right here where I'm pointing. He's burned bad. When we found him, the rest of my crew wanted to get a shovel from the truck and hit him over the head to put him out of his misery, but I said no. That's when I told them about you guys. I told them you would know what to do."

"How badly burned is he?" I asked, still struggling with the memory of the dead dog.

"He can't walk. All four of his legs are burned. I didn't want to get too close and scare him, so I can't tell you much more than that," he said, using his blackened hands to adjust the goggles that hung around his neck.

"What color is he?" Sharon asked.

"Orange, I believe. He's pretty dirty, so it's hard to tell," the firefighter responded.

"When did the fire pass through this area?" I asked, trying to get a sense of how long the cat had been lying there.

"Probably two, maybe three days ago," he guessed.

"So he's been lying there at least two days." I said, more to myself than to anyone else. That was a long time to be in that condition, undoubtedly in a lot of pain.

"Probably so," the man concluded. "It's amazing a bear or fox didn't get him."

"Is this a lake?" I asked, looking at the map more closely to be sure I understood the directions.

"Yeah, that's Lazy Lake," he said. "The cat more than likely caught on fire, cause there wasn't much of anything out there that didn't burn, and then he must have got into the water to put out the fire. Somehow he managed to get back on shore, but since his legs were so badly burned, he couldn't walk."

"Well, we'll go find him and see what we can do," I said to the firefighter. "Thanks for tracking us down and letting us know."

"Hey, I'm glad I found him and that I knew about you guys. It would have killed me to use the shovel on the poor thing."

The drive out to Lazy Lake took us about 20 minutes. The firefighter had been right, there was not much left. Here and there a house still stood, untouched by the flames. The homeowners, fortunate to still have their houses, had already put up handwritten signs on the roadside thanking the firefighters who had somehow managed to save their places.

We passed mop-up crews as we wove our way down the narrow, winding dirt road, the once-luscious forest on either side now nothing more than charred wood. One of the crews stopped us and warned us to stay alert, that the fire could easily come back to life again.

Fire is a very intimidating force of nature, for which I have a world of respect. Our intent was to grab the cat and get out of there as quickly as we could. Continuing to use our crudely drawn map as a guide, I drove along, wondering what it had been like when the deadly inferno had roared through this area. I wondered, too, how many other animals had been left behind to fend for themselves, not to mention the wildlife in the path of the fire, with few places to run.

"This looks like the place," I said, pulling up a steep driveway, at the end of which was a two-story house that had survived the intense heat and flames. The firefighter's landmarks had been right on: a burned Volvo, an untouched blue house, a mound of sheet metal that had been a shed three days ago, a child's swing set with melted seats—all of these things led us to the right address.

Getting out of the van, we stood still for a minute as I re-examined the map to get my bearings. "Okay, here's the house," I said, pointing to the X on the map with the letter H next to it, and then looking at the house straight ahead of us.

"There's the car with the flat tires," Wendy said, pointing out another one of the landmarks.

"Do you see the garden hose?" I asked, walking closer to the house to get a better look.

"There it is," Sharon exclaimed.

"So the cat should be in that direction," I said, pointing to our right. "The firefighter said that if we followed the hose, it would lead us to the lake."

"What's that?" Sharon asked suddenly. "Listen."

"It sounds like a cat meowing," Wendy said, after hearing the sound, too. "But it doesn't sound like it's coming from the direction of the lake."

"Maybe the cat's not as badly burned as the guy thought, and he's moved," Sharon said with optimism.

"Nope, I'm afraid not," I said, as I spotted a tortie-colored cat making her way through the junk-cluttered yard toward us, continuing to welcome us with her soft meow.

"Looks like we have another survivor," Wendy said, re-lieved that when she got closer, the cat appeared to be just fine.

"Do you want something to eat?" Sharon asked, picking up the skinny cat.

We returned to the van and filled a paper bowl with Meow Mix and another one with water. Then the three of us headed toward the lake, anxious to find the cat and get him to a veterinarian. We had been working with Dr. Lorelei LaMere, who was with the Alaska State Veterinary Associa-tion. After we located the cat, we would contact her to see where she suggested we take the cat. We would need a veteri-narian who specialized in severe burns.

I was in the lead as we carefully made our way down an embankment. The brush in this area had not burned, so we grabbed on to branches to keep from sliding. It was indeed amazing that the fire crew had found the cat because the undergrowth got thicker when we got to where the ground leveled out again.

"See the cat yet?" Wendy asked, bringing up the rear.

"No," I replied. "But I can see the lake between the trees up ahead, so we have to be getting close."

"Maybe if we call for the cat, he'll respond," Sharon suggested.

"It's worth a try," I said.

Sharon called, "Here kitty, kitty, kitty." Then we stood still and listened, but we heard nothing. She tried several more times, but there was no response.

"Let's move closer to the lake," I said, careful where I stepped for fear I might step on the cat as we cut a path through the bushes.

Coming to a clearing, I scanned the bushes for anything that looked like an animal.

"There he is," I said softly, so as not to frighten the orange cat lying on his side in a bush just feet from the shore. "He really didn't make it very far once he got out of the water."

"How bad does he look?" Wendy asked, trying to peek around me to see the cat.

"I can't tell yet," I said, sliding my cat gloves on. "But I can see that he's covered with flies."

"Why don't you two stay here and I'll move a little closer," I said, taking my first step.

The next thing I determined was that the cat smelled disgusting. I was about 20 feet away from him and, even at that distance, I had to pull my bandanna over my nose to block out the stench of burned fur and flesh.

I began to talk softly to the cat as he tilted his head in my direction, his big yellow eyes watching my every move. He made no attempt to get up and move, either toward me or in the opposite direction, which either meant he was too injured to walk or he was a friendly cat, welcoming my help. The firefighter had kept his distance when he found the cat, so he had been unable to tell us if this was a friendly feline or one that would use whatever fight he had left in him to try and convince me to leave him alone.

My next observation of the cat led me to believe the cat was glad to see me and had no intention of doing battle with me. When I got within 10 feet of the injured animal, I could hear him purring.

Knowing that even the nicest animal can bite when he's in pain, I kept my cat gloves on as I crept toward the cat, all the while talking to him in a reassuring voice. When I was within reach, I slowly bent down, not wanting to make any sudden moves that would frighten the cat. Sharon and Wendy remained 20 feet behind me, and silently watched me lower my hand and finally pet the cat on the top of his head, causing the flies to scatter. My touch was welcomed with even louder purring.

I didn't want to rush picking up the cat, but I knew from looking at my watch that it was already four o'clock. If we were going to get him to a veterinarian, we probably had about an hour before they closed.

"Okay, fella, I'm sure this is going to hurt, but I've got to move ya," I said, working my hand down his side. "You can't stay out here, that's for sure, or you may become some bear's dinner."

When I got my hand midway down the cat's back, I very gently rolled him more onto his back, so I could see his legs, which he had pulled up underneath him. I didn't want to touch them until I absolutely had to, but it didn't take moving them to see what the fire had done. His front paws no longer had any pads and I could see charred bones where they had once been. The back feet were in far worse shape, having been the last thing to go into the water as the cat was fleeing the fire. Both legs were burned and at the end of each was a stump of melted skin. His right paw was still attached, but the other one was hanging by a sinew of blackened tissue.

The marmalade cat had to be in incredible pain but, as I kneeled next to him trying to decide the best way to pick him up, he just looked at me and purred.

"You want the Evacsack?" Sharon asked.

"Yeah, I think he'll be most comfortable in there. You want to bring it over here?"

"Sure," Sharon said, coming up behind me, careful not to make any noise that would scare the cat.

"Why don't you hold the Evacsack flat and, when you get it open, I'll pick him up and slide him in on his side. You're going to have to be sure your hands support him from underneath until I can let go of him, though," I said, still stroking the cat's fur. It surprised me that the only part of the cat that had burned was the bottom of his legs. If you didn't see his feet, you'd never know there was anything wrong with him.

"I'm ready," Sharon said, standing to my left with the Evacsack opened.

"Okay, fella, this is it," I said, putting my hand under his chin so that I could tilt his head up. "I promise you we're going to take you some place where they'll make you feel better." What ran through my mind at that point was "I hope he can be saved."

The cat was a real trooper, as I ever so carefully lifted him off the ground and slid him into the Evacsack. He didn't fight me at all, and the only sound out of him was more loud purring.

"He sure stinks," Sharon said, as I secured the end of the bag that held the cat.

"I know. Here, let me carry him," I offered, taking the cat from Sharon.

We took the climb back up the hill at a slower pace, my fear being that every step I took caused the cat to cringe in pain. But there were still no complaints from the feline. When we got to the van, Sharon climbed in the back and took the bag from me, placing it on the carpeted floor between her feet.

Looking at my watch again, I saw that it was 4:15. We had to get moving.

"Dr. LaMere, this is Terri Crisp," I said, backing down the driveway as I spoke into my cell phone. "We've just picked up a severely burned cat. I need to know where I should take him."

"Where are you?" Dr. LaMere asked.

"We're at Lazy Lake, not too far from Houston," I said, as I put the car into drive and retraced the route we had taken to get to the lake.

"Hold on," Dr. LaMere said. "Let me make a call."

"How's he doing?" I asked Sharon, as I waited for the doctor to come back on the line.

"He's just lying here, purring," Sharon told me. "If I'd had all my feet burned, I sure wouldn't be this calm about the whole thing. He's a truly amazing cat."

"Terri," Dr. LaMere said.

"I'm here."

"Take the cat to the Susitna Veterinary Hospital in Big Lake. It's on the main road, so you can't miss it," Dr. LaMere assured me. "Dr. James Leach will see the cat."

"How late are they open?" I asked, knowing we would be cutting it close if they didn't stay open past five o'clock.

"They said they'd stay open until you got there."

"Thanks, Dr. LaMere," I said. "I'll call you tomorrow."

"Sounds good, and I hope the cat will be okay."

"Me, too," I said, far from certain that the cat could be saved.

We arrived at the hospital at 5:05. One of the veterinary technicians met us at the door and immediately took the cat into one of the examination rooms, so she could begin cleaning his feet before the doctor took over.

When the doctor was ready to see us, we joined him in the examination room, where the cat lay on the table. "Hi,

I'm Dr. Leach," the man with the kind smile said, as Sharon, Wendy, and I crowded into the tiny room. After we introduced ourselves, he began to deliver the bad news. "He has third and fourth degree burns on all four legs," the doctor began. "The pads on his front feet are burned to the bone. Some, if not all his toes are gone, and it's pretty hard to tell for sure at this point how many of them might be saved."

Moving the cat slightly so we could see his back feet better, Dr. Leach explained that the paws on the back feet could not be saved. "His feet will basically have to be amputated at the ankle," he said, pointing to the place he was talking about.

"Would he be able to walk if the paws were amputated?" I asked, fearful of where this conversation was headed.

"I really don't know for sure," the doctor said, as he stroked the purring cat's fur. "A lot will depend on him."

"What about his legs? Will he stand on them okay? How about his balance and his ability to jump? Will he be able to dig in the litter box?" The questions just didn't seem to end, and the answer to each one kept coming back, "It depends on the cat."

"Dr. Leach, we want this cat to survive, especially after what he's been through, but we're also concerned about the quality of his life," I said, hating to be in a position of having to choose the fate of this cat. Of course, I wanted him to live, but I kept asking myself, *What kind of life would he have?*

We left the cat with Dr. Leach that evening so he could run further tests to determine if the cat had suffered any internal damage from breathing smoke. Sharon, Wendy, and I all agreed that we wanted some time to think before making a decision.

A good night's sleep is always advised when you have a tough decision to make, and this was going to be a really difficult one. We knew that the tragedy we had learned of that morning was influencing us. Losing two animals in one day was too much, but we couldn't keep this cat alive just for our own peace of mind. We had to do what was best for him.

We returned to the hospital after the morning debriefing at the command center. When we walked into the reception area, we were quiet, each of us wondering if what we had decided was the right choice. None of us had gotten much sleep as we lay awake in our tent at the campground in nearby Wasilla, which was our home away from home during this disaster. We talked a lot about the cat and the dog, and it was the process of talking it out together that brought us to our conclusion. We would leave the decision up to Dr. Leach. All of us were too emotionally tied to this cat, and all the other victims that he represented.

"The doctor can see you now," the technician told us from the doorway of the examination room where we had left the cat the evening before.

We waited only a minute before the doctor joined us, carrying in his arms the marmalade cat, whose legs were now covered in purple bandages. Somehow, he looked better than he had when we last saw him. There was one thing that had not changed, though. He was still purring.

"Well, I have good news and I have bad news," the doctor said, as he lay the cat on the examination table. "Which do you want first?"

Looking at Wendy and Sharon, I said, "The good."

"Okay," he said, and referred to the medical chart on the counter. "We ran some tests and the cat doesn't appear to have any internal damage from the smoke. That doesn't mean something may not appear later, but at this point, his lungs—which were what I was most concerned about—look okay."

"How old is he?" I asked.

"Our guess is maybe six or seven, which is working in his favor. If he were an older cat, I'm sure we'd be seeing a whole different picture."

"Any more good news?" Sharon asked.

"Yes," Dr. Leach said with a smile. "He's eating well, probably because he's gone for some time without a decent meal, and I mean longer than just the past few days. My suspicion is that this cat was dumped out there by the lake and he's been doing an adequate job of surviving on his own. He's about 7 or 8 pounds underweight."

"That's a lot!" I exclaimed.

"That is, so we've got him on some good fattening food," Dr. Leach said, lightly ruffling the fur around the cat's neck.

"So what's the bad news?" I asked, wanting to get past this part of our conversation.

"I think we can work with what's left of the cat's feet to give him something sturdy enough to stand on," Dr. Leach answered. "My guess is that it will take at least six or seven surgeries and, even giving you guys a discount, it's still going to be expensive."

"What's expensive?" I asked.

"Maybe five to six thousand dollars," he said.

"What's the rest of the bad news?" I asked, expecting to be told something a lot worse.

"That's it," he said.

"That's it?" I blurted out. "Nothing more?"

"Well, these things can always be risky because he's going to have to be put under for each of the surgeries, but I have no reason to believe at this time that he won't make it through the surgeries just fine."

"So let me understand this," I said, with growing enthusiasm. "The cat's feet can be fixed and it's going to cost somewhere between five and six thousand dollars to do it. I take it you can do the surgeries?"

"That's right," he replied.

"How long a period of time are we talking about to complete the surgeries?" I inquired.

"Three to four months," the doctor said.

"Can he stay here during that time and, once he's through, we'll figure out what to do with him?" I asked.

"Sure, he can stay," he said, patting the cat on the head.

"One last question. What kind of life will he have?" I wanted to be told normal, but deep down I knew that would be unlikely.

"I've seen lots of animals come through this hospital. There is something very special about this cat," Dr. Leach said, looking at the cat with the purple-wrapped legs. "He obviously has an incredible will to live or he would not have survived what he has so far. If he continues to be such a fighter, I suspect he'll find a new way to live life, and he'll do a damn good job of living."

"You fix those legs then, and we'll find a way to pay for it," I said with a smile.

WE NAMED the marmalade cat, with the most unique paw prints in the world, Bumpus. Our fighter remained in Alaska under the excellent care of Dr. Leach and his staff for three months. It ended up taking eight surgeries to repair all four of his legs. A day after his back legs were amputated, he was standing up, digging in his litter box, a sure sign that he was going to triumph over his handicap.

We all decided that Bumpus might need some extra help getting around, so we ordered a specially made cart that would support his hindquarters. When it arrived, the staff put him in it. As soon as they turned their backs, he managed to wiggle his way out of it. During one of my follow-up phone calls, Dr. Leach's wife, Annie, told me, "He was like Houdini. We still can't figure out how he got out of that contraption. When he managed to get free of if, he looked at us and meowed, as if to say, 'Are you guys crazy? I'm not dragging that thing around.'"

Before Bumpus left Alaska, he was walking, running, jumping, and purring louder than ever. When Dr. Leach released his patient, it was decided that he would go to St. Louis to live with Sharon while we searched for the perfect home for our survivor.

Bumpus arrived in St. Louis, escorted by Dr. Leach, who felt that this was a cat who deserved a first-class seat and not a spot in the plane's cargo hold. After getting Bumpus settled into his temporary home, Sharon called me and said, "I can't believe it's the same cat we left in Alaska three months ago. He's gorgeous, and his legs are so cute."

We never had to find Bumpus that perfect home. He found one for himself. Our fantastic, fearless, fireproof feline moved in with Sharon and her family, and *he* decided he wasn't leaving.

There are people and animals put on this earth for very special reasons. Dr. Leach is one of those people and Bumpus is one of those animals. In addition to free housing and free staff time, Dr. Leach donated $1000 of the vet bill back to the EARS fund. Bumpus is now a pet therapy animal. Sharon has seen him work his magic with patients who are ill, seriously burned, or have had limbs amputated. He brings hope into people's lives, and he doesn't stop there.

I have a cat named Minus who knows Bumpus's power to motivate. When she and her littermates were about eight weeks old, they had limbs and tails bitten off by a Rottweiler. After Minus's front leg and tail were amputated, she was not responsive to the TLC being given to her by volunteers at the St. Charles Humane Society in Missouri. She and all her littermates had given up. When they were left alone with Bumpus, at the recommendation of Sharon, things began to change.

Bumpus saved those kittens' lives, and I'm grateful for the role EARS played in keeping him alive.

CHAPTER TWENTY-ONE

Sharing

Every time I've returned from a disaster in Alaska, I've brought an extra special memento back with me. I'm not talking about the kind of souvenirs that you can get at the airport gift shop either. After the Exxon *Valdez* oil spill, it was Ken Crisp; we were married in October 1989. From the Miller Reach Fire, I brought back a young cat and her four kittens. The petite feline, with fur like a chinchilla, ended up being adopted by my parents, Mac and Ginny McKim, who named her Ashley. Ashley was my parents' first disaster-rescued companion. In January 1997, they went to their first disaster with me and finally understood why they had to share their daughter with the animals.

I had just started taking ornaments off our Christmas tree. Ken and the girls cuddled together on the couch, watching the Rose Parade, a New Year's Day tradition in our house. I momentarily stopped what I was doing when the description of one of the lavish floats was interrupted by a special news report, which told of flooding in Northern California along the Russian and Napa Rivers. Days of continuous rain were the cause of this disaster. These rivers flood, it seems, every year, so this was nothing out of the ordinary; it was just happening a little earlier than normal. As I returned to un-decorating the tree, I told myself, *The people who live along those rivers are no strangers to floods, so they certainly should have figured out by now how to keep themselves and their animals safe and alive.*

"So, are you going to go check it out?" Ken asked after the news report ended.

"Mommy, are you going to go save the animals?" Amy asked from under the quilt she had pulled up to her chin. "Will you bring me home a puppy?"

Ken glared at me with a look that said, "You better not!"

"No, Amy, I don't think I'm going," I said, more to reassure Ken. "I responded to a flood up in that area once before and found out things were under control." As I carefully wrapped a glass ornament in an old sock and put it in its designated box for safekeeping until next Christmas, I added, "The animal shelters have heard of EARS. I'm sure they will page me if they need help. I can get some volunteers and be there within three hours."

My pager went off for the first time just before the parade was over, and it beeped several more times during the next hour. EARS-trained volunteers who lived near the flooding areas were concerned that the animals were not adequately being taken care of, and I knew they were also anxious to go to their first disaster. Their persistence convinced me to go see for myself what was going on. Besides, I figured this was a way to delay taking down the Christmas tree, a job I didn't enjoy.

It took me less than an hour to pack my van with what I would need for my trip to Guerneville, a community about two hours north of where we lived in Santa Clara. The news report had said that this area had seen the most water, so it seemed like a good place to start. As I was packing, I called Shirley Bollinger, who had become an EARS coordinator following the flood in Texas. She and two EARS volunteers who had called me agreed to meet me in Santa Rosa.

"I suspect I'll be home later this evening, but I'll call and let you know for sure," I told Ken, as he helped me carry a few last things to the car. "If you want to finish taking down the tree while I'm gone, I won't be disappointed."

"Ha, ha! You think you're getting out of that, but you're not. It'll be waiting for you when you return," he said, hugging me.

"Gee, thanks. I'll be sure to hurry home."

"You be careful, okay," he said, walking back toward the house to watch the first of several football games that would keep him glued to the TV for the rest of the day.

"I will," I said, realizing how fortunate I was to have him. He is incredibly supportive of what I do and never complains when I take off on such short notice, leaving him to take care of the girls and the animals. It is a lot of work being mom, dad, and animal caregiver, but he does it, and he does it well.

After saying good-bye to the rest of the family, I drove off in the pouring rain, uncertain what the day would bring. I felt pretty certain, though, that this would be a quick one-day, maybe two-day, assessment trip. Then I'd be able to go back home to pack away the last remnants of Christmas. Mother Nature proved me very wrong. It was 30 days before I saw home again.

The flooding along the Napa and Russian Rivers was as bad as what I had seen on television, but everywhere we went that afternoon, we found that the animals had already been moved to safety. One of our stops was the command center and they were glad to see us, but they didn't think there was anything for us to do. They had not received any requests for help with animals, which I knew was unusual, but it confirmed my earlier suspicion that people in this community really did know what to do. As they say, "Practice makes perfect."

To be safe, I decided we would stay overnight. If in the morning I found that nothing had changed, then Shirley and I would head home. We came close to doing that, but a page from Deanna at United Animal Nations changed our plans.

"There are levees breaking all over the place," Deanna said, as I listened to her tell me what was happening in the

Sacramento area. "When I got into the office this morning, there were all kinds of messages from people needing help and volunteers wanting to know what they could do. And the phone hasn't stopped ringing."

"When did this start?" I asked, as I sat in my van watching the rain pelt the windshield.

"Late yesterday," Deanna said. "They're calling this the Pineapple Express. The warmfront that moved across the Pacific from Hawaii is causing the snow in the Sierras to melt quickly, and all that water has nowhere to go. Hold on, I have to get this call."

While I was on hold, I looked at Shirley, seated in the car beside me, and said, "Well, it looks like the disaster has moved to Sacramento."

SHORTLY AFTER arriving at the UAN office, which was a safe distance from the overflowing rivers and creeks, I got a phone call from Dr. Vicky Joseph, a veterinarian in neighboring Roseville who was the Placer County coordinator for the California Veterinary Medical Association's disaster program.

"Owned and stray animals started arriving from Yuba County late yesterday," Vicky explained, following our brief introductions. "The Placer County SPCA was willing to put up temporary kennels to house them in their shelter, but they're running out of room real quick."

"Why are animals coming from Yuba County?" I asked. "Isn't there someplace in that county where they can be housed temporarily?" EARS always prefers to keep animals in the same county where they originated. If they're taken too far away, it's difficult for their owners to find them.

"The only shelter in the area has already flooded," Vicky explained, her voice emphasizing how serious the situation was becoming. "The SPCA was the next closest place that was prepared to take in the animals, so I took what I could get."

"How far is Roseville from where the flooding is?" I asked.

"Maybe a half-hour to 45 minutes," Vicky estimated.

"That's not too bad," I said. "And, like you said, you have to take what you can get at the time."

"What I want to know is if EARS is willing to take on the responsibility of housing the animals," Vicky said. "The manager of the Placer County Fairgrounds has gotten approval for flood animals to be kept there. The ones that are already at the SPCA would be moved, and any new arrivals would be taken directly to the fairgrounds, so that they'd all be in one location."

"Of course we'll do it," I was quick to assure her. "We've done seven or eight workshops in the Sacramento area, so we have lots of trained volunteers. We can bring in more volunteers from other areas if we have to. Just tell me when you want us to start setting up."

"You really will do it?" Vicky asked.

"Yes," I said, laughing. "We'll do it."

"Oh, thank you," she said excitedly. "If you couldn't do it, my only other choice was to start sending the new animals to the local vet clinics that had agreed to house animals during a disaster. In a small disaster, that would probably work, but I think this is going to be a big one."

We began setting up a temporary shelter at the Placer County Fairgrounds on Friday, January 3. After talking to Vicky, I contacted EARS coordinator Dean Richman and asked him to come up from Southern California to facilitate the setup, so I could remain in the UAN office for another day coordinating people and resources from there. He arrived Friday morning and went directly to the fairgrounds, along with a team of eager volunteers. Their job was to turn the place into an evacuation shelter, a transformation that took just over four hours.

"It's perfect," Dean exclaimed, when he called me at the office to give me my first update. I was anxious to see the place, but it would be several more hours before I could escape the office and the endless phone calls. It was amazing how many people wanted to help. I was learning that that's what happens when a disaster occurs practically in your own backyard. We were known in this community and it was a case of friends helping friends.

When I finally saw the fairgrounds late in the afternoon that first day, I had to agree with Dean. There could not have been a more perfect place to take care of animals. The fairgrounds' manager had given us the use of one enclosed barn and three open-sided barns, plus a grassy area large enough to set up at least half a dozen tents. There were already existing pens and cages in some of the barns, and we could get more portable ones if we needed them. As I walked around the property in the drizzle that had replaced the downpours, which had brought more unwanted rain all day, I estimated that we could easily house up to a thousand animals. We came very close to doing just that.

For 22 days, we took care of 878 animals: 571 dogs, 156 cats, 65 horses, 21 goats, 11 pigs, 10 chickens, 8 pheasants, 6 calves, 6 ducks, 3 potbellied pigs, 3 cockatiels, 3 wild rabbits, 2 bulls, 2 cows, 2 doves, plus 1 burro, 1 domesticated rabbit, 1 magpie, 1 quail, 1 parakeet, 1 iguana, 1 rat, 1 hamster, and our first emu. Dr. Joseph had been right, this was a big disaster, and there was no way that the many animals who needed care could have been squeezed in local veterinary clinics.

In order to take care of this many animals properly, we required a lot of help from people, and we had plenty of that. There were over 600 volunteers who gave generously of their time, in addition to 87 veterinarians who helped treat the sick and injured animals. Dr. Joseph was one of those, along with Drs. Forney, Gunther, and Lux, who showed up almost every day to do a thorough veterinary check on every incoming animal. To help them were veterinary technicians along with students from the veterinary school at the University of California at Davis. What an incredible learning experience it was for these future veterinarians, and what exceptional care the animals received because of all these people's willingness to share their talents.

For many of the animals, it was the best medical care they had ever received.

When I saw teams of vet techs working their way through the kennels one afternoon, brushing the teeth of the dogs and cats, I realized what an exceptional job we were doing of caring for these animals. We were not just giving them the basics. They were getting so much more. This was a major improvement over Hurricane Andrew when those of us who were there were pleased just to get all the animals fed every day.

To help me supervise this many people required the efforts of EARS coordinators Raquel Aluisy, Debi Crane, Wendy Borowsky, Dara Hoffman, Deborah Horn, Sharon Maag, and Kim Mester, all of whom arrived shortly after Dean and Shirley came on site. They all put in some long and demanding hours, and handled their varied responsibilities like real pros. When I would stand back momentarily and watch them caring for the animals and interacting with the people, I'd smile inside. They were a big reason why EARS was becoming so successful at helping animals during disasters. I was incredibly proud of them. I could not have asked for a finer group of truly dedicated people to share my dream with me.

My dream of ensuring that animals received the help they deserved during every disaster was kindled by my compassion for them. I have to thank my parents for doing whatever they did to make me one of those people who can't imagine going through life, or even a day, without the absolute pleasure of sharing as much time with animals as possible. Since I started doing animal rescue work, I have spent a great deal of my time making a difference for animals, but it has meant that each disaster, each workshop, each speaking engagement, each conference, takes me away from my entire family. This disaster was one they got to share with me, though.

When my parents came to the fairgrounds in Roseville as trained EARS volunteers, they saw for the first time what I really did in my animal rescue work. They say the result of what they had helped to create and it was their hugs, distant winks, and overheard conversations where they boasted about me that told me they were proud of what I was doing. And they enjoyed themselves. My dad was an excellent gatekeeper, making sure that only those people who were allowed in the shelter entered. The front office was a perfect spot for my mother, her calming nature often keeping the craziness of this hectic area from getting totally out of control.

Ken and the girls joined me for two of the weekends that I was in Roseville. This was not the first time Ken or Jennifer had been to a disaster, but it served to remind them why I needed to keep doing this work—even if it meant more absences from the family. As Ken told me during one of the rare moments that we were alone in my trailer at the fairgrounds, "We're just lucky to have as much time with you as we do because we know this is what you were really put here for."

Amy and Megan had never been to a disaster. When I called to let them know their dad and I had decided they were ready for this new experience, Megan got on the phone first.

"Megan, guess what?" I said, with as much excitement as a child who has a special secret to share with a friend.

"Do you have a surprise for me, Mommy?" she asked, her voice matching the look of anticipation I could imagine on her face.

"I do. How would like to come see me?" I asked. "We have some really cute puppies we rescued from the flood who would love to have two little girls to play with."

There was a pause before Megan answered. When she did, she said in a worried voice, "Oh, Mommy, I can't."

This was not the response I expected. It occurred to me that she was afraid. A flood must sound like a very scary thing to a six-year-old. *Maybe she isn't ready for this,* I thought.

I was wrong, though. When I asked her why she didn't want to come see me, she said in a very matter-of-fact way, "Mommy, I can't come to the flood because I don't have a lifejacket."

Only a child of mine would have thought of that.

That was one of my most favorite memories from this disaster. There are several others that I want to share from a disaster that deserves a book of its own, so all the stories can be told. One day I will write the entire story of the New Year's flood, but for now I want to tell you about two cows and the man who came into their lives unexpectedly. Theirs is a story that cannot wait.

Crossing Paths

A S I'VE said, every disaster brings animals and people into my life who leave permanent imprints on my heart. During the flood in Roseville, there were two cows and a 68-year-old man whose shared story will forever make me glad that I was at the fairgrounds that January in 1997.

This is Derrold R. Daly's account of how he came to cross paths with a cow named Tar Baby. He sent this letter in November 1997 to the United Animal Nations' office.

Dear Friends: I wrote a little about my experience during the flood in January that I am ready to share with you now.

While watching news coverage of the flood, my wife and I learned about EARS and their need for supplies, cages, and other items at the Placer County Fairgrounds in Roseville to take care of the animals that were being rescued. The next day we filled our pickup with poultry cages that we use in our waterfowl egg and rescue operation.

When we arrived at the fairgrounds, we were amazed at the number of people delivering supplies and making other donations for the welfare of the animals. After unloading what we'd brought, I inquired if there might be a need for someone experienced at transporting large animals. Three hours later, I was at the Feather River Animal Hospital in Marysville, where all the rescued animals were taken before being transferred to the fairgrounds. I had my pickup truck and horse trailer, and I was ready to work.

My first job was to transport a cow who I was told could not stand up. I unhooked my horse trailer, since they felt it would be easier to get the cow in the back of the truck, and headed out. Following the directions I'd been given, I traveled through stagnant floodwater up to two-feet deep to get to the site. When I arrived, the cow was lying down, her feet tucked up under her, on a steep gravel embankment. This was the first time I met a young lady by the name of T. J. Johnson, who was volunteering, too. She was sitting on the ground with the cow's head resting on her lap, attempting to give her some water from a plastic water bottle.

T. J. and another volunteer named Tom Dugally, had found the black cow on their way to rescue some dogs and cats. They stopped to help her, determining that she wasn't hurt, but rather, too exhausted to stand up. Tom figured the only way they were going to be able to move this cow was if he could find someone with heavy construction equipment to pick her up and place her in the bed of a truck. He got in his vehicle and went in search of what he needed, leaving T. J. to comfort the cow. Amazingly, he found a local farmer farther down the road, with a front-end loader, who was more than happy to help out. Meanwhile, more volunteers had arrived, after getting a call on their radios that assistance was needed. Someone contacted EARS coordinator Shirley Bollinger at the Feather River Animal Hospital and told her to send a volunteer with the biggest truck she could find. That was how I got involved.

Using heavy canvas straps the farmer brought with him, five of the male volunteers managed somehow to get them positioned under the cow. Then Tom directed the farmer as he slowly inched the bucket on the front-end loader up against the cow's side. Using the straps, the five men pulled her into the bucket, which was no easy task. All the while the cow went along with what was being done to her, as she had no energy left to fight.

When everyone thought she was secure in the bucket, the farmer raised her off the ground, taking it real slow. I got the signal then to back up my pickup truck directly under the elevated cow when she was just high enough to clear the side of the truck. The farmer then slowly lowered her into the bed. She ended up lying down, her legs tucked up under her again, with her head toward the cab.

T. J. climbed into the truck next to her, so she could hold the cow's head up, while a young man sat alongside the cow to keep her from rolling too far over. We then left for the Feather River Animal Hospital, retracing my route that once again took us through the slowly receding floodwater.

Once we got to the hospital, we had quite a time freeing the young man who had been riding in the back, as the cow had rolled to one side during our return trip and pinned him against the side of the truck bed. While T. J. remained in the truck, Dr. Goemann checked over the cow and did what he could to help her. The decision was to move her to the fairgrounds where they were better suited to treat her through the night. Before we left, the doctor gave T. J. a special kind of water for the cow and instructed her to tell the veterinarians at the fairgrounds to get as much of it down her as they could.

T. J. insisted on riding in the back of the truck with the cow, so that she could begin to administer the fluids and keep the cow's head elevated as we drove to Roseville. We stacked several 50-pound bags of dog food along the cow's side to keep her from rolling. It was getting late and very cold, so we found some horse blankets that someone had donated and put two over the cow and one over T. J.

Just before we got ready to leave, I questioned whether we should tie the cow down, but the volunteers assured me that she could not stand up. I told T. J. that if she wanted me to stop once we got started, she should bang on the back of the cab.

We got on the freeway, which was the only possible route back to Roseville. I had barely gotten up my speed when I could feel the pickup beginning to rock back and forth. I looked in my rearview mirror and saw the cow moving. She was trying to get up. T. J. started banging on the cab window about then and I immediately pulled over to the side of the road and stopped. By the time I got out of the truck and alongside the bed, the cow had settled down. To be safe, I decided to tie several lengths of rope loosely over the cow. After I made sure T. J. was okay, we started off again, going slower this time.

The rest of the ride went pretty smoothly, but it seemed to take forever to get to the fairgrounds. I was worried about the cow and concerned about T. J. It was starting to get even colder. About halfway to Roseville, I glanced out the back window to see how my two passengers were doing. I couldn't believe what I saw. T.J. had taken the horse blanket that I'd given her and placed it over the cow. The cow now had three blankets and T. J. had none. I wanted to stop and do something to make her more comfortable, but she motioned for me to keep going. It would have killed T. J. if anything had happened to this cow before we got her back to the fairgrounds and the team of veterinarians who were waiting to take care of her.

We arrived at the fairgrounds just as it was getting dark. T. J. was soaking wet from the waist down from the fluids that she had tried unsuccessfully to get into the cow. She had to have been freezing cold, but all she was worried about was the cow.

Great care was taken unloading the cow from my pickup, as her condition had deteriorated since I first saw her. We had left the straps under her when we loaded her, so they were used again to guide her onto the front end of a forklift. There must have been 20 men helping, each of them being extremely gentle as they handled the cow. She was raised out of my truck and then lowered onto a bed of straw. Volunteers placed bales of straw behind her, again to keep her from rolling too far over. As soon as the cow was safely on the ground, the veterinarians began treating her. I stayed around for as long as I could to watch. Something told me, though, it didn't look good for the cow.

I KNEW the cow was coming before she arrived. Someone from Dr. Goemann's hospital had called to warn us to be prepared to treat a very sick cow, and we were. I watched as the 1965 yellow Chevy pickup came through the gate and stopped next to the stables. As Derrold said, there were at least 20 men standing by to assist in whatever way they could, in addition to the large-animal veterinarians and veterinary technicians. The care given to that cow by everyone was by far the tenderest thing I have ever watched, and I knew it had to be helping to keep her alive.

Throughout the night, veterinarians and techs took turns tending to the cow, doing everything medically possible to make her as comfortable as they could. Her breathing became increasingly more labored as the night passed, though. What I heard first when I went to check on her the next morning was the wheezing. When I saw the cow, she was still down on the ground, surrounded by two veterinarians, a tech, several volunteers who were helping to keep the straw clean, and T. J., who was seated on the ground with the cow's head in her lap. She had sat up with her all night.

Later that morning, the owners arrived and the decision was made to transfer Tar Baby to the veterinary school in nearby Davis. The couple who owned her was torn up over their sick cow. They sat with her while volunteers arranged to get the forklift again and the truck to transport her. As I waited with the owners, I learned from them that Tar Baby had a calf, who had not been found.

Watching her being lifted off the ground again was even more moving than it had been the night before. Everyone who had worked so hard to save her took turns wishing her well and, I think, saying good-bye in their own way. I, too, said good-bye, trying to remain positive as I whispered a few comforting words in her big black ear. When I stepped back, I could not ignore the ache in my heart. None of us could bring ourselves to tell Derrold Daly that the cow died the next day, despite his valiant effort. It was several weeks before he learned the truth.

Although I made several more trips to the fairgrounds to volunteer, I never saw the cow again. The day after she arrived, she was transferred to the veterinary hospital at the University of California at Davis, where she continued to receive the best of care, but it came too late.

It was a while before I found out that the cow was put down. No one had the guts to tell me what had happened to her and I was afraid to ask. They told me what killed her was the diesel fuel she had ingested while she was in the water swimming for her life. The people who owned the cow were heartbroken. It turned out she was a pet and her name was Tar Baby.

Thanks again for letting me help.

Your friend,

Derrold R. Daly

IN FEBRUARY 1998, Northern California flooded again. This time it was Yolo County that felt the full impact of too much rain. A small team of EARS volunteers and I helped out at a temporary shelter set up in a barn at the fairgrounds in the town of Woodland. There were no dogs or cats to take care of in this disaster. Instead, we mainly had sheep, most of which had newborn lambs.

For almost two weeks, we cared for the 34 sheep and their offspring along with 10 chickens, 5 rabbits, 2 goats named Nannie and Billy who loved to go for walks on a leash, an extremely overweight potbellied pig named Earl, a turkey named Big Bird who wore himself out strutting his stuff, and one very sick calf.

As we were parking next to the barn on a cold and damp morning, I spotted a blue packing blanket spread on the ground in one of the pens we had set up in case we received any dogs.

"That blanket wasn't there when we left yesterday, was it?" I asked EARS coordinator Cindy Samuelson, who was seated in the car next to me.

"No, it wasn't," she replied.

"I don't remember seeing it either," Wendy Borowsky, another one of the EARS coordinators, commented from the backseat.

"Does it look like there's something under it?" I asked, turning off the car's ignition. "There seems to be a mound in the middle of it."

All three of us got out of the car and walked toward the pen, watching carefully for movement under the blanket. When nothing happened as we got closer, we decided that if there was an animal under the blanket, it was either sleeping really soundly or it was dead.

Standing outside the pen, we talked louder to wake up whatever it was. We got no response.

"I'm going to get a broom and use the handle to lift a corner of the blanket," I said, as I stepped backward to go to the shed where we kept our supplies. "I don't particularly want to walk into the pen and pull the blanket back with my hand, not knowing what's underneath."

When I returned with a push broom, I slid the wooden handle through the chain-link fence and very carefully used the end to lift the corner of the blanket closest to us. What I saw underneath was not what I had expected. Lying on its side, its dark brown eyes wide open, was a calf who could not have been more than a day or two old—and he was alive.

I got into the pen to get a better look at our discovery. Cindy and Wendy followed. I pulled the blanket back and ran my hand over the calf's shoulder. The little guy was freezing cold. "We've got to get him warmed up," I said, quickly pulling the blanket back over him, leaving just his head exposed.

"I'll go set up a stall in the barn and plug in one of the warming lamps," Cindy said, backing out of the pen. "It won't take me but a few minutes. Then I'll come back to help you carry the calf."

While Cindy was gone, Wendy and I sat in the straw next to the calf, stroking his head. I didn't know a lot about cows, but I could tell this guy was in bad shape. I figured we'd get him warmed up and wait for the vets from UC Davis who were due within the hour for their daily check on the animals.

"I'm set," Cindy said, as she rejoined us. "Do you think it will take three of us to carry him?"

"Probably so," I said, as I stood up. "Why don't I support the head, Wendy you take the middle, and Cindy you grab the rear end."

"Gee, I guess when you're the newest coordinator that's the end you get," Cindy said with a smirk.

"No, if you want, I'll take that end," I offered.

"I'm just kidding," Cindy said with a laugh. "Let's just get him moved and warmed up."

We had just lifted the calf and moved him out of the pen when he arched his head backward and his body started to shake uncontrollably. It scared all three of us, but we didn't let go of him.

"What's happening to him?" I asked, as we supported his wrenching body.

Wendy, a former nurse, said, "My guess is it's a seizure. We've got to get him to a vet immediately."

"Let's put him in the back of the Cherokee," I said, altering our course. "Cindy, you got a good hold on him?"

"Yeah, I think so," she said, as she slid her hands further under the calf's rear end.

"Wendy, let go of the middle part and get in the back of the car. Do you mind riding back there with him while I drive?"

"No, that's fine," Wendy said. She let go of the calf, once she knew we had hold of him, and ran to the car. The cow was not shaking quite as much as Cindy and I carried him the rest of the distance to the car. We would have preferred to put him down until the episode passed, but we knew the calf was running out of time.

"Here, put his head on my lap," Wendy ordered, as we lay the calf down in the flat cargo area of my car. "And, Terri, step on it. This calf is fading fast."

"Cindy, can you stay here and wait for the volunteers who are scheduled to show up to clean?" I asked, as I ran around to the driver's side of the car.

"Sure," she said, closing the back and moving out of the way.

"We'll call from the vet school and let you know what's going on," I said, as I jumped in the car and slammed the door.

It was normally a 20-minute ride from the fairgrounds to the vet school at UC Davis, but I did it in 15 minutes. The calf had quit shaking, and was just lying next to Wendy, his head still on her lap, and those big eyes of his staring up at her. Every minute or two, I'd ask Wendy for an update, and when she'd tell me he wasn't doing great, I'd push the accelerator closer to the floor.

Thank goodness I knew exactly where I was going. I had been to the large animal clinic of the vet school just a few days before to drop off Earl, our potbellied pig. Dr. Madigan, the veterinarian who had been working with us at the fairgrounds, suggested that we take Earl to the vet school, where they could put him on a very stringent diet. His owner had decided she didn't want him anymore. Earl was so fat that he could barely open his eyes, due to his fat rolls. If losing some weight didn't take care of the eye problem, Dr. Madigan recommended surgery. "You mean you're going to give Earl a face-lift?" I asked.

"Yeah, something like that," Dr. Madigan replied. "We'll do a few tucks here and a few tucks there, and he'll be as good as new."

When I pulled into the receiving area of the large animal clinic, I honked my horn several times in the hopes of getting the attention of someone inside the massive building. I backed up to the loading dock, put the car in park, and jumped out. As I got around to the rear of the vehicle, a man in green scrubs came out the emergency room door. I had seen him when I dropped off Earl.

"We've got a very sick calf," I told the man, as he walked quickly toward us. "We think he's a flood evacuee, but we don't know for sure. He was at the fairgrounds when we got there this morning."

"About 20 minutes ago, he had a seizure, or at least that's what we think it was," Wendy explained when the man reached the car.

"Let me grab a gurney," the man said, after giving the calf a visual once-over.

"Hold on, little guy," I said, stroking the calf's head. "These people will take good care of you."

A second man returned with the gurney. The two men lifted the calf out of the car, laid him on the metal surface, and then tied him down with two straps. We followed as they wheeled him through some double doors into a large sterile room, well stocked with state-of-the-art medical equipment.

Wendy and I stood back while a team of veterinarians went to work on the calf, hooking up IVs, giving him a shot of something, drawing some blood, and checking his temperature. He hadn't been on the table but five minutes when his head once again tilted backward and he began to shake. It was horrible to watch him struggling, but I was relieved that he was in the hands of people who knew what to do.

We waited around for nearly half an hour. During that time, the calf had another shaking episode, which was worse than the ones before. The staff was still doing everything they could to save him, but we guessed that his prognosis was not good. Finally, one of the vets came over to where Wendy and I were standing, and filled us in.

"He's definitely a very sick calf," the man said, removing his plastic gloves. "I don't know if we'll be able to save him. It's way too early to tell, and we won't know for sure what all is wrong with him until we get some lab results back."

"We sure appreciate what you're doing for him," I said.

"I understand you don't know who his owners are," the vet said.

"No idea," I told him. "When we get back to the fairgrounds, we'll see what we can find out."

"So you want us to do what we can to keep him alive?" the vet asked. I think he was pretty certain what my answer would be.

"I trust you to do what is best for the calf," I said, looking past the man for a moment to where the little guy was lying. "We don't want him to suffer, so if it gets to the point where putting him down is the most humane thing to do, then do it."

"How can I reach you?" he asked.

Handing him my business card, I said, "The pager is the best way to get me, and don't hesitate to call, no matter what time it is."

I called Cindy when we got back into the car and gave her an update. I also asked if she had learned anything about where the cow had come from.

"I did," she told me, as I drove out the gate of the vet school. "Ken, the maintenance man, said that a truck pulled up just after he got here this morning. The two men in the cab—Ken thought they were probably Mexican farmworkers—didn't speak English very well, but Ken was able to figure out that they found the calf along the road near some flooded farmland. They had seen on the news that we were here at the fairgrounds taking care of the disaster animals, so they brought him to us."

"Did Ken tell them to put the calf in the pen?" I asked.

"Yeah, and he got the packing blanket to put over him," Cindy explained.

"He didn't by chance get their name or a number did he?" I asked.

"No, I'm afraid not," Cindy said. "At this point, we have no idea who the calf belongs to."

We got our first update on the calf that afternoon. He was still alive, but everyone at the vet school was finding it hard to believe he had survived. When the doctor started reading off the list of everything that was wrong with him, I, too, couldn't believe that he had lasted this long. I didn't understand half of what the doctor was telling me, but when he said the calf had meningitis, I knew that was serious.

Later that afternoon, I talked with Vicky Fletcher at Yolo County Animal Control, the agency that we were assisting, and told her about the calf.

"He's probably too young to have a brand is my guess," Vicky said, after I finished filling her in.

"Yeah, I didn't see one," I told her.

"Well, I'll have to call the brand inspector and report him as a stray," she said. "Will you keep me updated on his condition?"

"Sure," I replied. "Hopefully, he'll make it, but it's still very much touch and go at this point."

When it came time for us to close our rescue site at the fairgrounds, the calf was still at the vet school. He'd had some really bad days. The vet in charge of his care came very close to calling me on several occasions to say, "I think it's time." But each time, the calf would suddenly begin to show signs of improvement, so the vet postponed the call.

Three weeks after we found the calf, I did get a phone call, but it wasn't from the vet school. It was the brand inspector calling to tell me that she had been to see our calf and he did not have a brand.

"So what does that mean?" I asked.

"Once he's healthy enough, he'll be transferred to the auction yard and sold," she explained. "And from what the vet told me, he should be able to leave there in about a week."

"What if I want to buy him?" I inquired.

"You'll have to go to the auction and bid on him," she told me.

"Where is the auction?" I asked, never having been to one.

"He'll probably go to the one in Petaluma—that's my guess," she said.

"My guess" made me really nervous. It sounded as though once he left Davis we might easily lose track of him. After everything this calf had been through, I wasn't about to let someone else buy him and have him end up at a grocery-store meat counter.

"There's no way we can buy him now and save everyone a bunch of trouble?" I asked, almost pleading.

"Nope, things don't work that way," she said.

I then tried to work on her sympathy, telling her the calf's whole story and how the staff at the vet school was calling him The Miracle Baby. The woman was sympathetic, but she had a job to do, and what she could and could not do was clearly outlined.

"Okay, tell me everything I need to know so that I can be at that auction to buy the calf," I said, reaching for a piece of paper.

For the next few days, I worked on an elaborate, hope-fully foolproof plan to buy the calf at the auction. I consulted regularly with the brand inspector, each time calling with a new list of questions. It was absolutely necessary, I thought, to understand every step of the process in order to safeguard the calf. My fear was that if I made just one mistake, it could cost the calf his life. There was one thing that I had not planned on, though.

Three days before the auction, I found myself on a plane headed for Florida. Tornadoes had struck near Orlando, and EARS had been mobilized, thanks once again to Mother Na-ture. As I was packing to leave, I was on the phone with Jim Edon, an EARS coordinator who lives in Roseville. I put him in charge of buying the calf.

"Jim, do whatever it takes," I told him during my first con-versation with him. "And here's the brand inspector's name and phone number. Be sure you call her first thing tomorrow and let her know you are now in charge of this for me."

"I will," Jim assured me. "I promise you, your calf will be waiting for you when you return."

"You know, Jim, I still don't know where he's going to live," I confessed. "But I'll worry about that once we've got him."

Two days later I was still in Florida, standing in the park-ing lot in front of Osceola County Animal Control, when my cell phone rang.

"Hello," I said, plugging my other ear so that I could hear over a very loudly barking dog who had just been brought in from one of the neighborhoods leveled by the tornado.

"Terri, it's Jim."

"Jim," I yelled. "Did you get him? Is the calf okay?"

"You're not going to believe what happened." The sound of Jim's voice made me nervous. I needed him to tell me that the calf was safe; only then would I relax.

"I got a call this morning," Jim began. "The woman said she was calling about the calf at UC Davis."

"Yeah, so," I said, prompting Jim to hurry.

"She told me the calf had died."

"What?" I yelled. "Yesterday you said he was doing great."

"Wait, wait, wait," Jim repeated. "The woman said she died and they needed me to come and remove the body."

"I don't understand," I interrupted.

"Well, I didn't either, at first," Jim said in a calm voice, which made me feel a little bit better. "I told the woman that I had talked to the vet school no more than an hour before and the calf was fine. The woman just said again, 'No, the calf has died and you need to remove the body.'"

"Terri, I was tongue-tied at that point. I didn't know what to say. All I could think about was how was I going to tell you that the calf didn't make it."

"So, go on," I said, anxiously.

"The woman said again that I had to go get the body and dispose of it," Jim told me. "So I agreed to do it, but I had to ask just one more time if this person was sure they were talking about the calf who was rescued during the flood."

"And she said yes?" I asked.

"Not only did she say yes, she said very distinctly, 'Jim, the calf died, so remove it today!'"

Jim went to pick up the body as soon as he got off the phone. Never having had to deal with a situation like this before, he made some phone calls from his cell phone on the way, trying to figure out what to do with a deceased cow. He hadn't gotten an answer by the time he got to the vet school. As it turned out, he didn't need it. At the large animal clinic, a very much alive calf was waiting for him. Jim asked no questions and took the "body" away.

Tar Baby II now lives in Live Oak, California, with his new owner—Derrold R. Daly.

CHAPTER TWENTY-THREE

Nothing Else to Give

PEOPLE WHO attend the EARS Disaster Preparedness workshops do so because they care about animals. During the section of the workshop when I talk about the realities of doing disaster work, there is one really important point I make. I tell the volunteers who are seated in front of me, "In this kind of work, you have to have as much compassion for the people as you do for the animals, because we're constantly interacting with the human victims who have hit bottom and have a long way to go to pull themselves back up."

A group of us at the fairgrounds in Roseville got a really good reminder of how true this is.

We were still in the process of getting things organized the first night when an older couple arrived with their middle-aged son and three mixed-breed dogs. One look at the people instantly told us that they needed as much help as their animals.

"Is there something I can do for you?" I heard one of the volunteers ask when the family approached the row of tables that had been set up under an awning to process all incoming animals.

"We need a place to keep our dogs," the man said, struggling to get the words out.

"That's what we're here for," the intake worker said, with all the enthusiasm of a first-time volunteer. "If you want to leave us your dogs, you just need to fill out some paperwork."

At this point, I decided to step forward and offer to help them complete the forms. I easily had two dozen things to do, but all of a sudden this became more important than everything else on my list. I could tell that asking these people to complete paperwork on their own was something they just weren't up to. It was taking everything they had just to stand there, facing the fact that they were about to be separated from three dogs who they obviously cared very much about.

As we sat and completed the paperwork, I learned that the levee near their farm had broken the day before. A 20-foot wall of rushing water had wiped out everything they had in just a matter of minutes.

"We nearly didn't get out ourselves," the man said, rubbing his dirty, callused hands together. "There was just enough time for the three of us to grab the dogs and jump in the car and get out of there before the levee broke. If we'd lingered another ten or 15 minutes, we'd have been killed for sure."

"Were the dogs the only animals you had?" I asked. "If there were any left behind in your haste to escape, we'd be glad to send a rescue team out to look for them."

"We had over a hundred hogs, but I reckon they're all gone," the man said, massaging his neck with his hand. I noticed that it was very hard for him to sit still. "It's not likely they could have survived in all that water."

"That's how we made our living," the woman said quietly, and patted her son's hand, which was resting on her knee. "I don't know what we're gonna do now. I just don't."

At moments like this, I want to say something to give the disaster victims hope, but what can be said? It's not fair to lie to them, and false hope doesn't provide any lasting comfort. The harsh reality for disaster victims is hard to escape. Speaking the truth is the best approach in supporting survivors of a disaster, but you must do so very carefully. If you don't know what to say, I have found it can be just as helpful to listen.

In talking more with the family, I learned that life had not been kind to them, and now the flood had made things worse. It had been a constant struggle for this man and woman with the parched and wrinkled skin to make a living on their small farm. Undoubtedly, it was the constant exposure to the hot summer sun of the Central Valley that had weathered them, aging them too fast. The clothes they were wearing were worn and patched and not heavy enough to protect them from the cold January night, but they had nothing else. This was it. The flood had stolen everything but their lives, their three dogs, a beat-up car, and the clothes on their backs.

"How will you be taking care of our dogs?" the woman asked. I sensed she changed the subject to refocus the conversation on something besides what she and her husband had just lost.

"If you want, we can keep the three of them together in a large dog run," I explained. "I'd be happy to show you where we'll put them."

"That would be good," the woman said, reaching down to pet the dog closest to her. "They've been together a long time, so I'd hate to separate them, especially now. I suspect they're as confused as we are."

"Are you sure they'll be safe?" the son asked. It was the first thing I'd heard him say since they arrived.

Looking him straight in the eye, I placed my hand on his shoulder, and said, "I promise you, nothing will happen to them. We'll have volunteers take them for walks, make sure they get plenty to eat, give them toys to play with, and find them three comfortable dog beds to sleep in, and the veterinarians will keep an eye on them to make sure they stay healthy. They will be fine."

"Maybe we should stay here, too," the man said, so softly I barely heard him. At that time, I didn't realize how close to being serious he was.

"Does this cost?" the woman wanted to know.

"No, it doesn't. Everything is free," I assured her.

When she heard that, she started to cry. After a few moments, she was able to say, "Thank you."

Putting my arm around her shoulder as we headed to the barn, I said, "It's our pleasure."

The family followed me to the open-sided barn where we were sheltering the large dogs, using chain-link panels to create pens large enough to house a horse comfortably. We hadn't had many canine arrivals yet, so these guys got the pick of the place. We found a nice roomy run in a quiet corner that would give the three dogs more than enough space to stand, play, sleep, and eat. As the family was saying their good-byes, volunteers spread a thick layer of straw in the bottom of the pen and found three beds, just the right size for the dogs. They filled food and water dishes and placed them near the pen door. It wasn't home, but it was a pretty nice substitute.

"They'll be fine," the woman said, trying to reassure her son, as I closed the door of the pen. "We'll come and visit them every day."

"I know they would enjoy that," I said, watching the man petting the dogs through the chain-link fencing as he said good-bye one last time. "Please know that you can come by anytime."

As I was walking toward the office the next morning, they were the first people I saw. They were standing at the front gate, waiting to come in. When they recognized me, they asked, before I could say a word, "How are our dogs?"

We all walked back to the barn where we'd left the dogs the night before, and the morning hellos were terrific to watch. This was truly a family who meant the world to one another. When I finally had to leave them to attend to my ever-growing list of "things to do," I expected that the next time I walked through the barn they would be gone. But I was wrong. At noon, they were still in the pen, asleep, with their dogs curled up between them.

It was nearly 10 o'clock that night when the family finally walked out the front gate with the promise that they would be back first thing in the morning to check on their dogs. This became a routine that they stuck to for three days, spending between 10 and 12 hours with their dogs. They would have made terrific volunteers, even if they spent most of the morning asleep in the pen.

"Terri, can I talk to you?" It was a volunteer who had been helping since the first day. She stopped me on my way to get my morning glass of freshly squeezed orange juice. At this disaster, we ate really well. The caterer was especially considerate of us vegetarians. Every day for lunch, we actually had honest-to-goodness, made-from-scratch vegetable soup that didn't taste a bit like Veg•all. The caterer served us three meals a day from the converted snack bar, which became known as the Bowwow Café.

"Sure," I said to the volunteer, stopping to see what she needed.

"You know that family who spends all day with their three dogs?" she started out.

"Yes," I said. "They arrived the first night."

"Well, I think they are spending all day here because they don't have any place to go."

"What makes you think that?" I asked.

"I've noticed for the last two days that their car has been in the same parking spot. When I get here in the morning, it's where it was the night before. You know how busy the parking lot gets, no matter what time of day it is. You leave, and there's no way you're going to get the same spot again." The volunteer lowered her voice and said, "I think they're living in their car."

I thought about what she said for a moment, and then asked, "Are they here now with their dogs?"

"Yes," she replied. "Just like clockwork, they arrived at 7:30."

"Okay. Let me do some checking on this," I told the volunteer, who was obviously very concerned about the family. "I'll get back to you."

I'd had numerous occasions to talk with this family since first meeting them and I'd come to realize that they were proud people. They had worked hard their whole lives and had probably never needed to ask for help, until now. I suspected that they didn't even know how to go about doing it either.

I took a walk out to the parking lot to find the car the volunteer had described to me before she returned to her duties. When I peeked in the window, it was obvious to me that the family's car had become their temporary home. I knew this was no way for these people to be living. Something had to be done, but how was I going to help them without offending them?

It was a group of volunteers, which included my mother, who came up with a solution. They decided to take up a collection, with my approval, to get the family a hotel room near the fairgrounds. That way they could visit their dogs during the day, and at night take a shower and sleep in a real bed. There would also be money left over for food. Another volunteer offered to go to the Red Cross and gather some clothing and toiletry items for the family, all those things that had been left behind when they fled for their lives. We had done a great job of replacing what the dogs had lost. Why couldn't we do it for the rest of the family, too?

The group then picked the person they thought should approach the family. I agreed that the person they chose would know how to handle this very delicate situation—and she did. Gwen was a volunteer we'd seen handle other delicate situations and had proven that she was compassionate and that people were receptive to her.

As we suspected, the family admitted that they had been sleeping in their car at night, or at least trying to. They would not go and look for another, more suitable place to stay because they wanted to remain close to their dogs. The human evacuation shelters were too far away. And, as I'd suspected, they had no money for a hotel or another place to live.

When Gwen found me, she said, "The hardest thing about telling them what we had for them was doing it without crying. My heart went out to them. I can't even imagine what this must be like for them."

"Did they accept the money?" I asked.

"Yes, but it took some convincing," she said. "When they finally did take it, they were very gracious. They actually didn't say very much, but I know how much they appreciated it. I just wish we could have given them more."

"I think you all gave them more than you realize," I said, as I gave Gwen a hug.

The family's routine did not change much after they moved into a nearby hotel. They still spent most of the day with their dogs, but now they would take them for walks, play fetch with them, and spend hours brushing them. I never saw them sleeping in the pen again.

We'd had the dogs with us for just over a week when I heard that the family had come to reclaim them. I wanted to say good-bye and find out what their plans were, but an urgent situation that I had to tend to intervened, so I missed their departure. EARS coordinator Wendy Borowsky came to me later with tear-streaked cheeks to tell me about her last words with the woman. When she told me what had happened, I was truly sorry I hadn't been able to say good-bye myself.

"I had just completed the paperwork on the dogs, releasing them to the family," Wendy explained. "We hadn't said anything about the money and the hotel room, which was okay. I knew how much they appreciated our help. I didn't need to hear her say it."

"Did she say where they were going?" I asked.

"They're going to live with a relative who has enough room for all three dogs. That was what mattered to them the most. The dogs had to be okay, too," Wendy said, her eyes beginning to tear up.

"I wonder if they will be able to rebuild," I said out loud, more to myself than to Wendy. "Well, I hope it works out for them. They deserve only the best."

Wendy could only shake her head.

"Are you okay?" I asked her, sensing there was something else she wanted to tell me.

"Uh huh," she said in a whisper.

"What is it, Wendy?"

It took her a moment to share with me the details of her last few words with the woman. When she did, I, too, could not speak.

"While I was finishing up the paperwork with the woman, the husband and the son took the dogs to the car," Wendy explained. "I'd just handed her copies of the forms when she looked at me. What she did next, I will never forget."

I was still, waiting for Wendy to continue.

"She said to me, 'Ma'am, I want to thank you and everyone else for taking such good care of our dogs. Not only did you do a lot for them, but you also helped my family when we were having a really hard time. We'll be eternally grateful.'"

"I told her we were happy to do it," Wendy explained. "I thought she would turn around and leave then, but she didn't."

"What did she do?" I asked.

"She said to me, 'I've seen all the people come here to bring those things that you need to take care of this many animals. I wish I could have brought something for the animals, too, but that's just not possible right now. Someday I hope I can be one of those people that can help. I never want to be a victim again.'"

"I didn't know what to say to her," Wendy said, wiping away a tear with the back of her hand. "And then, what she did next left me completely speechless. I have never been so moved by something so simple."

Wendy went on to tell me what happened next. "The woman said to me, 'I just wouldn't feel right leaving without giving you all something to show my appreciation. So I want you to have these.' I looked at this woman standing in front of me, and I thought, *She has nothing left to give.* But I was wrong.

The woman reached into the pocket of her worn sweater and pulled something out, clutched in her fist. She took Wendy's hand and placed in her palm what she had removed from her pocket: a mound of rusted safety pins.

"This is all I have to give. It's not much, but I wanted you to have them," the woman said before walking away.

CHAPTER TWENTY-FOUR

The Boxed Cat

W E CLOSED down our site at the fairgrounds in Rose-ville on Saturday, January 25, but the work did not stop then. EARS volunteers Tom Dugally and Molly Tobias and I spent the next month wrapping up all the loose ends, which included working to place the remaining unclaimed dogs. The last animal adopted was a Pit Bull named Guy, who went to live with an EARS volunteer a year and a half after the flood. It was a perfect match for a very special dog.

Out of the 878 animals we cared for in the New Year's flood, 404 of them were reclaimed by their owners, most going back home before January 25. For the people who still did not have a place to keep their animals, we arranged for foster homes until the families were ready to take them back. Some of those animals remained in their temporary homes for months as their owners worked on getting resettled.

That left us with 474 unclaimed animals. We lost nine of them to illness or injuries after doing everything medically possible to save them. There were three extremely aggressive dogs who had to be euthanized, something we rarely do. The animals we help during disasters are frequently traumatized when we first encounter them, so it's not unusual for them to behave differently than they would normally. They often try to bite when they get really scared. We always give the animals time to calm down and adjust to their temporary surroundings before we do a temperament assessment for adoption. Most of the animals end up being just fine within a day or two, but the three dogs in Roseville were definitely too dangerous to place.

On that last Saturday, a team of us packed up a 27-foot U-Haul truck with all the supplies and equipment that would go back into storage to wait for the next disasters, while several of the volunteers worked to find homes for the remaining dogs. When it came time to leave, there were just 12 dogs left. We took them to Classic Kennel in Roseville, where owners Joann Caetano and Barbara Junior agreed to house the dogs until permanent homes could be found for them.

This was not the first time Joann and Barbara had been there to help us. The first night we were at the fairgrounds a family arrived with their 25 high-maintenance Chihuahuas. I used to always say that when we have to set up a temporary shelter what we hope for is a bunch of Chihuahuas because they don't require a lot of space. But after taking care of this bunch, I'll take Great Danes any day.

As the owners of the Chihuahuas were filling out their paperwork, I went in search of cages, something we were short of at that moment. I didn't have to go far. I was stopped by a woman who said, "I have some crates in my van I thought you could use. Where do you want me to put them?"

Joann and Barbara pulled out of their van the exact number of crates I needed for the Chihuahuas. Once again, the guardian angel had perfect timing.

The follow-up to a disaster this size generated activity clear into early March. There were still calls coming in from people wanting to tell us how much they loved the animal they had adopted, or disaster victims thanking us again for our help. There was also the person who found one of the reclaimed dogs because it still had our ID collar and tag on it and the elderly woman who called one day looking for the red feeding dish that she had loaned us. I couldn't believe it when I actually dug through the thousand-plus bowls we had in storage and found the bowl that she absolutely had to have back, though it was nothing out of the ordinary.

With each new phone call, I wondered if the New Year's flood was ever going to end. Eventually, the calls did taper off. It was a good thing they did, because on March 5, EARS responded to flooding along the Kentucky and Ohio border. Waders were becoming my fashion statement for 1997.

Once again we ended up at a fairgrounds, this time in Clermont County, located east of Cincinnati. A phone conversation with Kim Naegel at the humane society in Owensville, Ohio, had resulted in the mobilization of EARS. Coordinators Wendy Borowsky, Deborah Horn, Sharon Maag, Michele Richmond, and I, along with our two newest additions, Tom Dugally and Cindi Fanchier, got a shelter up and running in one of the enclosed exhibition buildings at the fairgrounds within a few hours of our arrival, thanks to the work Kim had already done getting permission to use the facility.

This was not another Roseville, though. We ended up staying in Ohio for only eight days. We took care of 121 animals with the help of over 100 volunteers, who once again put in some long hours making sure the animals along the flooded Ohio River were not forgotten.

There was a very brief period of normalcy in my life after I returned from Ohio. In those four and a half weeks, I managed to attend a Yuba County follow-up meeting to the January flood, dye Easter eggs, attend an EARS fund-raiser at a Sacramento restaurant, take Megan to her first karate lesson, attend the annual EARS coordinators' meeting in St. Louis for three days, bake a cake for Jennifer's seventeenth birthday, and teach two workshops. It was while I was doing one of those workshops in New York City that my life got immersed in a flood yet again.

My pager went off just before I was getting ready to dismiss the workshop participants for lunch. Instead of spending that hour having something to eat, I sat in my hotel room making phone calls to Grand Forks, North Dakota. It seemed the Red River was getting ready to spew over its banks, taking direct aim at this city, which sat right on the normally tame waterway.

Prior to leaving New York, I was able to make contact with Arlette Moen, the executive director of the Grand Forks Humane Society. I was relieved when she told me that the shelter was not at risk of flooding. The disaster was preventing seven members of her staff from getting to work, however, at a time when they needed all the help they could get to deal with the growing number of requests for help from worried pet owners who had left their animals behind. Never having been through something like this before, Arlette was very receptive when I offered her our help.

The first to arrive were EARS coordinators Raquel Aluisy, Tom Dugally, and Kim Mester and me, along with EARS-trained volunteers Ellen Brown and Chris Loudon, who had driven up with us from Minneapolis. Over the next few days, we were joined by other coordinators—Shirley Bollinger, Wendy Borowsky, Valerie DeMesa-Bruemmer, Dara Hoffman, Michele Richmond, and Cora Tyson.

During the 12 days we remained in Grand Forks, we recruited over 50 local volunteers, which included several veterinarians and one of the city's animal control officers, plus members of the National Guard and air-force personnel from the base in Grand Forks. In spite of having no previously trained EARS volunteers in the state of North Dakota, we wasted no time pulling together a dedicated team that did a tremendous job of working with the humane society staff to save the lives of 768 animals.

After our arrival at the shelter on April 20, I assessed the situation, and Arlette and I determined that EARS could most effectively assist the Grand Forks Humane Society by responding to the growing number of requests to retrieve stranded animals from homes that were surrounded by water. This would be in addition to helping at the shelter.

Our next step was to get permission from the Emergency Operations Center to gain access to the evacuated neighborhoods, which covered 85 percent of Grand Forks. Jim Campbell, the incident commander, realized immediately the need for EARS. He proceeded to introduce us to representatives of the fire department, law enforcement agencies, search and rescue, Coast Guard, National Guard, plus the city attorney, who had overseen the evacuation of Grand Forks. Confident in our experience and emphasis on safety, all of them agreed that EARS should be given access to the flooded area, except for one piece of land that jutted out into the river.

"That is where the levee broke," the Coast Guard commander explained, pointing to the place on a map taped to the wall, "and the entire area, a total of about four blocks, is sitting right now under 20 feet of water. It's going to stay that way for some time because that water has nowhere to go."

"He's right," the city attorney confirmed. "And there's no way any animals left in that area could have survived. The force of the water alone was enough to kill them. So you're better off directing your efforts at helping the ones farther away from the river; they may still be alive."

With the approval we needed, and more than enough rescues to keep us busy, we went to work. First, we had to prioritize the many rescue requests. Before we had arrived, Arlette and her staff had been taking down information about animals who needed to be rescued. As we went through the piles of paper, we had to determine which animals were at greatest risk.

We were particularly concerned about birds and reptiles, since temperatures were getting down into the low thirties at night. With all the electricity turned off in the flooded areas, the animals had no heat to keep them warm. Our other priorities were animals who had been left in confined spaces such as closed rooms, cages, pens, basements, or even chained outside. There were also a number of sick animals in need of medical attention, who were only going to get sicker if they didn't get their medicine.

Beyond all these special considerations, there were still lots of other priority rescues.

FOR 10 days, we maneuvered our fleet of boats through the flooded streets of Grand Forks, retrieving 75 dogs, a variety of domesticated birds, snakes, iguanas, frogs, fish, hamsters, ferrets, rabbits, hedgehogs, rats, and 503 cats. This is the largest number of cats EARS has ever had to take care of during a disaster.

When the floodwaters got too shallow for boats, we arranged through the command center for the National Guard to loan us one of their two-and-a-half-ton flatbed trucks and Staff Sergeant Jonathan Simmonds to drive it. He was picked for the mission because he was known at the armory as the person who would go out of his way to help an animal. While he was waiting for the truck that had been assigned to him, his buddies joked, "Hey, Simmonds, we hear you've been assigned to the Bunny Hugger Mission."

After two days of Jonathan working with us and returning to the armory with stories to tell, the same guys that gave him a bad time were now asking him if he needed any more help. It seemed that rescuing animals was a pretty cool thing to do after all.

Once we got Jonathan and the truck, along with another flatbed truck that belonged to a man whose fish we rescued, the rescues went much faster. It was so much easier filling up the back of the trucks with cages, rather than trying to work with the limited space of a boat.

We took all of the animals we rescued to the humane society, where many of the owners were anxiously waiting in the parking lot to be reunited with their pets. When a rescue vehicle would arrive with a load, people would swarm around it, peering in the windows to see if their animal was inside. Many of the people were able to immediately take their animals with them, but some needed us to take care of them.

There were a few times the shelter got too full to take in more animals, so we transferred some of the ones who had been there the longest to a temporary animal shelter at the air force base. Several military veterinarians had set up this facility to house animals belonging to enlisted personnel who lived off base and had to be evacuated.

~~~~

IT WAS during one of my trips to the base to check on the animals that we had moved there, a Red Cross mental-health worker told me about a cat who needed to be rescued immediately.

The brown Tabby belonged to an 80-year-old man who lived in a cramped, one-room apartment above a coffee shop in the business section of downtown Grand Forks. As the floodwaters were rising, the National Guard had evacuated the frail gentleman, taking him to the temporary shelter at the air force base. His rescuers forced him to leave his cat behind. Five days later, the mental-health worker spotted the old man hunched over in a chair, alone in a shadowed corner of the gymnasium where rows of cots had been set up for the evacuees.

The woman had just arrived in town that afternoon, providing relief for several of her colleagues who had been comforting the evacuees since the first day and were in desperate need of some time off. Concerned about the man, the woman approached to make sure he was alright. Not wanting to startle him, she cleared her throat as she got near, then asked in a caring voice, "Sir, is there anything I can do for you?"

The man said nothing. He just raised a lit cigarette to his lips and inhaled, never looking up to acknowledge the presence of the woman.

"Sir, are you alright?" the woman inquired, as she bent down to get a better look at his face.

The man blew out a cloud of smoke through barely opened lips. Then, as if trying to get rid of an annoying headache, he rubbed his forehead with nicotine-stained fingers.

Once again, the woman repeated her questions. Finally, the man spoke, in the raspy voice of a longtime smoker, as he continued to massage his creased forehead. "I'm going to die if I don't get my cat."

When the mental-health worker told me this story, I moved his rescue request to the top of my stack. I fully believed, as she did, that this man was not exaggerating.

The apartment we were looking for turned out to be located right around the corner from the block of buildings that had caught fire in downtown Grand Forks shortly after the flooding began. All the national news broadcasts had featured dramatic footage of fire trucks being transported in on flatbed trucks that could just barely make it through the still-rising water. As Jonathan Simmonds and I got out of the truck that we had been using to pick up animals all morning, the smell of smoke was still strong, even though the fire had been extinguished days before.

"This one's going to be an easy one to get to," Jonathan said, as we approached the entrance to the building. "Someone's already broken out a window for us."

People had granted us permission to force our way into most of the houses we had been to because they didn't have a key to give us and they wanted their animals. Jonathan had become a real pro at using a credit card to unlock doors and at breaking windows with one swift tap of a boat oar. On one occasion, he had sprung a door lock by lightly tapping the doorjamb with the bumper of the truck. The solid metal, dead-bolted door stood in the way of our reaching half a dozen apartments, each one of them with animals inside.

Squeezing through the narrow window frame to the right of the locked door, Jonathan and I stepped into a dark, musty foyer. The carpeted floor made a squishing sound as we walked toward the stairs, anxious to get this cat so we could continue with the rest of the rescues we wanted to complete before it got too late.

"Looks like the water was about four feet deep in here," Jonathan said, pointing to the brown waterline that circled the room.

"Yeah, it got just high enough to get into the mailboxes," I said, as I passed the black letter holders lined up on one of the water-stained walls.

We climbed three flights of squeaky wooden stairs to apartment number 312. Tucked away in my pocket was a key ring with a miniature Lucky Lager beer bottle and a single key dangling from it—our access to the apartment.

Standing in front of a masterfully carved wooden door, one of the few remaining clues to what a fine building this once had been, Jonathan and I read a three-by-five-inch handwritten note pinned to the door, intended as a warning.

"Oh, this is great," Jonathan said, after reading the sign. "As if we haven't had to deal with enough mean dogs already."

The words "Beware of Mean Cat" prompted us to put on our protective gloves.

Unlocking the dead bolt, I pushed open the door just far enough to poke my head inside, and at the same time slide my leg between the door and the frame, hopefully blocking a potential escape route for the cat. Checking the floor first, I was relieved to see there was no cat waiting to attack me, or to dart into the hallway, escaping the apartment where he had been confined for five days.

With no cat in sight, I opened the door a little farther so I could get a better view inside.

"I can tell by smelling that there's a cat in here," I told Jonathan, who was standing behind me, ready to grab the cat should he get past me. "I don't see him, but then it's real dark in here."

We stepped inside, still being careful to guard against the cat making a sudden run for it while the door was open. Once inside, the door shut behind us, we stood still as our eyes adjusted to the gloom. As I began to see more clearly, I dreaded taking another step. I had already pulled the collar of my sweatshirt over my nose in hopes that it would block out the horrible stench, but it didn't.

It looked as though the cat had decided to quit using the litter box after it got too full, choosing to leave his messes scattered across the matted, orange shag carpet. Adding to the nauseating smell were the yucky contents of a saucepan on top of a compact stove just inside the front door. Our guess was that the concoction had at one time been cream of mushroom soup.

"Wow, this is really disgusting," Jonathan commented, taking a few more steps forward.

"Yeah, and the flood's not to blame," I said, trying to right a chair lying on its side in my path. "No wonder this chair won't stand up. It's only got three legs."

"If I didn't know better, I'd say a tornado hit this place." Jonathan's description could not have been more accurate. Throughout the one-room apartment were stacks of un-evenly-cut scrap lumber, some piled as high as six feet. They looked just like the remnants of houses collected after a tor-nado had done its demolition job.

"Why would someone have all this wood in such a tiny apartment?" I wondered.

"Beats me," Jonathan said, moving toward the window so he could raise the yellowed window shade.

Peeking in the bathroom, which was to the left of the front door, I found more lumber piled in the rust-stained bathtub and on both sides of the toilet. *This is really strange,* I thought to myself, as I wandered back into the room that served as the man's living room, kitchen, and bedroom. There wasn't much there besides the piles of wood. I suspected that even the Goodwill would turn down the few pieces of mismatched furniture. The only thing on the peeling gray walls was a framed photograph of a barn, which reminded me of a picture you would see on the top of a jigsaw puzzle box.

Stacked next to an overstuffed chair no longer able to contain its protruding springs was at least a week's worth of TV dinner trays holding fuzzy green leftovers. On a wooden crate to the left of the chair were half a dozen nearly empty buttermilk cartons that were most likely contributing to the sour odor in the stuffy room. The smell of stale smoke was thrown into the sickening mix, the strongest odor emanating from an assortment of plastic ashtrays filled to overflowing with unfiltered Camel cigarette butts.

On the floor, below the room's only two windows, was a narrow mattress. There were no sheets or pillows on it, just a thin avocado-green blanket wadded up in a heap. With some help from the faint rays of light poking their way through the dirty windowpanes, I saw something that I recognized sticking out from under the blanket. It was the tip of a tail that undoubtedly belonged to a brown Tabby.

"Jonathan," I whispered.

When he looked at me, I pointed to the blanket. He nodded when he, too, recognized the sight.

Tiptoeing toward the bed, I used two gloved fingers to gingerly lift the corner of the blanket. When the cat's face came into view, I instantly knew he was not pleased to see his rescuers. His quick departure was a pretty good clue that we had our work cut out for us. This one wasn't coming willingly.

The cat took refuge behind one of the many piles of wood. Jonathan and I began to dismantle his hiding place, one piece of wood at a time. When we got down to the last few boards, the cat made a mad dash for the next closest pile.

He was fast and determined. But we were, too. After an hour of playing hide-and-seek, though, we began to think that we were going to have to bring in reinforcements, and a humane cat trap. But then the cat chose the wrong place to hide.

As we were getting down to the last few pieces of wood in the pile nearest a junk-filled closet, the cat made his predictable move and shot past us. Instead of heading for another pile of wood, this time he disappeared into the closet, Jonathan hot on his trail. Using the clothes that hung in the closet as a ladder, the cat clawed his way up to the lowest shelf and dove into an empty Crock-Pot box.

Having him where he wanted him, Jonathan quickly grabbed the box with both hands, and in one swift motion, picked up the box and slammed the open end up against the shelf above, taking away the cat's only way to escape. Then he looked over his shoulder at me and asked, "Now what, rescue expert?"

As we discussed our options, keeping in mind the kind of damage the cat could do to us with either his teeth or claws, Jonathan kept a firm grip on the box. Meanwhile, from inside the box, the cat showed his discontent at being confined and his growing dislike for us. As he performed continuous somersaults in the box, he let out howling screams that could have served as chilling sound effects for a scary movie. He was warning us to beware!

"We need a board just a little bit bigger than the box—heaven knows there's enough wood in this place to choose from. I'll slide the wood between the shelf and the box opening, creating a top for the box," I suggested. "Then we'll find some rope or a cord or something to secure the board in place."

"So you want to take him back to the shelter in this box?" Jonathan questioned.

"Yeah," I said. "I don't want to take the chance of transferring him here and having him get loose again. We'd never get him and I sure as heck don't want his owner dying because we couldn't bring him his cat."

"Okay, it sounds like we've got a plan," Jonathan said, still battling with the angry cat.

After locating the perfect board and a roll of duct tape, I cleared a pathway on the floor of the closet, so Jonathan could back out of it and not trip once we had the board in place.

"Okay, I think that does it," I said, as I deposited on the mattress the last armload of dirty clothes from the closet floor. I picked up the board. "Let me just squeeze past you," I said to Jonathan.

"You better not bump into me," he warned. "If I lose my balance and let go of this box, this cat's coming out fighting. And, at this point, I think he's more determined to win."

"Don't worry," I said, as I carefully moved into position.

As planned, Jonathan lowered the box just an inch and I slid the board into place. Then we counted to three, at which time he lowered the box another inch, giving me just enough room to place my hands on top of the board. My job was to hold down the board so the cat couldn't push it aside and escape while Jonathan backed out of the closet carrying the box.

We walked very slowly across the room, as if we were carrying a bomb that would explode with one wrong move, and placed the Crock-Pot box on a waist-high stack of wood.

"So far so good," I said, and took a deep breath.

Meanwhile, the boxed cat grew angrier.

Imagining what the cat would do to us if he escaped, I put more weight on the wood lid as Jonathan grabbed the duct tape. He had just pulled a long strip off the roll when his foot accidentally hit the pile of wood the box was resting on, causing the pile to shift and my hand to slip just enough to give the cat the space he needed to escape.

What happened next was pretty much a blur, but I do remember moving out of the way of the falling pile of wood, hearing an angry meow, and thinking, *I'm going to have sharp claws latch onto some part of my body at any moment.* When the commotion was over, I saw Jonathan crouched down on the floor, one of his gloved hands holding down the back end of the cat while his other hand pressed the cat's head against the carpet.

"God, this sucker's strong," Jonathan said, as he struggled to maintain control of the cat. "Quick! Grab the Evacsack."

With the open rescue bag in my hand, I stood next to Jonathan, waiting for his signal that he was ready to give this a try. There was no time to say anything, but I knew both of us had our doubts that this was going to work. We had already struck out once, and if we did again, I was almost certain Jonathan and I would end up with scars to prove that our plan had failed.

"You ready?" he asked, as he got his legs in position to be able to stand up quickly and basically slam dunk the cat into the bag.

I pulled my cat gloves as far up my forearms as they would go. "I think so," I said.

"Okay," Jonathan said, never taking his eyes off the cat, who was still struggling to get free. "You're going to have to move real fast to get that bag closed. I know we normally put the cats in feet first, but this time the head's going first, which will give you an extra second to pull that bag closed before he can flip around and try to come out of there the same way he came in."

"Let's do it," I said with as much confidence as I could muster.

"Here goes," Jonathan said, and quickly stood up. "Pull!" he hollered, as he released the cat.

With one swift tug on the drawstring, I closed the opening, and much to our surprise . . . the cat was in the bag.

CHAPTER TWENTY-FIVE

Bottomless Pit

I MISSED THE reunion between the 80-year-old man and his cat. There was still a stack of rescues to do, preventing us from spending many daylight hours at the humane society. Jonathan and I were actually quite relieved to drop off the feisty cat and join the other teams working to save the animals still waiting to be rescued. Hopefully, those animals would be a lot more cooperative.

A volunteer told me later that when the old man arrived, it took him 10 minutes to walk in a slow shuffle back to the cat room, as no one wanted to take the cat out of the cage and bring him to his owner. Once two volunteers had managed to get him out of the Evacsack and into a cage, they decided that was where he was going to stay.

The volunteer who was telling me the story said she put a chair in front of the cat's cage, and then stepped out of the room to stand with the Red Cross volunteer who had driven the man over from the base. Through a window in the closed door, they looked on as the man slowly unhooked the latch on the cage and opened the wire door.

"It wasn't but a second before that cat was out of the cage and sitting on the man's lap, rubbing his head against his chest," the volunteer said. "When the man started crying, I started bawling, too. They definitely missed each other."

The cat stayed at the shelter, since the man was still living at the base. Various volunteers drove him to the humane society once a day to visit. I did finally have the opportunity to see the two of them together. As I watched the old man and the cat interact, I found it hard to believe this was the same cat Jonathan and I had tangled with.

⟿

IT'S ALWAYS interesting to see how animals react to different people. There are the animals who prefer women to men and vice versa, and those who dislike children. I got another reminder of these varying preferences while I was doing more rescues with two teams of volunteers in an area where all the water had receded. An official-looking man, carrying a clipboard, flagged me down when he saw the Emergency Animal Rescue Service placards on the side of my Cherokee.

"Hi," he said, walking up to the passenger window, which I'd electronically lowered. "Are you the people rescuing the animals?"

"Yes, we are," I replied.

"Well, that's great," he said. "My partner and I are tagging the condemned houses. About an hour ago, we came across a dog inside one of the houses we were inspecting on this block. When we were walking around the place, he was at every window, barking and growling and basically being really nasty."

"Does it look like anyone has been back to the house since the flood began?" I asked.

"No one's been there. In fact, we confirmed that the owners are in Minnesota staying with relatives and they're not sure when they're coming back to town," the man explained.

"Do you have their name and a telephone number for them?" I asked.

"Not on me, but I sure could get that information to you if you give me a number to call you later," he offered.

Handing him my business card, with the humane society's number written on the back, I told him how much I appreciated him taking the time to let me know about the dog. The length of time the dog had already been on his own concerned me, and it sounded as though his owners weren't coming back for him anytime soon. I needed to get him out of the house and taken care of. Then I would try to make contact with the owners to let them know that their dog was safe at the humane society. I wondered if they would even care.

"I wasn't about to go in the house and get bitten, but I do feel sorry for the dog," the man said, as he secured my card on his clipboard. "He looks real skinny. When I peeked in the window, I could see a bag of dog food torn apart, but there was nothing left. I suspect he finished it up days ago."

"I'll go check it out," I said, reaching for a rescue request form. "Do you know the address of the house?"

"Yeah," the man said, and flipped through the papers on his clipboard. He gave me the address, along with his name, official title, and a way to get hold of him, too. Then he left to catch up with his partner and resume the tough job of deciding which houses people could and could not return to. They had already designated the house I was headed to as one of those no longer safe for people or animals to live in.

I radioed one of the rescue teams and told them to meet me at the location the man had given me. If this dog was as mean as he said, I was going to need some help. I drove to the house and waited for my backup.

"The inspector told me there was just one dog inside and he's not exactly friendly," I told Jonathan and Cindy, the two volunteers who joined me. "Let's walk around and see if there are any more animals inside the house first. If there is more than one mean dog in there, I want to know it before we do anything. I don't want any surprises."

The house was not very big. It had a living room, a tiny kitchen, a bathroom, and one bedroom, all of which we could get a good look at by peeking in the windows. It was obvious why the inspectors had condemned the place. The house had slid at least eight inches off its foundation, and there was other visible structural damage as well. As the three of us looked in the windows, searching for any other animals, the dog would jump up and put his front feet on the window ledge, behaving exactly as the inspector had described. I noticed, though, that he seemed to get more upset when Jonathan looked in the window. This made me think this dog did not like men.

By the time the three of us had returned to the front yard, I had decided how Cindy and I were going to try and get this dog out of the house. I was almost positive that the dog was more partial to women, so I said to Jonathan, "I hate to say this, but I don't think he likes you. So why don't you take the truck and head back to where the rest of the team is. Cindy and I can handle this one. When we're finished, I'll radio to find out where you are and drop her off there."

"That's fine," Jonathan said, as he started to head back to the truck. "Radio if you need any help. You know I'm used to dealing with the feisty ones. After that cat today, I can handle anything."

"Something tells me that this dog will be just fine once you're not around," I said, as Jonathan was about to climb into the driver's seat. "Hey, Jonathan, wait a minute. There is something you can do before you leave. See if you can use your talents to get us in the front door."

The front door turned out to be unlocked, so Jonathan left Cindy and me to convince the medium-sized black dog that we meant him no harm.

"I'm sure he's hungry," I said to Cindy, as we walked to my car. "The only thing I've got to give him is canned cat food. I think it'll be exactly what we need to become this dog's best friend." I grabbed four cans of cat food and a can opener, along with a slip leash and a muzzle.

"So what are we going to do?" Cindy asked, as we headed for the front porch.

"I'm going to open one can of food at a time, push the front door open just far enough to slide it in, then close the door fast," I explained. "Then we'll peek in the window and see how the dog responds after he's had something to eat and doesn't have any men to bark at."

The first can of food went through the narrow opening in the door. By the time Cindy and I got around the corner of the house to where we would have the best view into the living room, the can of cat food was empty.

"I'd say he was hungry," I said, as we returned to the front porch to open another can of food and repeat the process.

Not only was the food gone when we looked through the window a second time, but the dog was standing on the floor in front of the window, looking up at us and wagging his tail. We never heard the dog bark again.

I opened the third can of cat food and slid it through the opening, but this time I kept the door partially open. As the dog inhaled the food, I talked to him in a soft voice, hoping to reassure him that we were only there to help. Once the food was gone, the dog walked over to me, his tail still wagging, and allowed me to pet the top of his head. If I had let him, he would have also planted a nice, juicy cat-food-breath kiss on my cheek, but I decided to wait a little longer before I got that friendly with the dog.

Closing the door, careful not to pinch the dog's nose in it, I grabbed the fourth can of food and the slip leash, deciding that the muzzle wouldn't be necessary.

"This time I'm going to slide the food in and, while he's eating, I'll slip the leash around his neck," I explained to Cindy, as I was putting my gloves on just to be safe. "Why don't you go open the back door of the car. I'll just lead him in there and take this dog for a ride. I suspect he'll be real happy to get out of the house once and for all."

Just before I reached for the door handle, I asked Cindy to get a red "Notice of Removal" sign and fill it out, so we could post it on the house, just in case I didn't reach the family by phone. The inspector did not know how long it would be until the people who lived in this house returned from Minnesota, but when they did, I wanted them to know exactly where to find their dog.

Opening the door slowly, the can of food in my left hand and the leash in my right, I bent down and slid the food about two feet into the room. The dog was waiting and, as I expected, it took no time for him to finish off this can, too. Before he was finished, I gently slipped the leash over his head and pulled it just tight enough so he could not get away. After he finished licking the can clean, he walked right up to me, tail wagging again. This time, he planted a real juicy kiss on my chin.

"Well, fella, you ready to go for a ride?" I asked, running my fingers through the fur on his head. "I bet you've been really lonely in here all by yourself."

A second kiss seemed to confirm that I was right.

"Okay, then, let's go," I said, beginning to back out the door.

The dog started to follow, but paused for a moment to pick up the empty can with his teeth. Once he had it in his mouth, he was ready to leave.

"It's all gone. You don't want that," I said. "Once we get back to the humane society we'll give you a real meal."

I reached for the can, but the dog quickly turned his head away from me, as if to say, "Don't you dare."

"Okay, you can keep the can," I assured him, fully expecting him to drop it on his own once we were outside and he got sidetracked by other things.

But I was wrong.

The dog carried the can across the front yard, and when he jumped into the backseat of the car, he still had the can in his mouth. I closed the door behind him, got into the front seat, and waited for Cindy to post the notice on the house. When she got in beside me and saw the dog still had the can in his mouth, she asked, "Do you want me to try and take that can away from him?"

"For some reason, he seems to want to hang on to it, so let's just let him have it for now," I said. I got on the radio to call the other team and dropped Cindy off a few houses away from where they were, so the dog wouldn't see any men. When she got out of the car, the dog was still holding the can in his mouth.

It took about 15 minutes to get to the humane society. During the drive, the dog walked back and forth in the backseat, as if uncertain which window he wanted to look out. As he paced, there was one thing he was certain of—he wasn't about to let go of the can.

"Cora, this is Terri. Do you copy?" I said into the radio when I was about five minutes from the shelter.

"This is Cora. I copy," came the response.

"Cora, I'm bringing in a dog who isn't real fond of men, so I want to drive up to the side gate. Could you please make sure there are no men around when I get there?"

"Can do," Cora said. "How close are you to the shelter?"

"Just a few minutes," I told her.

"I'll be ready when you get here."

"Thanks." I signed off.

"We're almost there, fella," I said to my passenger, who I could see in the rearview mirror, still had the can in his mouth.

I spotted Cora waiting for me as I drove past the parking lot full of vehicles, and people who were still anxious to be reunited with their animals. When I stopped the car, Cora came over to my window and asked, "Do you need any help getting him out?"

"No, he'll be fine, just as long as there are no men nearby," I said, getting out of the car.

"What's that dog got in his mouth?" Cora asked.

"An empty can of cat food," I said as though it was no big deal.

"Why don't you take it away from him?"

"Because it's his and he's not about to give it up," I explained, as I reached for the backseat door handle.

"How long has he been carrying that thing around?"

"Ever since I gave it to him," I told her, reaching inside the car and grabbing the end of the leash.

"Why'd you give it to him?" she asked, as I led the dog out of the car.

"When I gave it to him, it had cat food in it, and when he finished eating everything inside, he decided he didn't want to leave it behind."

"He's probably trying to tell you something," Cora said, petting the dog, but being careful not to get too close to the can.

"What?" I asked.

"That he wants more," Cora said with a laugh.

And that's exactly what the dog got.

CHAPTER TWENTY-SIX

Beyond Their Reach

EVERY CREATURE, domesticated or wild, is a life worth saving. As we were sorting the rescue requests early one morning, I said to Shirley Bollinger, who was going to be on one of the field teams that day, "Here's one I think you can handle."

In the house on South Ninth Street, there was a single goldfish and a pet snail, whose owners were very anxious to have them rescued. When they got the call later that morning that both the goldfish and the snail were alive and ready to be picked up at the humane society, the family was as thrilled as the people we called to tell that their dog or cat or bird was safe. They reminded me of the man in Florida whose fish we rescued after Hurricane Opal. When I handed him the bucket with five-inch Oscar inside, he immediately put the bucket on the ground and proceeded to pick up the squirming fish and kiss it on its lips.

While Shirley was rescuing the goldfish and snail, I was in a boat with Rick Schuchart and Arlette Moen, headed to a house on Sunset Drive in search of Silver. The owners had come into the humane society late the day before to complete a rescue request form. Before they were finished, they needed a second piece of blank paper to write down all the information they thought we would need for the rescue to be a success. When Wendy handed me the completed form, with the one-page attachment, I looked at her and asked, "Are these people serious?"

"I'm afraid so," Wendy said, trying to keep her emotions under control.

"Let me read this again to make sure I understand," I said, thinking I must have missed something. When I finished reading though the information a second time, I still could not believe what I had read.

"Okay, let me see if I got this straight," I said, looking at Wendy and then referring back to the form.

"When these people evacuated, they got a ladder and leaned it against the outside of their house. Then they went back inside and got the cage that their cockatiel was in, carried the cage up the ladder, and left it on the roof. Am I right so far?" I asked Wendy.

"That's exactly what happened," she said, urging me to continue.

"Okay, let me see. Then they decided to open the door on the birdcage. Do you know why they did that?" I asked.

"If the water got higher than the roof, they didn't want the bird to drown in its cage," Wendy informed me.

"Did they cover the cage with a heavy blanket or something to give the bird at least a slim chance of surviving the cold nights?"

"No, they didn't," Wendy said. "And they told me they regretted not doing that."

"Is that the only thing they regret?" I asked, trying not to judge these people, but I was finding it really hard to understand how these people ever expected this bird to survive.

"They did say they were sorry they didn't put extra food and water in the cage before they left," Wendy said, obviously as upset as I was.

"I don't understand. Why didn't they just bring the bird with them? It's not as if he would take up a lot of room or cause a big mess."

"The people they were going to be staying with were afraid the bird would make too much noise," Wendy said, her voice trailing off.

"Do they really think we are going to find their bird?" I wanted to know.

"They haven't given up hope, they told me before they left yesterday." Wendy was obviously not as hopeful as they were.

"So all this stuff that is written on the back is how they want us to call the bird, *if* he's not in his cage?" I said, glancing at the instructions again. "Do they really think that Silver may still be sitting in his cage, waiting for us? I don't think so."

When Rick, Arlette, and I turned the corner onto Sunset Drive, we couldn't help but see the gold cage that had been left on top of the turquoise-blue house. It was hard to tell from a distance, but it didn't look like there was still a bird inside. When we floated up to the fence at the edge of the neighbor's yard, there was no longer any doubt. Silver was gone.

"So what do we do now?" Rick asked.

Turning to the second page of the rescue request form, I read what the paper said. "We're supposed to give one sharp whistle, and if the bird can hear us, they think he will whistle back. If that doesn't work, then we're supposed to try a shriller whistle, repeating it multiple times."

"They really do think this bird is still around?" Rick asked, scanning the bare trees lining both sides of the street. "My guess is he's in the Bahamas right now enjoying the sunshine."

"They seem to think so," I said. "And, they go on to say on this paper that if the whistling doesn't work we're to try calling his name."

"Somehow I don't think this bird is going to come swooping out of the sky when he hears us call his name," Arlette said, shading her eyes from the sun that was just beginning to peek out from the clouds for the first time that day.

"I don't either, but let's give it a shot," I said, putting the rescue form back into a plastic sealable bag to protect it from getting wet.

The three of us gave it our best shot, whistling in a manner that we thought would convince Silver to either respond to us, or to fly down and land within our reach so that we could capture him. Fifteen minutes of trying resulted in nothing but us feeling light-headed from blowing so much, confirming that none of us were very good whistlers.

"I think you're right, Rick. Silver's not anywhere near here. He got smart and flew south while he had a chance," I said, looking up into the sky one more time, just in case there was a gray and yellow bird circling overhead. This is one time I would have loved to be surprised.

"I agree," Arlette said, as she pulled her collar up on her coat. Even though the sun was now out, it had not warmed up. If Silver was still anywhere in North Dakota, I suspected he wouldn't last long. The last thing Silver's owners had put on their extended form was "Please check on our bird soon because he does not do well in cold weather." If they knew that, how could they have left him out in the cold to begin with?

SILVER WAS not the only bird we went in search of during the Red River Flood. Over 150 domesticated birds needed rescuing in Grand Forks. Some of them we found in time, but as the days passed, we found more dead than alive.

As our bird population began to increase at the humane society, we were going through the bird food like crazy, all the feathered evacuees making up for the meals they had missed. One of the afternoons when Jonathan and I were on our way back from doing some rescuing, we noticed that one of the pet stores in town appeared to be open. Through the front window, we could see people standing inside. Knowing that we were running low on bird food, we stopped to see if we could buy some.

When we walked through the front door, the store was dark, which led us to believe the electricity was still off in this part of town, even though the water had not quite reached this block. Behind the counter was a middle-aged man who was speaking to a young couple. When the woman turned slightly, we saw a cockatoo perched on her arm.

While I went to look for some bird food, Jonathan walked over to the counter, unable to resist saying hello to the bird.

"What a nice bird you've got," Jonathan said, when there was a break in the conversation.

"Oh, he's not our bird," the woman was quick to explain. "He belongs to some friends of ours. They were out of the country when the flood came and we were taking care of the bird. We couldn't get to their house to grab him when the water starting coming, so he's been there alone for eight days. We just picked him up a little while ago when the authorities finally opened some of the roads."

As the woman was talking, the bird worked his way up to her shoulder and extended his neck, as if trying to reach for Jonathan. That was when Jonathan realized how emaciated the bird was.

"They came in here to find out if they should give him as much food as he wants or if they should gradually give it to him. They were afraid too much food too fast might not be good," the man behind the counter explained.

Jonathan was about to ask a question but, before he could, the bird started squawking and fussing to get to him.

"The people who own him are in the military, so I think your uniform reminds him of them," the woman said. "Do you want to hold him?"

"Sure," Jonathan said, putting his thumb and index finger out for the bird to step on.

"What's his name?" Jonathan asked, stroking the bird's head.

"Baby," the woman said.

"Well hello, Baby," Jonathan said in a soothing voice. "I bet you're happy to be around people again who can feed you and take care of you."

Just then the bird reached for one of the buttons on Jonathan's shirt, but when he brought the bird closer to his chest he was not the least bit interested in the green button. Instead he bent his head down slightly, turned it to the side, and laid it against Jonathan's shirt. Then in a very distinct voice, he said, "Thank you."

We didn't rescue this bird, but maybe he knew how hard we were working to save other ones.

SOME OF the birds listed on our rescue forms lived in a recently built senior apartment complex in town where the only kind of pet the tenants were allowed to have were small birds, such as canaries, parakeets, or finches. When the water began to rise, the elderly people were some of the first ones to be evacuated, and once again, they were told they had to leave their pets behind. Most of the people had put in extra food and water and covered the birdcages before they left, so we weren't as worried about the birds at first.

When it was time to go and retrieve these birds, we called the phone number that the tenants had given us, which would put us in touch with the company that managed the complex. After two days of calling and leaving messages, we had not heard back from anyone. It was essential that we talked to them because they were the only ones with the key that would unlock the solid metal front door. Without it, we would be unable to access all the unlocked, one-room apartments that had birds in them.

"Jonathan, why don't we swing by that senior complex and see if there might just be someone there from the management agency?" I suggested one afternoon when we were only a few blocks away from the place. "If not, I think I'll leave a note on the door in case they show up later."

"Good idea," Jonathan said, as he turned the corner and continued down the street that was still a foot underwater.

When we got to the complex, it was still deserted and locked up as tight as ever. Even with all the techniques Jonathan had recently learned to gain access to people's locked houses, this was a place we weren't getting into until we had a key.

"I'll be just a minute," I said, and jumped down from the cab of the truck to go post a note on the door. In big, bold red letters, I wrote:

URGENT NOTICE
TO PROPERTY MANAGEMENT

There are tenants who live in this building who were forced to leave their birds behind when they were evacuated. They are extremely worried about them, and they certainly don't need another thing to be worrying about right now. To rescue these birds, I need to have a key to the main door. I am working with the Grand Fork's Humane Society. Please call me at 775-3732, so we can arrange to meet here, and these birds can be rescued before they die.

—Terri Crisp, Director,
Emergency Animal Rescue Service

As I walked back to the truck in almost knee-high water, I thought of our guardian angel who had helped us so many times before. *If you're anywhere near here, could you maybe put a bug in these people's ears because the birds are running out of time.*

The apartment complex manager called the next morning. He had seen my note, and I think our pal had something to do with the quick response.

Jonathan and I were the ones who arranged to meet the man at the main door at 10 o'clock. As we drove to the location, Jonathan was not himself. I knew we were all getting tired, but there was something definitely bothering him.

Finally, I asked, "Are you okay?"

"Sort of," he said, continuing to watch the road directly in front of him.

"What does that mean?" I asked.

He didn't answer me right away, but when he did I understood better why he had been so quiet all morning.

"I'm not looking forward to going into this place," he said, turning to look out his window for a second. "These birds that we're going after have been in there for over a week."

We were both silent after that.

Jonathan was the first to speak again as we pulled into the driveway of the senior complex. "Something tells me we're not going to find many of the birds still alive, and it really stinks that we have to be the ones to go in and find them."

The complex manager accompanied us through the building as we went down the list of apartments that contained over two dozen birds. It wasn't until we got to the seventh apartment that we found one parakeet, barely alive. He was the only live bird we found in the building; Jonathan's prediction had been right.

When we got back into the truck, we put the parakeet in his cage, which we wrapped with a thick blanket, between us. Jonathan started to turn the ignition, but then stopped, grabbing the top of the steering wheel with both hands. He lowered his forehead onto his clenched fists and remained that way. I felt numb as I silently stared out the window, tears rolling down my cheeks. All I could think about were the dead birds.

We had removed them from their cages and put them all in a plastic grocery bag we found in the first apartment. The nearly full bag was now in the back of the truck. We decided we would bury them in the field behind the humane society because we didn't want the people who were so worried about them to return and find them lying on the bottom of the cages.

What Jonathan and I had seen was another one of those memories that will forever be tacked to my mental bulletin board. Those birds are another reason that I do what I do. Every one of them had run out of food and water, probably days before. As they slowly succumbed to starvation, they could see the seeds they had so carelessly thrown around when their dish was full, now lying under the metal grill that covered the bottom of their cage. Almost every bird we picked up, died with its beak tightly wedged between those thin metal rods, as they desperately struggled to grab the seeds just beyond their reach.

CHAPTER TWENTY-SEVEN

Why?

I HAVE KNOWN from the beginning that when you do disaster work you have to take the good with the bad. The happy endings are what I hope for, but that's not always how things turn out. There have been times when I just don't think I can bear to see another animal who died due to human indifference. It becomes a struggle to go back out on another rescue when you've already picked up one too many dead animals that day. The tragic discoveries tear me up inside, but I have to go on.

The volunteers are not sheltered from the tragedies either. They, too, see what happens when people don't care enough about their animals to evacuate them. During each disaster, part of my job is to keep an eye on the coordinators and the volunteers to make sure they're okay. Of course, we all watch out for each other, but through 46 disasters I've learned a few lessons, some the hard way, on how to survive what we see during or after floods, fires, earthquakes, tornadoes, and hurricanes. I wish I could say there was one easy survival technique that I've learned, but there isn't. I've gotten through the tough times in all different ways. One way that helps me is to write about my experiences.

Volunteers have also learned that writing can be an extremely effective way to bring closure to each disaster or to a particularly difficult rescue. EARS coordinator Michele Richmond shared a story with me from the flood in Grand Forks when I was working on this book. After she finished telling me what happened, I asked her if she wanted to write the story for the book. This is her story, which she and I worked on together.

PROTECTED BY my chest-high waders, the boots of which were three sizes too big, I was about ready to take a carefully placed step into the still water. My pounding heart reminded me that this was my first water rescue. If it weren't for my love of animals, there was no way that I would be doing something like this.

As I looked down the stairwell leading to the basement apartments, I was reviewing in my head the information from the rescue request form: two cats and four kittens. I couldn't delay it any longer. I had to go get them.

The pressure against my body is what I remember most about that initial step into the uninviting water. Slowly, I descended the stairs, holding on tight to the railing, as my waders clung to my body as if they were frightened of their surroundings. Every step added more pressure, not only physically, but mentally, too. By the time I reached the bottom step, I was submerged in dirty, cold water as high as my waist, and my heart pounded even harder.

Tom, another EARS coordinator and my rescue partner for the day, stood at the top of the small staircase. He had hurt his leg the day before and was unable to go back into the water for a few days, so I was on my own. Tom and I had worked well together in other disasters and I was counting on his assistance to get me through this rescue, even though he wouldn't be by my side. Eagerly awaiting my description of the scene in front of me, Tom asked, "Do you see the apartment?"

I looked down the hallway and on the right saw the number 3 nailed to the door. "It's right here," I answered with a slight quiver in my voice, as I waded through the water toward the apartment.

My arms were extended as I moved, as if I was walking along an invisible tightrope. I was really trying hard to keep my balance, a difficult task when you're wearing shoes that don't fit. Squeezed firmly between my index finger and my thumb was the key that would unlock the door to apartment number 3. I knew if I dropped the key it would be difficult to retrieve, and would delay rescuing the cats who had already been trapped for too many days.

Reaching the door, I grasped the doorknob with my left hand. I had a hard time getting the key in the lock. The bulky work gloves I was wearing to protect my hands, of course, didn't help. As I continued to fumble with the key, my heart raced in anticipation of what was waiting on the other side of the door.

I was relieved when I finally heard the lock click and I was able to turn the door handle. Before I went any farther, though, I had to find a safe place to keep the key because I really didn't want to go diving in this water to look for it if I dropped it. Realizing my waders didn't have pockets, I turned to the cameraman who had followed me down the stairs. He was from a local television station and had been assigned to document the rescue. When we first met at the humane society, he had said, "Just do what you do naturally, and forget that I'm here."

I had almost done that. "Do you have a place for this?" I asked, still holding the key firmly between my fingers.

"Yeah," he replied, reaching for the key while balancing his heavy camera on his shoulder.

My attention returned to the job I had to do. As I attempted to push the door open, I discovered it was hard to move. *Something must be blocking it,* I thought, as I pushed harder. The cameraman was about to help, when we heard a thump on the other side of the door. Whatever it was that was in my way, wasn't any longer. Tom heard the noise from the top of the stairs and yelled down to me, "Is everything okay?"

"Yeah, there was something blocking the door, but I got rid of it," I said, as I used my shoulder to give the door one more big shove. The door gave way. "I got it. I'm in," I called to Tom, proud of my accomplishment.

My mind slowly took in the scene in front of me as I remained in the doorway. The sunlight peering through the small windows to my right was brighter than what my eyes had been used to in the hall. I gave them a moment to adjust before I took my first step into the apartment.

When I could see clearly again, I saw directly in front of me a huge mirror hanging cockeyed on the far wall. I was in the main living area and everything was out of place. Tables, couches, trash cans, laundry hampers, and crumpled cardboard boxes were some of the floating objects I would have to maneuver around. Nowhere did I see the cats.

I started moving forward, concentrating on planting each foot firmly on the floor. I heard myself saying, "Balance. I have to keep my balance."

Much to my relief, a loud meow broke my concentration. It startled me at first, but it was a good feeling to hear the cry of the first cat.

"Yes. One survived," I said for the benefit of the cameraman.

The cat continued talking to me as I moved in its direction, still unable to see the feline. When I turned the corner into a part of the living room I couldn't see from the door, I saw the cat crouched on a ledge that ran the length of the wall at a height of about four feet. The waterline on the wall showed that the floodwater had reached higher than the ledge. I could only guess how the poor thing had survived the rushing water. I know it was not on that ledge.

Not wanting to scare her, I began softly talking to her from a distance. "It's okay, sweetheart. You're all right," I repeated.

The female cat had long black fur with a white face, chest, and stomach. I could tell she was beautiful, almost elegant, even though she was now drenched with dirty floodwater. She had to be really cold; even with my waders to keep me dry and warm, I was beginning to get chilly.

I continued to talk to her in a soft voice, in much the same tone as you would use to reassure a small child, "You're fine. I'm here to help you."

She watched me, without moving a muscle except to let out an occasional meow. When I finally approached her, I extended my hand to pet her. She responded by immediately raising her head to welcome the touch of my fingertips, even flattening her ears so I could scratch more of her damp head. Seeing her delight, I continued to pet her, something I'm sure she had missed. I, too, would welcome the attention after being alone for five days. I could have pet her all day without her tiring of the affection, but I still had another cat and her four kittens to find.

After a few moments, when I felt she trusted me, I scooped her onto my shoulder. She was just as eager to leave as I was to get her to a safe place. With her comfortably situated on my shoulder, I called to Tom, "I'm bringing you one of the cats."

I heard Tom's reassuring voice in the distance, "I'm ready for ya. Take your time."

With the cat's rear end resting on my bent arm, I used my other hand to hold her by the scruff, just in case she tried to get away from me. You never know what will scare an animal, so I'm always prepared for the worst. As I continued to retrace my path to the staircase, I could feel the cat's claws sink into my shoulder. I didn't mind, though. It was almost a comforting feeling to know she was holding on tight.

To reassure both her and me, I continued my one-sided conversation, "Just a few more steps. Hold on, sweetheart. We're almost there."

When I reached the hallway, I could see Tom at the top of the stairs ready with a cage, the door open to receive her. "Hi there, sweetie," my rescue partner said, as we started up the stairs. "Oh, aren't you beautiful!"

When we reached the top, I slowly released the cat's tight grip on my shoulder and gently used both hands to put her into the cage. When she was safe inside, Tom closed the door. She peeked at us through the bars and I petted her nose—one last reassuring gesture.

"How bad is it in there?" Tom asked, as he picked up the cage to take it to the truck.

"It's bad. They've lost everything," I replied, seeing the picture in my mind. "I've got to get back down there and find the others now."

"You're doing great, kiddo. Just take your time. I'm here if you need me," Tom said with his familiar smile. "Just holler."

I reentered the apartment. The cameraman had worked his way to one of the back rooms. "There's one in here," he yelled when he heard me.

"Great. I'm heading your way," I said, loudly, to be heard over the swishing sound of the water.

As I neared the bedroom, I heard a terrified meow from another cat, which had to be the male I was looking for. The haunting sound of his long, drawn-out cries made me wonder if he was injured. When I entered the room, his intense meows changed to small little chirps, almost as if he were talking to me.

The male cat was mostly black with white blotches scattered through his slick, short fur. His white whiskers accentuated a cute black nose. He was drier than the first cat, but still visibly shaken from his ordeal. The room he was in appeared to be a weight room. Exercise equipment tossed around by the water formed barriers that would make it difficult for me to reach the cat on the ledge where he had sought refuge. An accumulation of feces piled along the ledge indicated that he had been there for a while.

As I tried to figure out a path to reach him, he continued chirping, like human disaster victims who want to tell everyone about their ordeal. I wondered if he was trying to say to me, "So where have you been?"

I tried to get closer to him, but the exercise equipment was making it difficult. The heavier stuff was shoved into the corner where the cat was perched. I would have to move it if I was going to reach him. Pushing as much as I could out of the way, I barely squeezed through some weight-lifting bars popping up out of the water. I was finally able to reach the ledge, but not the end where the cat was.

"Please come to me," I said, resting my outstretched hands on the ledge, hoping to coax him to me. "Come here, honey, it's okay," I assured him, lightly tapping my fingers on the ledge.

The cat just looked at me, unwilling to give in to my coaxing. He appeared to be uncertain of my intentions, just like a little child who has been told not to talk to strangers. I continued my efforts, knowing that moving the exercise equipment would be too difficult. Even if I could move it, the commotion would likely scare him even more. I had learned when I worked for an equine veterinarian that the slow way is often the fast way. It was a valuable lesson, one that was proving true again.

"It's okay, sweet pea. I won't hurt you," I said, continuing to talk to him while my fingers danced on the ledge.

I finally extended my arm toward him and wiggled my fingers, trying to entice his curiosity. He responded by cautiously creeping forward to sniff my fingers, but then he retreated back to his corner. I continued to talk to the cat, who just wasn't sure if he could trust me, while I extended my arm a couple more times. Every time I stretched my arm toward him, I would shorten my reach a little to encourage him to come closer. My persistence paid off when he finally got close enough for me to lift him up and place him safely on my shoulder. I stood there for awhile, stroking his fur, until I felt he was ready for me to take him upstairs.

As I exited the apartment, I called to Tom, "I got another one."

My reliable partner was again waiting with an opened cage. Together we put the cat inside, and I said a few more words of comfort before Tom carried him to the truck to be with the other cat.

"How are you doing? Holding up okay?" Tom asked with his comforting grin.

"As long as I don't trip and land headfirst in the water, I'll be just fine," I replied, as I started down the staircase. I realized that my heart wasn't pounding anymore. Each time I went down the stairs, my confidence grew.

When I reentered the apartment, I saw the cameraman. He wasn't able to direct me to another meowing cat this time, though; he broke the news when he said, "I found the kittens."

It was the way he said it that told me we already had all the survivors.

I tried to prepare myself for what I was about to see, but I knew nothing could make the sight any easier. I peered into the bedroom and my heart stopped when I saw four little kittens who couldn't have been much older than six weeks. They were mirror images of their parents, all covered with black-and-white fur. They were lying on the bed next to a box, which is probably where they had been born. The box was now nothing more than a pile of soaking-wet scraps of cardboard. As I moved toward the bed, the only movement was from the small wave that I created in the water. Standing next to the bed, I looked at the lifeless bodies. I was sad, but I was also angry.

It took a few minutes before I was able to return to the front door to share my unfortunate discovery. "Tom," I yelled. "The kittens didn't make it."

I heard Tom take a deep breath, which was followed by silence. I knew what he had to be thinking. The kittens were the first fatalities so far in this disaster, and we hated being the ones who found them.

"You have to remove the kittens, Michele. We can't let the owners find them that way," Tom said.

I could hear the frustration in his voice, which echoed what I was feeling, too. There was so much I wanted to say, but I just yelled back, "Okay."

"Can you find a bag or something?" Tom asked. " If not, I'll run out to the truck."

"I'll look around," I said, as I headed back into the apartment.

I looked through the kitchen first, thinking I would find something there that would hold the kittens. Wanting a dry bag, I looked on top of the refrigerator, but I didn't find anything. The counters had nothing on them but a thin layer of dirt, left behind when the water receded. I continued my search, and a floating grocery bag caught my eye. *I guess this will have to do,* I thought, picking up the dripping bag.

The cameraman, who had been quietly filming all this time, stood in the hallway as I made my way to the bedroom, dreading what I had to do. This is the difficult part of disaster work, but it's inevitable that not every animal is going to survive.

Taking a deep breath, I reached for the first kitten. My gloves still protecting my hands, I grasped the little kitten at the base of her neck and picked her up as a mother cat would carry her baby. This time the kitten's stillness was permanent, not just a relaxing reaction to a mother's firm grip. The kitten was soaked. As I stared at her, I knew Tom was right. The owners shouldn't have to see this. They had lost everything, and this would be too much.

I held the bag open with one hand and carefully lowered the kitten into it. Repeating the painful task three more times, I took the same gentle care with each one of them. My mind was full of questions as I finished what I had to do, but the one that still haunts me today is "Did they suffer?"

I walked through the now-empty apartment, holding the bag of kittens tightly against my chest. Even though they were gone, I gave them the same treatment as I had their parents, keeping them close to me.

The cameraman, who was standing in the doorway, broke the silence. "I guess I'll leave the kittens out."

Disappointment crept into my face as I looked at him. He wanted to show the successes and leave out the tragedies. If this story was going to be accurate, it would have to show both. I also felt I had an obligation to the animals who lost their lives during disasters, to make sure people knew the truth.

I paused for a second to gather my thoughts, then I very calmly stated, "This is the most important part. The reality is that animals die in disasters. A small amount of preparation and knowledge of what to do to protect them when a disaster strikes could have saved these kittens. By showing what happened to the kittens, you can help other people to understand and keep this from happening again."

The cameraman thought about what I had said for a moment, then nodded, and walked into the hallway. I'd said everything I could. I just hoped he heard. As I headed for the door, I could hear him climbing the stairs. I never saw him again.

I took one last look around the apartment, trying to absorb all that had happened there that afternoon, and then I closed the door.

THE ANIMALS' innocent and loving spirits are what drives me to continue to work so hard for their survival, no matter how difficult it becomes. They give me more than I sometimes think I give in return, but that's only because they ask for so little.

When I think about the mother cat I carried out of that basement apartment in Grand Forks, I wonder what she must have felt as she watched her kittens drown. If she could ask the people who left all six of the cats behind in a basement apartment just one thing, I guess it would be, "Why?"

That is my question, too.

CHAPTER TWENTY-EIGHT

Too Many

PEOPLE WHO rescue animals never have just one animal of their own. Someone asked me once, "Why don't you spend more time in the kennel during a disaster?" My response was, "Because I'll get attached and want to bring them all home."

There is a point where one more animal is just one too many. Not realizing this can defeat a person's initial intention, which is to help an animal. Having too many animals can result in jeopardizing an animal's health when you can't afford another veterinary bill, needing to cut back on the quality of food when food bills get too costly, not having enough time to give each animal the attention they need, and having to leave some or all of them behind when you evacuate because you don't have a vehicle big enough to get them to safety. When people are responsible for more animals than they can evacuate, what often ends up happening is: Animals die.

There was a woman in Grand Forks who learned this the hard way.

When I saw the rescue request form, I thought, *We're going to need the two-and-a-half-ton flatbed truck the National Guard has in Grand Forks if we're going to get all these animals.* Aloud, I said to Wendy, "Are you sure about the number of animals on this request?" We were prioritizing the rescues for that afternoon. "I can't believe they all live at this one address."

"They're all there," Wendy replied. "And if you look at the sheet of paper attached to the rescue form, you'll see that the owner has provided a detailed map showing us where each one of the animals is located in the house."

"You're kidding?" I said, turning to the next page.

"No, I'm not," Wendy assured me. "She was afraid if she didn't give us a map we wouldn't find them all."

"What are the chances they are still alive?" I asked, as I glanced at the map. "Does the owner know if her place flooded?"

"She knows the water got in the house. She just doesn't know how much," Wendy answered.

"Didn't she take any animals with her when she evacuated?" I said, putting the papers on the table in front of me.

"She had room for a few dogs, but that was it," Wendy told me. "Apparently she wanted to go back for more, but the police wouldn't let her past the roadblock."

"I can see why," I concluded. "If they had, she'd still be making trips back and forth to get this many animals."

Rather than tie up all the rescue teams on this one request, which is what it would take to retrieve this number of animals, I decided I would go to the house first to see if any of them were still alive, then I would know how many teams to send.

I anticipated finding more dead animals than live ones when I got to the house. It was pretty unrealistic to expect over a hundred birds to survive four days in a freezing cold, damp house, with little or no food. Then there were the snakes and lizards who didn't do well in the cold either. If anything made it, my guess was that it would be the remaining assortment of fish, rats, turtles, and the cats. We were about to find out for sure, as our boat turned onto North Fourth Street.

"It says on here the side door is unlocked," Arlette read from the rescue form, as Rick and I looked for the most unobstructed path up the driveway of the house.

"From out here, it looks like there's probably still a foot of water left inside," Rick said, as he waited for me to use an oar to push an aluminum lounge chair out of the way of the boat. "And my guess is it got as high as five feet."

"Well, the animals who were in cages on the floor are gone then," I said, having succeeded in removing the obstacle in front of us.

"I'm afraid so," Rick said, from the rear of the boat, where he was using the trolling motor to push us forward again.

When we reached the carport, I spotted the first animal. On the top of a four-by-four gatepost, with barely enough room to stand, was a drenched kitten.

"See it?" I said, pointing to the pathetic feline. Arlette and Rick confirmed that they had. "Let's get it before we go in the house." I reached for my waders.

"Do you think it'll dive in the water when you head for it?" Rick asked.

"Maybe, but my guess is this cat has had its fill of water." I pulled on my waders and fastened the suspenders. Ready to get into the water, I leaned forward, grabbed on to the carport post that was within my reach, and pulled the boat closer to where I guessed the steps to the porch and the side door were. Then I grabbed on to the next post, which got the boat as close to the porch as we were going to get.

I slid the oar, paddle end first, into the water to check the depth and to feel around for any objects hidden under the surface. At least in this flood we didn't have to worry about water moccasins because it was too cold for them to be slithering around. There were still lots of other things we had to be on the lookout for, though. The one that concerned me the most was uncovered manholes, especially when a person was wearing waders. If someone had a pair of chest-high ones on and stepped into one of those holes, chances were they weren't coming back up alive. Once the waders filled with water, which would only take seconds, it would be the same as having lead weights tied to their feet.

Feeling with my oar where the porch steps were, and finding nothing hidden in the water between me and them, I pulled the oar out of the water, and said to my two team members, "I'm ready to go in."

"The kitten hasn't moved, but it's sure watching you," Arlette informed me, as I swung my legs over the side of the boat and slowly lowered myself into the water, which was up to my waist. Grabbing the oar and the Evacsack that Arlette handed me, I was ready.

Using the oar as a blind person would a cane, I had to walk only a yard or so to reach the first step. My plan was to climb the stairs to the submerged porch, and then determine if there were steps on the opposite side that I could climb down to get to the cat, who was about seven feet beyond where I guessed the porch ended.

With no railing to hold on to, I very carefully climbed the three steps. Depending on the oar again, I directed it through the water, looking for any hidden obstacles on the porch. When I determined there were none, I stepped forward, still using the oar to feel my way to the other end of the porch. When the oar suddenly dropped and there was nothing below to stop it, it was clear there was not another set of steps, which meant I'd have to lower myself to the ground. Before I did, I looked to make sure the kitten was still there.

The kitten still hadn't budged, but then it's only option was to go for a swim, something cats really don't like to do unless they absolutely have to. This kitten didn't have a good enough reason yet to take the plunge.

"I bet you're tired of standing up," I said to the kitten, to see how it would respond. In its own way—a meow—I think it said yes.

"Okay, you just stay put and I'll get you off that post," I said, as I began my descent into the waist-high water again.

As I got closer to the kitten, it began to meow louder, especially when I talked to it, which was a good sign. I didn't have but a foot or two more to go when I had to drop my oar suddenly to catch the kitten, who decided I was moving way too slow and took a flying leap in my direction. It was awfully trusting to think I would catch it. If it had known what a lousy job I do of catching a ball when someone throws one at me, it probably would have stayed put.

"Good catch," Rick said.

"Thanks," I said. The kitten climbed up on my shoulder and began to purr.

After the kitten was safe in a cage with a towel to curl up in, Rick and Arlette joined me in the water. We decided to bring only the map and our flashlights on this first trip into the house. Once we knew how many animals were alive, we would return to the boat for the Evacsacks and cages.

The back door gave us no problem; we pushed it open on the first try and stepped into the house, which did indeed have a foot of water in it. Straight ahead of us were the stairs to the basement, according to the map.

"Careful," I said to Rick and Arlette, as we turned right to go down a short, narrow hallway to the kitchen. "Stay close together next to the wall because you sure don't want to slip and end up tumbling into the basement."

We took steps like a baby who has not mastered the skill of walking.

"What we're looking for in here are three bowls of fighting fish; they're supposed to be on the counter to the left of the sink," Arlette told us when we had safely reached the kitchen and she could refer to the map again.

"I see the bowls," I said, moving toward them to get a better look. "But the fish are floating."

The next room we entered was the combined den and dining area. Arlette didn't have to tell us what we were looking for in this room because everywhere we looked there were cages and aquariums, some of them completely visible and some still partially submerged in water. Remembering what I had seen on the map, I knew there were also some fishbowls containing hermit crabs on the floor, but the water was too high to see them. There was no point in searching for the crabs.

"The rats made it," Rick said, lifting the lid on a partially submerged aquarium.

"How many are there?" I asked, going to take a peek.

"Just two," Rick said as I looked over his shoulder at them. They were both standing on their hindlegs, repeatedly scratching the glass with their front legs, relieved to see us.

"They have no more food or water," I said, backing up when I got a whiff of the urine-soaked cedar shavings. "If I had to live in there, I'd be begging to be picked up, too."

I went to the kitchen to look for some bottled water and something to feed the rats. When I opened the refrigerator, I found a pitcher of iced tea, which I figured was better than nothing, and in one of the higher cupboards I located a box of Wheat Thins.

As the rats drank their tea and feasted on the crackers, their first food in four days, I continued to search for more animals.

"Here's the parrot," Arlette said, lifting a blanket that concealed the wrought-iron cage placed on a milk crate on top of the dining-room table. The water had gotten into the cage, but one of the bird's perches and his food and water had stayed out of its reach.

"His feathers are all fluffed out, which means he's cold," I said when I peeked under the blanket. "We definitely need to get him out of here or he won't last much longer."

"Terri. Arlette. Come check this out," Rick called from somewhere in the front of the house.

Crossing the den to get to the hallway, we passed more aquariums, all of them sitting up high enough so that whatever was inside was still dry. When we passed an aquarium that had thick vegetation and clusters of rocks in it, Arlette said, "I think that's the one with two snakes and a lizard in it."

My toes immediately curled under. Just the mention of a lizard summons this response every time, as lizards are my least favorite creatures in the world, with snakes a close second.

When we reached Rick, he was standing outside a closed door.

"What did you find?" I asked, hoping he wasn't about to tell me more lizards, as I knew the one in the den was not the only one in this house.

"Look," Rick said, as he slowly opened the door and told us to follow, closing the door behind us.

What had been intended as a bedroom was now an aviary. On shelves, and nailed to the walls, were all different-sized bird-cages and wooden nesting boxes. As I stood just inside the door, looking around in amazement, a canary flew over my head.

"The cage doors are all open," Arlette said.

I looked in the cage closest to me, and counted three dead parakeets and two live ones.

There were more birds loose in the room, some sitting on top of the cages, and others on the shelves. On the window ledge was a pair of lovebirds cuddled with each other, probably trying to keep warm. I started to count the loose birds, but I was having a hard time because they wouldn't stay still, especially the finches. It looked as though there were close to 30.

"I count 26 dead birds," Arlette said when she had finished looking in every cage.

"Did you look in the nesting boxes?" I asked. "I suspect there'll be more in each of them."

Sure enough there were. The dead birds totaled 34, unless there were more who had died, fallen into the water, and sunk.

"How are we going to catch all these birds?" Rick asked.

"There must be a net around here somewhere," I guessed. "I can't imagine having all these birds and not having a net to capture any escapees."

"It's probably in the water somewhere," Arlette said, as she began to pass out rations of seed from the one partially filled coffee can with dry bird food inside.

"We'll have to get one then," I said, as I moved to keep from getting hit by a low-flying cockatiel, who was really struggling to stay airborne.

"This is really sad," Rick said, looking in one of the cages that had nothing but dead canaries in it.

"It is," I said. "We need to finish searching the house, but before we do, let's first close the doors on the birdcages so we don't have more birds to net."

The next room I found was the bathroom, and what I saw made me stop in the hallway outside. Lying on the toilet seat was a turtle the size of a catcher's mask. His head was partially extended, his legs were all completely out of his shell, and the only eye I could see was open, but I couldn't tell if he was alive. When I touched the tip of his nose, I got no response. I waited a few seconds and tried again, but nothing. Placing my hands on either side of the shell, I lifted the turtle and his legs went limp. Then I knew he hadn't made it.

The white mouse in the small aquarium on the bathroom shelf was still alive, though, and just as hungry and thirsty as the rats. Fortunately, there was still some iced tea and Wheat Thins left, which I gave to him, and then went to look for Rick and Arlette.

In the living room, we found all the aquariums that had at one time held tropical fish. Those high enough to keep out the floodwater had mostly dead fish in them. We did find three goldfish who had managed to survive. We scooped them up with our hands and put them in a Tupperware container Arlette found in the kitchen.

The lower aquariums were now filled with filthy floodwater, so it was hard to tell what they contained. Most of them did not have complete lids covering the tops. When the water had receded, there would likely be quite a few dead fish lying on the ground, those who swam out of the aquariums when the water was higher. At least for a brief time, they had been able to swim in what must have seemed like an ocean to them.

The only indoor cat we were looking for was supposed to be in the master bedroom. When we opened the door to that room, we saw that finding the cat was going to be like looking for a needle in a haystack. The bed was piled high with clothes that had been pulled out of the closet and the dressers had other belongings that had been tossed on them by someone who had obviously been in a hurry. The only thing missing in the room were piles of feces, which would have given us a clue as to whether or not the cat was in the room and still alive. Considering this was a cat who was frightened of everyone but one person, we decided to leave food and water out for it, even though we were pretty certain there was no cat in this room. If the food was gone when we checked later, we would know that our assumption was wrong and we would start hunting for the cat's hiding spot.

The rest of our search turned up two hamsters who had survived with the rest of the rodents, a frog who didn't seem the least bit concerned about all the water, a snake who we thought was dead until he stuck out his tongue, and more dead fish. The lizard in the den was dead, and I did actually feel sorry for him. We watched the two snakes in their shared aquarium for a while, and our conclusion was that they, too, had died.

WE MADE two trips back and forth to the house that afternoon, ferrying the survivors to the staging area where volunteers with transport vehicles were waiting to take them to the humane society. The kitten, the parrot, and 10 of the weaker birds were in the first load.

When we were making our second—and last—trip back to the staging area to unload more of the birds we had managed to capture with towels rather than a net, we spotted another rescue team who was also calling it a day. We only had about an hour of daylight left, so the remaining birds and rodents, who we determined could last one more night with the food and water we left them, would be the first animals we rescued the next morning.

Two Golden Retrievers stood on the bow of the boat headed our way. It almost looked as though they were directing the volunteers where to go, as they remained still, their noses pointed in our direction.

"So did you recruit some more help?" I asked, as we pulled our boat up next to theirs.

"Oh, the dogs," Tom said, when he realized to whom I was referring. "No, but if we had, we'd have fired them after what they did."

"What could they have possibly done wrong?" I asked, rubbing the muzzle of one the loveable dogs with both my hands.

"These guys are so well trained that for the three days they were in the house, they must not have peed," Tom told us.

"How do you know that?" I asked, as the second dog came over to get his share of attention.

"When we loaded them in the boat, they hadn't been onboard for more than two seconds when they both, at the same exact moment, started to pee," Tom explained with animated exasperation. "And they continued to pee, and pee, and pee, and pee. In fact, there was so much pee in the bottom of the boat we had to scramble to pick up these cages with hamsters, ferrets, and a hedgehog in them. It wouldn't have been too cool for them to survive the flood only to end up drowning in a boat that sank because it had too much pee in it."

Laughing at the exaggerated image Tom created, I said to both dogs. "It's not your fault. I'm sure your mom and dad never told you not to pee in a boat."

"Well, I wish they had," Tom said, chuckling.

We were all still laughing when we docked our boats 10 minutes later in the parking lot at Blockbuster Video. As I was helping to load the animals into the waiting vehicles, I thought, *I don't think we could survive all this if it weren't for the animals and the people who give us a reason to have a good, cleansing laugh.*

CHAPTER TWENTY-NINE

The Hitchhiker

MY LAST rescue in Grand Forks is how I would like all disasters to end. I was in the crowded lobby of the humane society, trying to talk over a yipping Poodle, a pair of meowing Siamese, and a parrot who could only repeat, over and over again, "Pretty Boy. Pretty Boy. Pretty Boy." At least a dozen people had all shown up at the same time to reclaim their animals, when I happened to catch sight of a thin girl standing just inside the doorway. I couldn't help but notice that she looked more bewildered than the people surrounding me did.

When I could, I worked my way toward the door to see if I could help the girl who couldn't have been more than 12 or 13. "Are you here by yourself?" I asked, coming to this conclusion after watching her for a few minutes.

Quietly, she said, "Yes," as she nodded her head up and down.

"Where are your parents?" I asked, concerned, but at the same time not wanting to scare her away with too many questions. She looked so frightened already, and I certainly didn't want to do anything to frighten her more.

She answered my question, somewhat reluctantly, by telling me that she had hitchhiked to the humane society without her parents knowing it.

"They're going to be worried when they can't find you," I said. "Can we call them and let them know you are here?"

"No," she replied immediately. "Not until we find my cats."

"Wouldn't your parents want to help you find them?" I asked, certain that they would.

"No," she said, fiddling with the silver ring on her finger. "They think my cats died, and they said you guys didn't have time to bother with dead animals, that you had to save the ones that are still alive. Is that right?"

When she finished, I reached out and gave her a hug, her tears darkening my red sweatshirt. "Please. If you find 'em, bring 'em to me," she said, then paused long enough to wipe her nose with the back of her hand. "I have to bury 'em. I don't want 'em out there in that scary house by themselves anymore."

I promised her that I would find her cats.

With all of our rescues completed for the day, the local volunteers who had been out in the field had headed home, probably to shower, change clothes, eat, and relax—all things I would have loved to be doing, but there was something much more important that I had to do.

The only rescue person left at the shelter was Jonathan, who I had seen earlier in the bird room, cleaning cages—a never-ending job when you have over 50 cages to keep clean. I got the young girl settled upstairs in the staff break room, and then I went to see if Jonathan wanted to go on one more rescue.

We drove to within three blocks of the house on Lincoln Street, which was one of the streets on a piece of land that jutted out into the river. This was where we had been told by the people at the command center nine days earlier that nothing could have survived the force of the water, which had risen to twenty feet deep and would not recede quickly because there was nowhere for the water to go.

I tried not to think about what they said, as Jonathan and I unloaded the boat from the back of the truck and set it in the water, a routine at which we were becoming experts.

"I'm not going to use the motor because there's still too much debris floating in the water around here," Jonathan said as he pushed the boat away from shore. "Why don't you grab the extra paddle and push anything in front of the boat out of the way, and yell if I need to stop."

"Aye-aye, captain," I said, needing to ease the seriousness of what we were heading to do.

"Very funny," Jonathan said with a laugh. "You keep that up and I'll throw you overboard."

The sound of the oar breaking the water was all that interrupted the silence that replaced the few moments of meaningless banter Jonathan and I had used to hide our feelings. Even the wild birds we saw perched in the trees were silent, as if they, too, were mourning all that had been lost. As we rowed past house after house, ruined beyond repair, I felt an all-encompassing sadness at the total loss. This was without a doubt the worst-hit area. The lives of the people who had lived along this street would never be the same again. I had heard at the command center briefing that morning that all these houses had been condemned and buyouts would be offered. Everyone who had lived here would be moving on, but it would be a painfully slow process.

I was absorbed in my thoughts, but Jonathan got my attention immediately when he warned me to duck so my head wouldn't snag the sagging power lines as we slipped underneath them.

"Thanks," I said, when I had straightened back up.

"Look at that." Jonathan pointed past me to a large tree ahead on the right. In the top of it was a metal storage shed, one of the things left behind in a strange new place as the water that had put it there dropped. Two doors down there was a picnic table likewise perched in a tree. We continued to see bizarre things as we traveled closer to the house we were looking for.

The girl's directions and mention of landmarks that might have survived led us straight to the slate-blue, two-story house. Finding a safe way to enter the house was more difficult.

"There's something wrong here," Jonathan commented, as we drifted while surveying the house. "How come their garage is a different color from the house?"

I looked at the garage for a minute, then turned around and looked at the house across the street. "Because that garage doesn't belong to this house. It came from that one over there."

Jonathan compared the two houses, and said, "You're right. The water pushed it off its foundation and that's where it came to rest."

WE FINALLY decided that our best choice for entering the house was to go in the back door. There was still part of an elevated redwood deck attached to the back of the house, providing enough height to allow us to walk in the water. There was no question that the ground was too far underwater for us to touch it with our feet and still keep our heads above water, even for Jonathan who was just over 6 feet tall. What remained of the railing would give us a place to tie the boat and then we could wade a distance of about seven feet to reach the door.

As we made our way through the cold water, we could feel the waterlogged deck boards sag under our feet. The thought of them breaking was not a thought on which we wanted to dwell. We made sure to find a secure footing before we picked up the other foot and moved another few inches forward. We stayed within an arm's length of each other in case one of us slipped.

When we reached the door, Jonathan handed me his flashlight and used his shoulder to lean into the door, which he expected to be difficult to open. His first attempt resulted in the door budging only a few inches.

"There's something in the way," he said, after trying it again.

"We need the truck's bumper," I said with a laugh.

"I'm afraid even it couldn't make it through all this water," Jonathan said. On his third try, the door opened a little bit more.

"Here, let me help," I offered.

It took a few more tries, but we finally managed to open the door far enough for us to squeeze through the opening. Inside, we discovered that it was a tipped-over refrigerator that had made our job so difficult.

The moldy odor that is inescapable during a flood was especially strong in the house, dashing our hope of maybe detecting the scent of cat feces. Entering through the mud room where the washer and dryer had also been rearranged by the force of the water, we pushed aside the contents of kitchen cupboards floating on the surface of the water, ruined from days of marinating in filthy floodwater.

As Jonathan and I cautiously made our way through the large country-style kitchen, still remaining within arm's reach of one another, we had to grab on to countertops and cabinet doors to keep from slipping. The buckled linoleum floor was as slick as ice and several times we nearly stumbled, something we both wanted very much to avoid. This was not the kind of water you wanted to go diving in.

I knew we had entered a very dangerous situation, but it was hard to make myself turn back. There was a 13-year-old girl anxiously waiting at the humane society for word of what we found. I so hoped we could tell her what she desperately wanted to hear.

My imagination told me that the dining room we were now attempting to cross had only weeks before been elegantly decorated. The floral-printed wallpaper had given up its fight, though. The penetrating moisture had caused it to slip into the water where it now lay crumpled and torn in a crisscross pattern on the water's surface, as if it were attempting to conceal what lay underneath. Pushing upholstered straight-back chairs out of our way, we crossed the room, pausing for a moment to admire the stately grandfather clock in the corner. The water had not knocked it over, but I wondered if it would ever keep time again.

A long solid-oak table, which could easily seat 10, lay on its side blocking our entry into the front hall, where we could see the steps that led upstairs. If by some miracle the cats had survived, it was likely we would find them up there. Unable to budge the table, we lumbered over the obstacle. As we raised our legs out of the water, we became aware for the first time that we were getting cold. The faint light coming through the broken windows on either side of the splintered front door reminded us that we had less than two hours of daylight left. We would have to try and move faster. This house was spooky enough now. I couldn't imagine what it would be like in the dark.

We used both hands to grab onto the railing that remained attached to one wall of the staircase. We did this not only to keep from slipping, but also to maintain our balance, as we realized the house was gradually shifting. We felt as though we had boarded a ship that was in trouble.

As we climbed slowly upward, we tried not to think whether the steps that seemed to moan from our weight were still strong enough to support us. I was distracted from the thought of the stairs giving out and us falling into the basement, which was still a pool of water mixed with fuel oil, another smell in the nasty flood mix. My distraction was the gold-colored nails sticking out of the buckled paneled wall, reminders of the pictures that had been carefully hung there. The water had not even spared them.

Relieved to reach the second-floor hallway, we clicked on our flashlights, since all the doors in the hallway were closed. The only natural light was mere slivers peeking out around the warped doorframes. As I moved my flashlight around to survey the hallway, the light found an obstacle course of assorted boxes, a Black and Decker lawn mower, a set of golf clubs, a microwave oven, a ten-speed bicycle, and a barbeque.

The family had obviously moved all these items to the second floor in hopes that the water would not find them. The water had won the game of hide-and-seek though. The beam from my flashlight found the telltale waterline—three feet up the stucco wall.

As we made our way down the hall, I found a litter box that had been put in a wagon. It was filled to the top with dirty water, in the middle of which was one large clump of cat litter. Next to it was a mound of disgusting, moldy cat food. In the muddy carpet surrounding the wagon, I looked for cat prints, but there were none. This was not a good sign, but I reminded myself it was too early to give up hope.

One by one, we opened the doors and searched for the cats, moving out of our way wet furniture, heavy, dripping blankets, and mattresses that had absorbed the floodwater before it retreated. We searched the bedroom closet, pushing aside clothes, all the longer-hanging ones bearing the marker of where the water had finally stopped. Stepping back into the hall, we realized we had only one more room to check. The perfectly dry poster of Leonardo DiCaprio hanging on the ceiling above the bed was a pretty good clue that we had entered a teenager's room. On the bed were a computer and a printer, put there with the hopes that they would be high enough to stay dry. The water was ornery enough to get just four inches above the bed, ruining both pieces of equipment.

While Jonathan checked the closet, I knelt down, my knees making a squishing sound as they sank into the Mother-Nature-dyed brown carpet. I leaned over so I could pull up the mildewed dust ruffle to get a look under the bed with my flashlight. This was a routine I had gone through in the other bedroom, and in every other house I had been in over the past few days as I searched for hiding cats.

Having a teenager of my own, I was not surprised by what I found stashed under the bed. I had to move mismatched shoes, discarded clothes, a tennis racket, an empty McDonald's soft-drink cup, a stuffed bear with only one eye, and a pair of roller skates in order to be sure I had scoured the entire space. Just as I was about to turn away, I spotted in the far corner, tight up against the saturated wall, a gray furry object, wet and splattered with mud.

At first, it was not clear if it was a stuffed animal or maybe one of the cats we were searching for. If it was one of the cats, I had the sickening feeling that it was dead, since it did not respond to the light from my flashlight. I let go of the dust ruffle and slowly got to my feet. Without a word, I motioned for Jonathan to help me pull the bed away from the wall. Having closed the hallway door to prevent the cat from escaping, just in case it was alive, I moved the computer equipment to one side, then got on my hands and knees, and slowly crawled across the bed. Each time I put my hand down on the pink quilt, brown water gushed between my fingers.

Suspecting I was about to see something I did not want to see, I paused and took a deep breath, thinking, *Here I go again.* If the cat was dead, it was going to be even harder this time because I was going to have to confirm for a 13-year-old girl, whose cats were her best friends, that her parents had been right about the flood taking their lives. At least they had been wrong about us—we did have time to help even the dead animals.

Knowing what I had to do, I finally peered over the edge of the queen-size bed. What I saw were two green eyes that looked up at me and blinked.

My own eyes filled with welcome tears as I slowly reached down between the wall and the bed, and with one hand scooped up the fragile cat. Tucking her up under my chin, I held her tight and kissed her damp head, my lips tasting her mud-caked fur. Whispering, I said, as I rocked her in my arms, "You're safe now. You're safe."

We found the second cat alive in a wicker laundry basket in the back of the bedroom closet.

When we got back to the boat, both cats secure in their own Evacsack, I pulled my cell phone out of my watertight equipment box and called the young girl.

Wendy answered the phone at the humane society. When she realized who it was, she simply asked, "Well?"

"They made it," I said, my lip quivering. Those were the words I had wanted more than anything to be able to say.

"Do you want to tell her?" Wendy asked.

"Yeah, I really do," I said, looking at Jonathan, who had a big smile on his face.

"Wendy, try not to give her any clue as to what I'm going to tell her," I said. "It may be selfish, but I really want her to hear the good news from me first. I want that memory."

"I will," Wendy said, completely understanding my request. "I'll take her the phone."

"Hello?"

There was apprehension in the questioning voice that answered the phone, which I knew would be replaced with shouts of joy and happy tears as soon as I said, "Call your parents and let them know your cats are alive!"

CHAPTER THIRTY

The Continuing Ride

I SPENT MY last night in Grand Forks at the humane society, alone. The shelter had also been our temporary home
during this disaster, and it deserved a four-star rating. Arlette
had given us permission to convert the upstairs office of the
Quonset-style building (used to store potatoes before it became an animal shelter) into one big bedroom where we'd
had as many as 20 people sleeping, along with a fluctuating
number of caged iguanas.

This was the only part of the shelter with enough electri-
cal outlets to plug in the heat rocks and lamps needed to keep
the reptiles warm, so I'd agreed to let them share our bedroom with us. In the cage closest to my staked-out piece of
the floor was a 30-inch iguana. The rescue team had almost
given up finding him, one of the volunteers told me, until
they discovered him sprawled on the back of his owner's
couch. "We must have walked past that couch two dozen
times and not noticed him," the volunteer said. "Who would
think to look there? Since no one had told us he was loose in
the apartment, we were looking for some type of cage."

It's a good thing that I was so tired each night or I would
have lain awake, letting my imagination run wild. I'm sure I
would have eventually convinced myself that the iguanas had

figured out how to unlatch their cage doors and were creeping across the floor, passing by everyone else, so they could crawl into *my* sleeping bag.

Fortunately, we didn't have a single escapee, or I would have taken up residence elsewhere.

With all the coordinators and volunteers from out of town en route to their homes, and the iguanas returned to their owners, I rolled out my sleeping bag on the floor, one last time. With no one to talk to and no iguanas to torment me, I fell asleep listening to the barking of the dogs downstairs. It felt good knowing that they were all safe, thanks to the incredible team of volunteers who had worked so hard to keep them alive.

There was no Red Cross mobile feeding truck waiting to serve me breakfast on my last morning in Grand Forks. After 11 days of eating cold, untoasted English muffins, minus any butter or jelly, followed by warm V-8 juice, I was ready for a full-course breakfast and a tall latte, which I would get at the airport during my layover in Minneapolis.

I was also overdue for a real shower, after leaning over the side of the shelter's grooming tub to bathe daily. That's not the easiest way to get your hair washed either. I'd end up spraying more water on the floor, walls, and ceiling than on my hair.

As I filled my bulging duffel bags with dirty clothes, muddy waders, knee-high boots, an assortment of other gear, and a plastic goldfish I had rescued, I looked around at the empty room. Only the day before, it had still been filled with tired volunteers, also packing to go home.

On our last night together, we all lay awake until long past midnight. We shared stories from the disaster that made us laugh and cry and giggle, sometimes all at once. It reminded me of the slumber parties I'd had as a kid, only this time there was no refrigerator to raid. A dry English muffin was not enough of an incentive to run downstairs.

Before we finally fell asleep sometime after midnight, we all agreed that this had been a successful disaster. We had worked our tails off, but the long hours had paid off. There were 768 animals who might not have made it if we hadn't been there to help Arlette and her staff, and every single one of them had an owner. This was the only disaster I had been to where there were no unclaimed animals, which eliminated the temptation to increase the head count at my house.

Before I dragged my stuff downstairs to wait for my ride to the airport, I said good-bye to the two shelter cats who had made the rounds every night, trying to decide whose bed was the most comfortable. When one of them would choose to curl up with me, it made me feel at home, and I was certain their presence would ward off any escaped iguanas. The only drawback to having two cats as roommates, we learned after our first night, was that air mattresses aren't a good substitute for a scratching post. We all woke up on the hard floor, where we remained every night after that.

I was sitting on my duffel bags in the parking lot when Jonathan arrived to take me to the airport at 7 A.M. Somehow we managed to cram everything into his Ford Mustang, thinking at one point that he would have to go and get the two-and-a-half-ton flatbed. During our short ride to Grand Forks' Airport, we didn't say very much. At this stage of a disaster, I'm usually physically depleted, the adrenaline has run out, and my mind is just beginning to play catch-up.

It was amazing how much had happened in 12 days. Aside from during the few hours of sleep I got every night, my mind was constantly processing new information. Before I could completely think through one thing, something else would demand my attention. It became necessary to prioritize and shelve a lot of information for later consideration. As I sat in Jonathan's car, staring out the window at the endless expanse of prairie, I began to sort through the leftovers that had accumulated, or at least as many of them as I could remember at that point.

I knew that over the next few weeks, when I would least expect it, more memories would pop up and I would find myself laughing or crying as I relived them. These are both healthy responses, necessary to bring closure to a disaster before facing a new one. And as I thought back to the miracles—and tragedies—I still felt a sense of accomplishment. And I realized with each tragedy, each animal lost, we gained a new guardian angel. Then it made sense to me why there was always one nearby.

⌒⌒◯

EARS RESPONDED to 11 disasters between May 1997 and the end of 1999, the last one being Hurricane Floyd, which struck North Carolina on September 16. Once again, EARS did a superb job; in this case rescuing and caring for 716 animals over a period of 18 days. This was possible thanks to a team of 636 volunteers and Cora Tyson.

Cora is one of the 15 EARS coordinators. She lives in Greenville, North Carolina, one of the cities hardest hit by the flooding that followed this category-four hurricane. After moving to the East Coast from Arizona, she began preparing her family for the next hurricane season, but she didn't stop there. She worked on getting the community better prepared to take care of animals, too, and it paid off. I believe more animals would have suffered and died during this disaster if it weren't for Cora's persistent message, "You've got to have a disaster plan for your animals, too."

Before our team arrived in Greenville, Cora had already set up a temporary shelter at the Life Sciences building at Eastern Carolina University. After having that state-of-the-art facility, setting up in open fields during future disasters is going to feel a little more difficult. We were definitely spoiled by our accommodations during Hurricane Floyd, and, boy, did the animals get first-class service.

As I'm completing this book, we're heading into another hurricane and fire season, both predicted to be bad. When and where the disasters will hit is guesswork. One thing is for sure, though—EARS will be there to help the animals.

Though I am ending this book here, there are still a lot of stories left untold, and there will be more to add to the collection with each new disaster. I imagine I will write a third book, but after spending five months on this one, I'm ready for a break and to spend some time with my family.

In October 1998, the Crisps left city life behind and moved to the Sierra foothills, about an hour west of Lake Tahoe. Ken, Jennifer, Amy, Megan, and I now share 10 acres on top of a mountain with 13 cats, 3 dogs, 3 parrots, 3 cows, 3 ducks, and 2 goats. It's the place I've always dreamed of having, and I'm looking forward to spending as much of my summer as Mother Nature will give me, exploring the countryside with my husband and kids, both the two- and four-legged ones, in addition to our three-legged cat, Minus.

My family, my parents included, is an endless source of support. They bring a healthy balance to the crazy lifestyle I've created for myself. When I leave for a disaster, they are there to wish me well. When I return, they welcome me back with open arms and the question, "Did you bring home any animals?"

More times than not, I return with nothing more than an accumulation of dirty clothes.

I am truly blessed that my family shares my love of animals and realizes that this work is what I'm supposed to be doing. Amy and Megan have both told me that when they grow up they want to be just like me. Jennifer is in college now, working on a degree in psychology. It will probably be good to have a shrink in the family to help keep us all sane.

I think back to when I was a kid and my parents would take my brother, Todd, and me to Disneyland. At that point in my life, I couldn't imagine there was anything more thrilling than the rides, the Matterhorn being my favorite. I now know there is.

The adventures that keep my life exciting and so incredibly rewarding have far surpassed my earlier expectations. Not a day goes by that I don't find myself hoping that the ride attendant will continue to forget to flip the switch, keeping this ride in motion—because I'm not ready to stop.

EMERGENCY ANIMAL
RESCUE SERVICE

I F YOU are interested in finding out more about the Emergency Animal Rescue Service (EARS) and how you can help, either by becoming a trained volunteer or providing financial support, please contact:

United Animal Nations
Emergency Animal Rescue Service
P.O. Box 188890
Sacramento, CA 95818
Phone: (916) 429-2457
Fax: (916) 429-2456
Web site: www.uan.org
E-mail: info@uan.org

In addition to information about the Emergency Animal Rescue Service volunteer program, United Animal Nations also has a variety of educational materials designed to prepare people to care for animals during disasters.

Another source for more detailed disaster preparedness information is the Appendix section of my first book, *Out of Harm's Way.*